INTIMATE WARRIORS

Intimate Warriors

Portraits of a Modern
Marriage, 1899–1944

Selected works by
Neith Boyce and Hutchins Hapgood

Edited by Ellen Kay Trimberger
Afterword by Shari Benstock

The Feminist Press
at The City University of New York
New York

Published by the Feminist Press at The City University of New York,
311 East 94 Street, New York, NY 10128
Distributed by The Talman Company, 150 Fifth Avenue, New York, NY 10011

94 92 93 91 6 5 4 3 2 1

Library of Congress Cataloging-in-Publication Data

Intimate warriors : portraits of a modern marriage, 1899–1944 /
  selected works by Neith Boyce and Hutchins Hapgood : edited by Ellen Kay
  Trimberger : afterword by Shari Benstock.
       p.   cm.
    Contents: Selections from The bond / Neith Boyce — Selections from The story
  of a lover / Hutchins Hapgood — Dialogue and Enemies — Two poems: Birds of
  passage, and Hutch — Letters.
    ISBN 1-55861-045-6 (cloth). — ISBN 1-55861-046-4 (pbk.)
    1. Boyce, Neith, 1872-1951 – Biography – Marriage. 2. Hapgood, Hutchins,
  1869-1944 – Marriage. 3. Authors, American – 20th century – Biography. 4.
  Intellectuals – New York (N.Y.) – Biography. 5. Greenwich Village (New York,
  N.Y.) – Intellectual life – 20th century. 6. Greenwich Village (New York,
  N.Y.) – Social life and customs. 7. Sex role – Literary collections. I. Trimberger,
  Ellen Kay, 1940–   . II. Boyce, Neith, 1872-1951. III. Hapgood, Hutchins,
  1869-1944.
  PS3503.0857Z73   1991
  810.9'0052 – dc20
  [B]   90-25531
                                                                                 CIP

Photograph acknowledgments
      Cover: Neith Boyce, circa 1898-99, courtesy of the Library of Congress;
Hutchins Hapgood, 1895, courtesy of Beatrix Hapgood Faust
      Page 39: Neith Boyce, circa 1898-99, courtesy of the Library of Congress
      Page 133: Hutchins Hapgood, 1895, courtesy of Beatrix Hapgood Faust
      Page 177: Hutchins Hapgood and Neith Boyce in *Enemies*, Provincetown,
Mass., circa 1915, courtesy of Beatrix Hapgood Faust
      Page 197: Neith Boyce and children, Miriam and Charles Hapgood, 1909,
courtesy of Beatrix Hapgood Faust
      Page 201: Neith Boyce, Settignano, Italy, 1923, courtesy of Beatrix Hapgood
Faust; Hutchins Hapgood, 1922, courtesy of Tim Bright

This publication is made possible, in part, by public funds from the New York
State Council on the Arts.

Text and cover design: Paula Martinac

Printed in the United States of America on acid-free paper by McNaughton &
Gunn, Inc.

Contents

ACKNOWLEDGMENTS

This book had its genesis in a year's fellowship for college teachers from the National Endowment for the Humanities in 1980–81. From an obscure footnote, I obtained a microfiche copy of Hutchins Hapgood's *The Story of a Lover*, written in 1914 and published in 1919. I was impressed that in the early decades of this century a man was probing his conflicted relationships with his wife and other women in contemporary psychological terms. I soon discovered the related novels of Neith Boyce, Hutchins's wife, and I was hooked on this couple. Nancy Cott helped me sublet an apartment in New Haven and find a babysitter for my infant son so that I could probe the letters and unpublished manuscripts in the Beinecke Rare Book and Manuscript Library at Yale University. The staff there has always been extremely courteous and helpful both in person and by mail. My parents, George and Eleanor Trimberger, provided support, including childcare, numerous times during this project.

I owe the greatest debt, however, to the cooperation of the two daughters of Neith Boyce and Hutchins Hapgood, Beatrix Faust and the late Miriam DeWitt. In 1984 Miriam invited me to her home in Provincetown, Massachusetts, to share her private archive (including typed copies of many of her parents' letters). Beatrix came down from New Hampshire, and the two sisters shared many stories about their parents. Before her sudden death in the spring of 1990, I learned much from Miriam's sharp memory and thoughtful insights. I benefited equally from Beatrix's generosity and from a perspective on her parents that often differed considerably from that of Miriam. That these two daughters were so open and undefensive about their parents' lives, and that they could both honor and criticize them, increased my respect for Neith and Hutchins. After Miriam's death her sons Tim and Ned Bright helped me obtain photos from her archives. Beatrix provided additional photos.

The intellectual and personal support of Ellen DuBois, Barbara Epstein, and Alice Wexler has been especially important in bringing this book to fruition. Other colleagues who have read parts of the manuscript and provided useful comments include Wini Breines, Naomi Katz, Kathy Peiss, Lois Rudnick, and Eli Zaretsky. Roz Baxandall and Dee Garrison contributed interesting discussion and insights. My agent, Frances Goldin, was a joy to work with. Jeffrey Escoffier, my freelance editor, helped me condense *The Bond* and *The Story of a Lover*, a strategy that was later abandoned, but I appreciate his efforts. Florence Howe encouraged this work from the beginning, but its final form owes most to Kathy Casto, my editor at The Feminist Press. Her creative ideas, efficiency, and enthusiasm have sustained me through the production process.

Finally, I dedicate this book to my son, Marc, in the perhaps idealistic hope that his struggles with a feminist mom may lead him to more equitable relationships in the future.

Intimate Warriors

INTRODUCTION

We tend to talk informally about other people's marriages and to disparage our own talk as gossip. But gossip may be the beginning of moral inquiry, the low end of the platonic ladder which leads to self-understanding. We are desperate for information about how other people live because we want to know how to live ourselves, yet we are taught to see this desire as an illegitimate form of prying. If marriage is, as Mill suggested, a political experience, then discussion of it ought to be taken as seriously as talk about national elections. Cultural pressure to avoid such talk as "gossip" ought to be resisted in a spirit of good citizenship.

—Phyllis Rose, *Parallel Lives: Five Victorian Marriages*

For a brief decade from about 1968 to 1978 the personal became political in the United States. Feminists and new leftists convinced a large public that sexuality, the structure of marriage, and intimate relationships were not universal, natural, or God-given but were socially constructed and hence could be reconstructed. Millions of people sought to create more equitable personal relationships where women would have room for autonomy, creativity, and achievement and men would participate more fully in emotional intimacy, child rearing, and homemaking.

As conflicts arose, however, and male resistance appeared, this vision of egalitarian relationships lost cultural ascendancy. In the 1980s the media was filled not with positive images of women and men struggling to live in a new way but with burned-out and disgruntled "superwomen" and "supermoms"; with neglected "latchkey children" and career women guilty about leaving their children in day care; and with successful professionals who had delayed marriage and motherhood too long and who now faced an unhappy life alone.[1] Discussion of men's ability or desire to change their personal lives was lost in the focus on women's frustration and guilt.

Missing from either the 1970s vision of more equitable personal relationships or from the 1980s backlash was the sense that women and men before us might have had similar ideals or dilemmas. I began to gain this historical perspective when I discovered the writings of a couple who in the first two decades of the twentieth century (a period that is increasingly seen by historians as formative of our own culture) wrote about their marriage in a manner that was eerily familiar and contemporary.

My study of Neith Boyce and Hutchins Hapgood, of their relationship, family, community, and culture, provided me with a small spur to help resist the contemporary erosion of the ideal of egalitarian relationships. It is not that I identified with them; my life is not like theirs. Nor was I inspired by their success in creating a satisfying relationship. If anything, their silences and failures were more meaningful to me. Rather, what impressed me about Neith and Hutchins was their ability to write about some of their conflicts and disappointments in ways that dignified the struggle without a nostalgic return to tradition. We expect attempts to alter power imbalances in the economy, polity, and social system to involve strife. Neith's and Hutchins's struggles signify the inevitability of conflict in attempts to change intimate and sexual relations—conflict that does not necessarily indicate failure.

Hutchins Hapgood (1869–1944) and Neith Boyce (1872–1951) were central figures in a group of intellectual radicals living in pre–World War I Greenwich Village in New York City. Hutchins was a journalist and essayist noted for his sympathetic ethnographies of underdogs, deviants, and radicals. Neith was a novelist and playwright whose fiction portrayed the difficulties of creating new forms of intimacy between middle-class women and men.

In the last years of the nineteenth century Hutchins and Neith gravitated independently from the Midwest to the bohemia of Greenwich Village. Before World War I this "village" in the city attracted writers and artists, along with a diverse group of reformers, socialists, anarchists, and feminists, all caught up in an intense period of political, social, and personal change. All the villagers—artists and intellectuals as well as activists and reformers—were in revolt against the human costs of the United States' emergence as a major industrial and world power.

These writers and artists created an alternative culture, a forerunner of the beat culture of the 1950s and counterculture of the 1960s. They started the bookstores, cafes, discussion groups, art galleries, little theaters, alternative magazines, and unconventional dress that characterizes (in more commercialized form) that area of New York City today. The men wore flannel shirts or brightly colored ties. The women bobbed their hair, smoked in public, and wore handmade Batik blouses. Both women and men wore sandals in the summer.[2]

Greenwich Village intellectuals were attracted to psychoanalysis and began to popularize it. They used Freud to argue for greater candor in life and literature and against puritanism and rigid moral judgments. Like Hutchins, many were attracted to immigrant culture and others to primitive art and spiritualism as an alternative to a bureaucratic and totally rational culture. For Village intellectuals writing poetry, novels, drama, or social and psychological theory was as important in transforming the consciousness and reality of the United States as labor union organizing or building an anarchist or socialist Left.

Unlike most of their counterparts in late twentieth-century countercultures, however, these cultural radicals were in close contact with activists. They discussed politics with the socialist Big Bill Haywood, the anarchist Emma Goldman, and the Industrial Workers of the World's Elizabeth Gurley Flynn. The most prominent Greenwich Village magazine, *The Masses*, integrated radical political analysis, cartoons, new art, poetry, and cultural commentary. Intellectuals participated in labor strikes, wrote about them sympathetically, and popularized them in the visual arts and plays like the large Madison Square Garden musical in 1913 in support of the Paterson (New Jersey) labor strike.

In the summers between 1910 and 1917 Neith and Hutchins and their group of friends (including John Reed, Mabel Dodge, Louise Bryant, Mary Heaton Vorse, Susan Glaspell, George Cram Cook, Eugene O'Neill, Max Eastman, Ida Rauh, Crystal Eastman, Floyd Dell, Theodore Dreiser, Carl Van Vechten, and Alfred Steiglitz) moved to Provincetown, Massachusetts, where they founded, wrote, and acted for the Provincetown Players to create a new American theater. Neith wrote the first play for the group, which was performed in the Hapgood-Boyce living room. The Provincetown Players produced short, realistic plays often about the personal conflicts between women and men in their group. It was here that Eugene O'Neill was inspired to write his family dramas. Many of the writers and artists in the Greenwich Village and Provincetown circle also spent time in Europe where they had friends among the more permanent expatriate literary and art communities. Neith and Hutchins were friends with Bernard and Mary Berenson, who were art historians and collectors in Italy, and with writers Leo and Gertrude Stein in Paris.

Hutchins and Neith met in 1898 when they were co-workers on a liberal newspaper edited by muckraker Lincoln Steffens. For "Hutch" it was love at first sight, but not for Neith. Friends agreed that they had very different personalities, which made a permanent relationship improbable.

Neith was a beautiful redhead with sleepy green eyes, but in other ways she was very "unfeminine." She was ambitious and willful, sophisticated and sardonic. People called her Sphinx-like because she was so quiet and self-sufficient. Although she was one of the first women to smoke in public, she was not demonstrative or very sociable. Hutchins on the other hand was an extroverted talker, eager for experience, with a genius for friendship. He was warm and sensuous, often childlike in his enthusiasm for life. It was Hutch who attracted intellectuals and activists from a wide range of political and social class backgrounds to the famous Fifth Avenue salon of the wealthy dissident, Mabel Dodge.

Despite his ardent courtship, Hutchins doubted that their relationship would prosper. He wrote to his mother in 1898:

> There is a girl in N.Y. who has been much more to me than any other girl I ever knew. We are not engaged and it is practically sure that we never shall be. She is a 'new woman,' ambitious and energetic, a hard worker, more or less disliked by all my friends that know her, and she has no idea of getting married, at any rate to me.[3]

Yet their differences attracted Neith, especially Hutchins's warmth and capacity for enjoyment. As she says in an unpublished autobiography (written in the third person):

> Having known H for nearly a year, seeing him almost every day, she had certain convictions about him. He was a good man, honorable, kindly, and she felt one could rely on him to the crack of doom. But it was not these qualities that made the strength of the current. It was the warm, life-quality in him, the capacity for enjoyment, the desire to enjoy and to have others enjoy. He loved pleasure, he was good company, he was charming. . . . He was unreasonable, unexpected, surprising; he insisted that life should be, and was pleasant, varied, rich. By now, it would have been very difficult for her to give up all this.[4]

Their attraction also rested on similarities and differences in their family backgrounds. Hutchins had grown up in Alton, Illinois, the middle of three sons of a plow manufacturer. Charles, his father, was a college graduate forced out of business in Chicago by the great fire to this small town exile. Although Hutchins characterized his father as a stern Victorian with a high regard for honesty, industry, exactness, and punctuality, Charles was no "captain of industry."[5] He never cared for money, and he communicated his dislike of the business life to his sons. In a history she wrote of the Hapgood family, Neith said of Charles: "He referred to himself merely as 'a link between generations of merit,' and he wrote: 'My paternal ancestors of three generations gave personal attention to the political questions of their day and my sons are giving attention to the social questions of the present day.' "[6]

All three sons attended Harvard University and were successful, although both the elder son, Norman, and the youngest, William, were more practical and conventional than Hutchins. Norman became an important liberal editor, most prominently of *Harper's Weekly*, and William became a progressive businessman who experimented with industrial democracy in a cooperatively managed canning company in Indiana. From childhood Hutchins considered himself "an odd stick," a dreamer. He was accepted by his father, but Hutchins identified with his mother in looks and temperament. A housewife, his mother was lively, charming, and emotionally expressive, with a zest for daily life. She also read Shakespeare to her sons.

While attending Harvard from 1889 to 1892 Hutchins finally found a niche for himself in the world of men. In the intense intellectual atmosphere created by William James, Josiah Royce, George Santayana, and others, he learned that men too could be emotional and introspective. As an undergraduate, he accepted the asceticism of the intellectual life, but it was his experience with alcohol and sex during his postgraduate study in Germany, and his growing attraction to the "underlife," that led Hutchins to leave the university for journalism after earning a master's degree in English from Harvard and briefly teaching at the University of Chicago.

Neith Boyce was born in Franklin, Indiana, the second of five children. Although her childhood also began in a small Midwestern town, it was much more mobile and tragic than Hutchins's. Neith attributed her unsocial and somewhat pessimistic character to the death of all her brothers and sisters in an epidemic when she was about six, the death of another baby soon after, and her mother's subsequent emotional withdrawal. Neith was a solitary child whose parents refused to talk about the deaths or to express much emotion toward her.

Neith admired her father, who was an active, extroverted Irishman, in contrast to her more rigid, New England–born mother. Yet he was also emotionally distant. When Neith was about ten (in the early 1880s) her father, previously a book publisher in Milwaukee, bought a ranch outside Los Angeles. Here Neith lived a solitary life, but she came to love both the out-of-doors and books. Around 1885 her father co-founded the *Los Angeles Times*, and they moved to the city. The success of the paper made the family temporarily rich, but Neith profoundly disliked their bourgeois family life, now enlarged by two baby girls. She retreated inward, writing stories and poetry, some of which her father published in the paper. Always striving, he soon bought a rival paper, the *Los Angeles Tribune*, and started real estate speculation, but his real estate failures forced him to sell their house and most of their newly acquired possessions. He left his family in Los Angeles to engage in speculative mining in Colorado but not long after moved them all to Boston where he bought a partial interest in the *Boston Traveler* and a socialist magazine, *Arena*.

Neith did not attend college, but as a teenager she became friends with a group of older writers, artists, and journalists in Los Angeles, and in Boston she met socialists and feminists connected with *Arena*. When her father moved the family again, this time to New York, she sold some of her stories to magazines and became friends with other young women writers and journalists. At the age of twenty-seven, Neith got a job as the only woman reporter on the *Commercial Advertiser* and moved out of the family home into a hotel in Washington Square.

As a teenager, Neith already had decided to forgo marriage in favor of independence and a career. As she wrote in her autobiography: "Children did not appeal to her at all and neither did the troubles and difficulties she had observed in marriage. . . . It was much better to observe other people's love affairs and write about them."[7]

Despite personality differences and professional commitments, Neith and Hutch were married in 1899 with the explicit understanding that she would retain her name and pursue a writing career. Although both left full-time newspaper work, in the next ten years they had four children and each published four books and numerous articles and stories. Hutchins's books have enjoyed a more lasting reputation, yet Neith's novels were as well known at the time.

A modest income from Hutchins's father made an independent lifestyle and some household help possible, but it was still unusual for both a husband and a wife to be as productive as Neith and Hutchins. Their productivity is even more impressive when one considers the unconventionality of their life. This family with small children was always moving—a six-month trip to Europe in 1903, a trip to Chicago in 1904, back to New York in 1905, to Italy, Switzerland, and Paris between 1906 and 1909, to Indianapolis in 1909, and back to New York in 1910. In 1911 they bought a big house in Dobbs Ferry, New York, where the family lived until 1922. Other exiles from the Village lived there, their friends from the city visited, and Hutchins commuted often into Greenwich Village for work and play.

Hutchins's early books were collections of his newspaper essays, focusing on people outside America's mainstream, whom he met in those places he felt most alive: "the ghetto, the saloons, the ethnic restaurants and among immigrants, radicals, prostitutes and ex-convicts."[8] Hutchins's sympathetic human interest stories were collected in *Paul Jones* (1901), *The Spirit of the Ghetto* (1902), *Autobiography of a Thief* (1906), *The Spirit of Labor* (1970), *An Anarchist Woman* (1909), and *Types from City Streets* (1910). Later he published two autobiographies, *The Story of a Lover*[9] (1919) and *A Victorian in the Modern World* (1939).

In contrast to her husband's books, Neith Boyce's novels were based on her own experiences in the middle class. Her first novel, *The Forerunner* (1903), illustrated the destructive impact of capitalist entrepreneurship on personal relations—a fictional recreation of her parents' marriage. The rest of her novels dealt with the marriages and personal relationships of her own generation, but like other implicitly feminist novelists in the early twentieth century—Edith Wharton and Kate Chopin, for example—Neith broke with the tradition of feminine romance to portray personal life in a more realistic manner. In *The Folly of Others* (1904), *The Eternal Spring* (1906), *The Bond* (1908), and numerous magazine stories, Neith dwelled on conflicts between women and men in their love relationships, conflicts that are never resolved in either a romantic or a tragic denouement. Like her husband, Neith published only two books after 1910, another novel, *Proud Lady* (1923), and *Harry* (1923), an autobiographical account of her first son, Boyce, and his early death at age seventeen.

Almost all commentators on Greenwich Village from 1900 to 1917 stress that its dissident intellectuals and artists, in addition to their political and cultural concerns, were committed to individual transformation and sought to alter their sexual and intimate relationships as an essential part of larger social change. Their writings and lives were important components of what cultural historians see as a major transition in American life—from the nineteenth-century ideal of self-sacrifice to the twentieth-century ideal of self-realization. As Warren Susman conceptualizes it, Victorians admired "character" defined by duty, work, conquest, honor, reputation, morals, and integrity, while twentieth-century Americans value "personality," which should be fascinating, stunning, attractive, creative, and forceful.[10]

The works by Neith and Hutchins in this volume demonstrate an emphasis on self-transformation. Writing about their internal conflicts and their relationship permitted Neith and Hutchins to hold personal contradictions in their consciousnesses and grapple with them. Through writing they struggled with changing ideals of sexuality, intimacy, and marriage in a manner that helped them begin to change their reality – to create and sustain a marriage that had the potential to be more equitable, richer, and more complex than existing cultural models.

The years from 1900 to 1920 were marked by a consolidation of ideals and practices of sexuality and intimacy that had developed throughout the nineteenth century and by the initiation of new directions. Significantly, the separation of sexuality and reproduction that began in the nineteenth century became a cultural norm in the first two decades of this century. A sharp drop in the birthrate in the United States between 1800 and 1900 resulted primarily from the widespread use of birth control among the middle class, despite its being neither culturally sanctioned nor publicly discussed. After the Civil War eugenicists became alarmed about the falling birthrate in the face of a growing influx of immigrants with higher fertility. The Comstock Act of 1873 for the first time limited access to contraception and led to an ongoing debate. The rise of a birth control movement around 1910 led by Margaret Sanger and inspired by Emma Goldman, both with close ties to the intellectuals in Greenwich Village, marked the transition to a society where birth control was culturally accepted and widely available.[11] (The question of abortion, however, was not addressed in these years.) In their writing both Neith and Hutchins describe the conflicts created by Neith's unplanned first pregnancy about 1902, indicating that the use of birth control was still problematic at this time for this upper-middle-class avant-garde. Neith's three other pregnancies seemed planned, however, and their intense discussion of sexuality never focused on issues of reproduction.

By the end of the nineteenth century sexual pleasure was seen as important to human health and happiness, but only if limited, controlled, and confined to marriage. A burgeoning advice literature, the women's movement, and religious and social reform movements accepted sexuality but argued over how to control, not repress, sexual desire. Men's sexuality had to be directed away from masturbation, prostitution, and pornography and toward their marital partners. Women had to be able to say no to excessive sexual demands by their husbands, and women's rights advocates argued that some women should be able to reject sexuality and marriage altogether in order to make a contribution to the public realm. Although there is considerable evidence that many nineteenth-century women enjoyed sex and had satisfactory sex lives in, and sometimes outside of, marriage, the accepted cultural norm was that women had less need and capacity for sex than men.[12]

Marriage for love and not for utility or to please one's parents became the cultural ideal by 1850. Love implied sexual passion, but nineteenth-century yearnings for physical intimacy were expressed in highly romantic—even spiritual—terms, in a language of "blending hearts," "holy kisses," "spiritual joys," "souls that entered paradise," and "communion with the beloved."[13] Husband and wife were supposed to be companions, but the increasing separation between men's public and women's private worlds meant that the "ideal of companionship was rarely achieved in married life; most [couples] found their relations with family and friends far more personally satisfying than those with their spouses. While they might subscribe to the ideal of conjugal love, they did not necessarily live it."[14]

In Neith Boyce's 1908 novel *The Bond* (and in many other writings in Greenwich Village a few years later), sex and intimacy were no longer written about in romantic and spiritual, but in psychological, terms. Being in love now involved a knowledge of the beloved's inner experience, an interpenetration that could be achieved not through a mystical union but by talking. The romantic vision of the fusion of two hearts into a unity was replaced by an ideal of deep communication that enhances two distinct selves who both expect sexual fulfillment.[15] Women and men now had comparable sexual needs and capacities. Thus, a new ideal of sexualized intimacy replaced the earlier romantic norm of spiritualized sexuality.

Feminism, as articulated in Greenwich Village, sought to link intimacy with the need for autonomy and creative work for women. Women in the Village were leaders in a transition from the nineteenth-century "woman movement" to twentieth-century feminism. The culture of the woman movement had emphasized the nurturing service and moral uplift that women could contribute to American society, based on their common domestic experience. In Greenwich Village from 1910 to 1917, Heterodoxy, an organized group of creative working women who met regularly for discussion about personal and political issues, took the lead in formulating a new feminist culture.[16] Feminism emphasized women's self-development so that women could do important work, experience sexual intimacy, and, if they wished, marry and be mothers without sacrificing their individual creativity to the family. A vision "combining equality of economic choice with heterosexual intimacy was essential to feminism in the 1910s. . . . Feminists assigned more libera- tory meaning and value to passionate heterosexual attachment than did any woman's right advocates before them. Seeing sexual desire as healthy and joyful, they assumed that free women could meet men as equals on the terrain of political representation or professional expertise."[17]

The importance of feminism is evidenced by the extent to which Greenwich Village women persuaded men to participate in relationships aimed at its egalitarian ideal. In numerous autobiographies, essays, and novels, women and men in Greenwich Village articulated their attempts to integrate sex, intimacy, and work in satisfying, equitable and stable marriages or personal relationships.[18]

On the surface, cultural emphasis on developing personal relation- ships that integrated satisfying sex and greater intimacy appealed to men who were breaking away from the Victorian work ethic and rejecting success in established institutions. Since work was no longer so central to their self-conceptions, the idea that women wanted to be more engaged with work was not immediately threatening to them. But nei- ther women nor men considered the potential difficulty of achieving an equitable integration of sex, love, and work in relationships embedded in a society in which men had greater power and privilege. This gender inequality made it easy for "feminist" men to interpret the new hetero- sexual ideal in a self-centered way by involving women in their personal development, rather than facilitating women's new work.

Looked at closely, writing by Greenwich Villagers reveals numerous difficulties in creating egalitarian relationships. Many of the substantive issues they discuss are similar to those articulated by Neith Boyce and Hutchins Hapgood—differences in women's and men's commitments to monogamy; anxieties about autonomy and dependence in relationships between strong women and men; disagreements about who is respon- sible for housework, childcare, and nurturing if both women and men were to have satisfying work.

Unfortunately, the European sexologists who so influenced the new ideal of sexualized intimacy also advanced ideas that reinforced tradi- tional male power and undermined the feminist ideal of autonomy and creative work for women. Between 1905 and 1915 Neith and Hutchins, along with many other Greenwich Villagers, read the *Psychology of Sex* and *Man and Woman* by Havelock Ellis, *Love's Coming of Age* by Edward

Carpenter, and Ellen Key's *Love and Marriage* (translated from the Swedish in 1911).

Ellis and Carpenter were English socialists who were associated in the 1880s and 1890s with the Fellowship of the New Life and the Men's and Women's Club in London, organizations that sought to change personal life (through diet and dress reform and open discussion about sexuality) as part of a larger political vision. Ellis and Carpenter wrote about the importance of sexual pleasure for women as well as men and openly discussed and validated homosexuality.

Ellen Key was a Swedish feminist and writer who broke with the Swedish suffrage movement to emphasize the importance of changing the personal relations between women and men. As a single woman, she shocked her Swedish contemporaries in the 1890s by discussing sex and marriage. Key believed that all women as well as men needed sensuality and psychological intimacy in their lives, and she advocated relationships based on "an increasingly soulful sensuousness and an increasingly sensuous soulfulness . . . in a union in which neither the soul betrayed the senses nor the senses the soul."[19] Such a relationship did not have to be confined to marriage since, for Key, the morality of sex depended on whether it enhanced the life of the individual. By 1912 the feminists in Greenwich Village who used to read Charlotte Perkins Gilman were reading Ellen Key.[20]

Ellis, Carpenter, and Key, however, held very conventional conceptions of gender difference. They believed that masculinity and femininity were biologically based and that women had a special need and capacity to mother. Ellis said, "Woman breeds and tends; man provides; it remains so even where the spheres tend to overlap."[21] While women had an equal claim to a good sex life, for Ellis female sexuality was passive and had to be aroused by a man. He believed that a youth spontaneously became a man but a girl must be kissed into being a woman.[22]

Even though Ellis, Carpenter, and Key all supported women's rights, they criticized movements that emphasized women's right to work outside the home. Carpenter stereotyped such feminists as being without strong sexual or maternal instincts, as "mannish" in temperament and "brain-cultured."[23] Key believed it was impossible for a woman to work outside the home and be a mother. A woman with children would have to have at least ten years free of any continuous outside work. Motherhood, she believed, brought great joy to women and was a more important way of exercising creativity than writing a novel or producing a work of art.[24] Ellis too saw women's creativity centered in their procreative abilities. "Women's brains, are in a certain sense, in their wombs," he said.[25] It is perhaps significant that none of these writers were parents.

These conventional gender ideals were attractive to many Greenwich Village men. In *Women as World Builders*, for example, Floyd Dell wrote an admiring chapter on Ellen Key's new sexual morality and conservative ideals of marriage.[26] In Hutchins Hapgood's writings about his marital conflicts, the stereotypic images expounded by Key, Ellis, and Carpenter keep intruding, hampering his struggle toward a more intimate and satisfying relationship.

Several contemporary feminist historians have argued that the increasing cultural discourse about heterosexuality in the United States between 1900 and 1920 was primarily male-defined, to the detriment of women.[27] Given the influence of Ellis, Carpenter, and Key on Greenwich Village intellectuals, such an interpretation seems correct. Feminists used the work of these sexologists to support their views of women's sexual needs and capacities, but they never criticized the writers' conservative gender ideals. Individual women thus had few cultural resources to help them understand the difficulties they experienced in their search for sexual fulfillment, intimacy, and an autonomous worklife and identity.

As a result, the feminist vision failed for many of these intellectuals as their conflicted relationships broke down. Many men sought women who would accept more traditional gender roles; many women became bitter.[28] An ideal of women combining satisfying sexual intimacy and creative work in the world also lost out culturally. By the 1920s the ideal of sexualized intimacy became the more culturally generalized and conservative ideal of companionate marriage. Here women's sexual fulfillment was still regarded as important, but intimacy was redefined to emphasize the husband's ability to confide *his* feelings and problems to a wife safely returned to her domestic sphere.

What was unusual about Neith and Hutchins among their contemporaries was their ability to sustain a high level of personal conflict without their relationship dissolving or reverting to more traditional gender roles. A closer look at their writings may contribute, therefore, to an attempt in the late twentieth century to revive a struggle to combine satisfying sex, love, and work for both women and men.

In the following pages I will draw out what are to me the important socio-psychological themes in Neith's and Hutchins's writings. As a starting point, I will use the poem Neith wrote for Hutchins on his forty-sixth birthday in 1915, printed here for the first time.[29] Written in the personal style of a journal entry, this poem in its structure, substance, and silences reveals much about their relationship as it both reflected and diverged from cultural ideals about intimacy, sexuality, and marriage.

TO H. H. AT 46

Nineteen years ago I met you—
You were then something incredibly fresh and young
Having lived twenty-seven years in the world
And known many men and women
And had many adventures in the byways
And embraced perhaps a hundred women
But you were still innocent
And there was an innocent corruption about you.

Your blue eyes were bright and ardent
And you came into my little room like a whirlwind
Like a spring gale, upsetting the furniture
And trying to upset all my ideas also—
Fain to persuade me that life was worth living—
Nay more, that it was a wonderful and beautiful invention.
And I denied it and said I hated life
And told you to go away—
But if you had gone I should have been much disappointed.

For you pleased me enormously—
I liked the shape of your hands and your ears
And the thickness of your neck where it joins the shoulders—
(I could not love a man with big ears or a thin neck
No matter how beautiful his soul)
And your soul was beautiful too
And I loved it.
It was warm and sensitive
Like your body.

One night you came into my bedroom
Where I was putting on my hat before the glass

And sat down on my bed and put your arms about my waist
And said in a thick voice
"Lock the door—don't be a fool—"
But I laughed and didn't lock the door
And was a fool—
Why didn't you insist?
So we lost at least a year.

During that year we made love and quarrelled
Of course, but incompletely—
And since then for seventeen years
We have made love and quarrelled
Pretty completely
And I suppose we shall go on doing so
Till one of us drops into the grave
Then we shall be peaceful
And lonely.

Meantime you will threaten about once a week
To leave me
And will tell me you hate me and that you are
Too tired
To struggle any longer with me—
And will tell me I have no soul, no heart
And no imagination
And that I never loved you
Nor understood you
Whereas many other women have done both
Only you did not love them
Though you tried hard—
But that perhaps some day you will find one
Warm and devoted and also beautiful
That you can love
And then you will desert me—
For five days a week
Anyway.

And I shall look at you coldly
Wishing you would try it
So that you could find out just how cursed

Other women can be
Then you might appreciate my virtues—
Wishing you were married to a *hausfrau*
Or to a woman who would talk you to death.
Or one who would make you come home
Every night to dinner—
Or one who was ambitious socially
Or had nervous prostration
And no sense of humor—
Or one who was sorry for herself
And would go about telling other men
How you had failed to appreciate her.

And I shall think what a good time
I might have also if I were free—
How I would go about and amuse myself
And have no one to find fault
With the cooking
Or the care of the children
No remarks about fresh eggs
Or soups
Or underwear with holes in it—
Yes, I should like that for a change—
I would not look for another husband either
Nor for some one to love me—
Except, of course, platonically
Or in some such way.

But these are only dreams—
As a matter of fact we are worse then married
For we can't get divorced—
So I suppose we shall go on
For twenty years more
Quarrelling and making love—
So cheer up, old sport!
Perhaps the worst is yet to come
Or possibly the best
I'm sure I don't know—
All I know is, you are still young,
In spite of what you say—

And still charming
I see no reason why you shouldn't live to ninety
And break the ladies' hearts
Right up to the last—
I shall be eighty-seven then
And we'll be a pair of turtle-doves—
Wise old birds.

"We Have Loved and Quarrelled"

Neith's poem depicts the emotional and sexual intensity of her relationship to Hutchins after more than fifteen years of marriage. We feel her physical attraction to him—to his thick neck—and her regret at her early sexual restraint. But sexual attraction is not obscured by romantic idealizing. Even earlier, in *The Bond*, we see that from Neith's point of view what held husband and wife was not mystical, romantic love but a clearly physical attraction and emotional interdependence. Yet before her marriage Neith foresaw that sexual fulfillment might conflict with her desire for autonomy and a career. For Neith, Hutchins "combined the life of the mind and the life of the body. . . . But she had a feeling that it might not be easy for her to combine them. A woman she felt might easily be swamped by the demands of physical and family life. And it was clear that H would be a demanding person, nothing half way would satisfy him."[30]

Neith came of age in the 1890s when, for the first time in American history, a small but significant number of middle-class women became independent career women and did not marry.[31] Because Neith did not meet Hutchins until her late twenties, after she was already established as a writer, and because she had the option to live as a single career woman, she could clearly see the dangers in marriage. She could impose conditions—that she would retain her name and pursue her writing—in order to maintain her independence within marriage. Moreover, Neith's "unfeminine" personality, her introversion and ability to distance herself as well as her sardonic and unsentimental wit, abetted her struggle for autonomy. She married too because Hutchins was emotionally available. Although his ideals about women and sexuality were often conventional and romanticized, an "unmasculine" personality that was sensitive, open, and warm made personal struggle possible.

Neith's and Hutchins's deviations from norms of gendered

personality—her autonomy and his emotional openness—can be seen perhaps as the psychological results of a breakdown of nineteenth century gender models in some middle-class families.[32] Neith did not have an engaged mother; in her unpublished autobiography she says: "Never that she could remember had either of her parents caressed her or really talked to her or made it possible for her to talk to them. Love? She did not know whether she loved them or not, nor whether they loved her."[33] Hutchins's close identity with his warm, expressive mother and his more distant relationship to his hard-working father suggest the source both of his nurturing personal qualities and the type of intimacy he sought. Because Hutchins's father disliked the business life and never cared for money, he made no demands for his sons to break away from their mother and develop competitive, masculine traits. Sons in this family— like more traditional daughters—could retain and internalize a more diffuse relationship to the mother, fostering greater capacities for emotional relatedness than the traditional male but also a less well-defined and clearly bounded self.[34]

Despite Neith's and Hutchins's more androgynous personalities, their writings document the tenacity of gender norms in shaping their sexual passion and maintaining a double standard. I link this conventionalism in large part to their reading of the early-twentieth-century sexual pioneers and to the cultural diffusion of the heightened notions of gender difference found in Ellis, Carpenter, Key, and others.

"Why Didn't You Insist?"

Neith's expression in her poem of her physical attraction to Hutchins is coupled with a traditional acceptance of his initiative in sexuality and several references to his greater interest in sex. Moreover, Hutchins's writing portrays his initial sexual attraction to Neith as a direct expression of a "natural" attraction of opposites. In his autobiography, *A Victorian in the Modern World*, published in 1939, Hutchins described how he fell in love with Neith at first sight without knowing that she was a colleague and an intellectual. He attributed his attraction both to universal differences existing between men and women and to the special distinction in their characters: Neith was "a foreign being, indomitable in her foreignness, but therefore contributing to me something distinct, unknown and beautiful" (158).

While Hutchins's attraction to Neith arose from their differences, he and Mabel Dodge saw themselves as very alike in personality, and they developed a deep intimacy. In her autobiography Mabel said of Hutchins: "He was one of the most attractive and lovable human beings I ever knew, and I soon became deeply attached to him and wanted to be with him all the time. I told him all about myself—everything—and oh how he sympathized. Tears stood in his eyes and he passed his hand tenderly over my hair. We spent hours and hours together in the white rooms, talking."[35] Yet Mabel did not appeal to Hutchins sexually because she was not really "feminine." As he says in his autobiography: "The normal way of a male is to fall in love with a woman who is like a plant, with roots in the ground and with a possibility of eternal flowering; a development from the physical into the conscious and the moral; the forming of the material of life. There are many beautiful sound women, whether they talk or not, who hold men with the power of the movement of life itself. But one of the most striking things about Mabel was that she seemed to lack this, root-like quality. . . . She is like a cut flower."[36]

In their unpublished *Dialogue*, possibly an early draft of a 1915 play, *Enemies*,[37] Neith and Hutchins attribute the attraction and the conflict between a woman and man to disparate and "essential" masculine and feminine natures. Neith is presented as the quiet, deep, and passive but morally superior female—the "nourisher of life." Hutchins is the talker, the restless doer and sinner—a man who wants a woman "to keep the old beauty, . . . to keep the old deep brooding charm, but somehow to combine with that free companionship and conscious self-development" (185). The *Dialogue* contends, however, that these traditional women and men no longer exist. That the play remained unpublished, that such gender stereotypes were absent from *Enemies*, and that none of Neith's fiction embodied such values testify, perhaps, to her at least partially successful struggle against the tendency to construct sexual passion through gender hierarchy. She was less effective in her conflict with the double standard.

"Many Other Women Have Both Loved and Understood You"

Neith adopts a sardonic tone in her poem in references to Hutchins's interest in other women, "his embrace of a hundred women" in his search for someone "warm and devoted and also beautiful" that he can love. Neith adopts the same tone of lofty unconcern in *Enemies*. Her letters, however, reflect a more complicated and painful reality.

In the second year of their marriage, during Neith's first pregnancy, Hutchins began a series of what he called "conventional affairs." Unlike his Victorian forefathers, however, he told Neith about them and urged her to experiment as well as a means of deepening their relationship. As he said in *The Story of a Lover*: "To have her know other men intimately, was with me a genuine desire. I saw in this one of the conditions of greater social relations between her and me, of a richer material for conversation and for a common life together" (146).

Despite an intellectual ability to envision a more open sexuality, Neith was still committed emotionally to monogamy. Her letters written during their courtship and in the early years of marriage express this strong feeling and her pain at Hutchins's affairs. In 1907 she wrote to Hutchins: "I have an abiding love for you—the deepest thing in me. But in a way I hate your interest in sex, because I suffered from it. I assure you that I can never think of your physical passions for other women without pain—even though my reason doesn't find fault with you. But it's instinct and it hurts. The whole thing is sad and terrible, yet we all joke about it every day."

Neith tried to adapt to Hutchins's view of sexuality. In about 1904 she began flirtations with other men—attractions that she revealed to her husband. Hutchins became very jealous, even violent, responses emphasized in both *The Bond* and *The Story of a Lover*. In provoking jealousy, Neith, like her heroine, Teresa, balanced the score: she rekindled his sexual attraction and enabled herself to forgive his affairs. Neith then abandoned her other relationships, got pregnant (for the third time), sailed off to Europe with the family, and translated her experience into *The Bond*.

In 1908, during their three-year stay in Europe, Neith began a flirtation with an old college friend of Hutchins's, Arthur Bentley, to overcome her hurt and depression after Hutchins again revealed to her some new affairs. In the beginning Hutchins encouraged the relationship, finding it sexually exciting, but he soon came to fear their intimacy:

> He liked her much as I liked her. She pleased our taste so utterly! And I loved to have him so perfectly appreciate her. . . . But then there came the old deep pain when I felt again the excluding movement of their souls. I felt near to them, but their growing affair steadily alienated

them from me. He withdrew from me and I was hurt and she in equal measure went farther and farther into that unknown land in which I had no home, and I was hurt more deeply still.[38]

In this quote and other passages in *The Story of a Lover*, Hutchins implies that Bentley and Neith became lovers, but in letters to a friend he said they did not have a physical affair. Both sources acknowledge, however, that it was a serious relationship and that Neith considered leaving Hutch or, at least, maintaining her involvement with Bentley. As Hutch said in a letter: "She has at least once (and I think only once, and that lately) wanted or thought she wanted for a time a life—another life—and this one too. A romantic feeling that she would like a double life—a double set of interests, complex and long sustained, with two men, and possibly two families."[39] *The Story of a Lover* details Neith's inability to leave Hutchins. At his insistence she broke with Bentley (who was also married), but then she had a nervous breakdown—and Hutchins both cared for the children and helped nurse her back to health.

Around 1910 Neith and Hutchins helped create a social circle in Greenwich Village and migrated with it to Provincetown in the summer. For Neith this involvement was intellectual, political, and social. Although Mabel Dodge and others mention men who were attracted to Neith, there is no evidence that she continued her spiritual infidelities or was motivated to experiment with physical affairs. For Hutchins, however, the attraction to the Greenwich Village circle was also erotic. He had at least two affairs in the Village that were more prolonged than those he described earlier. Neith, while hurt again, tried to accept Hutchins's idea that his love for her was not threatened by physical infidelities and to minimize the importance of his affairs. As she wrote to Mabel Dodge: "As to your famous question, 'Why do we want men to be monogamous?' I should respond, 'Do we?' So long as they won't be, why should we want them to be? Why want anybody to be what they are not? Perhaps we like the excitement of catching them in flagrante delicto—and then their excuses are so amusing! An absolutely faithful man, but what's the use of discussing him. He's a mythical creature. I don't want any mythical creatures. I like them as they are."[40] Her real feelings were more painful. Many years later, after rereading her letters about one of Hutch's affairs, Neith wrote again to Mabel Dodge (now Luhan): "How noble I was. How patronizing. And of course all the time I was nothing of the sort." Agonizing over her own lover's, John Reed's, affairs with other women, Mabel asked: "Women have always asked men to be faithful—will men change and become so if women won't take less? . . . Is it what feminism is all about?"[41]

Hutchins's adulterous sexual behavior was very common among men of the bohemian Left in this period. His emotional makeup, however, led him to value intimacy and domesticity. He could only have affairs with other women if he had a stable base to come home to. *The Story of a Lover* indicates that he regretted his affairs primarily because they did not involve a great meeting of souls, not because he valued monogamy. One concludes that Hutchins and his male peers would give up the pleasures of a sexual double standard only if forced to do so by Neith and other women.

Unlike a long-suffering Victorian wife who "overlooked" her husband's affairs and turned for affection to her children and women friends, Neith wrote—in published prose and her letters—about his affairs and those of his male friends. *Constancy*, a short play performed by the Provincetown Players in 1915 or 1916, depicted the conflicted relationship between John Reed and Mabel Dodge.[42] The dialogue between the man and the woman about infidelity clarified Neith's position:

MOIRA: In love one cannot be free. I was constant to you every moment while I loved you.

REX: While you loved me. That's not my idea of constancy.

MOIRA: No, your idea of constancy is to love a hundred other women and at intervals to come back to me.

REX: Moira, you drove it too hard. You tied yourself and me down hand and foot. And now you say it is ended for you. Now because I've been what you call unfaithful you throw me off. And that is your idea of constancy.

MOIRA: I can't endure love without fidelity. It tortures me. I don't want to be the head of a harem. Yes, it is ended.[43]

Neith remained sexually engaged with Hutchins for many years because she was able to struggle with his double standard, but not without damage to her own sexual responsiveness and her ability to combine sexuality and intimacy. In a 1916 letter Neith explained this to Hutchins:

I *know* that your physical infidelities (beginning very early) hurt that instinctive feeling for you in me—that I wished to be reasonable about it—that I therefore tended to be more aloof in my feeling about you because otherwise it would have hurt more—that I accepted your feeling about such things as reasonable—that I didn't blame you—but shrank from it. That as time went on I didn't feel it less, but came more and more to feel that you didn't belong completely to me *nor I to you*— that this gave me a more disengaged feeling to other men—that after the Indianapolis episode I did return to you in my feeling, bore you a child and did not think of any man for seven years—that the discovery of your long-continued secret relations was a blow to me deeper than you could realize—that I *did* then in my feeling really withdraw from you and by last summer had gone so far away that I could live without you, that after our break I felt free of you and could really love another man. This is my side of it. I know your side too—my failings toward you—that's why I've never *blamed* you—why I really have no resentment. I know I am just as much at fault as you and very likely much more, but it won't help us to feel we've both been wrong—for we have— we have *both* been ignorant and careless and reckless about our relation.

By withholding intimacy Neith retained some personal integrity and leverage against Hutchins. Yet she never directly confronted Hutchins in an attempt to force him to change his sexual habits. Even for an unconventional woman like Neith, Key's and Ellis's emphases on a woman's capacity for mothering and her passivity in sexuality had a powerful pull. In 1917 she wrote to Hutchins:

I would like to be your best, dearest, truest friend—your confidant and stay in time of trouble. I think I am capable of being good in that way. But I know I wasn't good to you in the way you wanted. I remember long ago my Danish friend, Laura, said to me "You will be a good mother, but a bad sweetheart." I guess she was right. I have not the amorous imagination as you have—so I couldn't be what you wanted. I am so sorry for you, poor infant, but it has been bad for me too.

Such submissiveness to Hutchins's needs undermined Neith's own sexuality. Hutchins, to his credit, recognized this: "Her deepest passion was to construct; she needed to build, to feel that of her own will she was bringing to the relation. Her personal work, her writing, had been the way in which she felt she was herself. There it was all her own doing; if she could have felt that our relation was her construction, not mine, she would have loved me more. . . . She did not so much want to be wooed as to woo!"[44] Nonetheless, he often treated Neith like a mother. For Hutchins communion between husband and wife depended on the presence of maternal love:

> Maternal love between husband and wife does not mean, in this connection, the love for the child, but for the man for whom the woman 'feels the maternal in a primary degree, while the man feels desire for maternal love in his wife. In this kind of love the deepest satisfaction lies. It is almost as if he were still enclosed in the womb. It tends to relieve him of all irritations, anxieties, and disappointed yearnings. It encloses him, cherishes him, soothes and satisfies. This she likes to give as much as he to receive. In this close relation they know each other, it would seem, as they really are.[45]

At other times Hutchins expressed a desire to merge with and be the mother. During Neith's pregnancy, he thought: "If I could only have been with child myself! If we could have been with child together! That would have satisfied my deepest instincts, would have made us one."[46]

Though Hutchins often proclaimed his desire for mothering, his writing suggests that another part of him preferred separation: "Whenever I felt the full pain of my dependency on her . . . I had an excess of hope of attaining aloofness for myself through relations with other women—a hope, however, that has never been realized.[47] Neith's reserve and her ability to struggle with him prevented maternal merging. If she had really given in and become the mother Hutchins craved, he probably would have run away for good, afraid of his own dependency. She would have lost her sexual appeal.

Rather, Hutchins eroticized their conflicts. "The deeper relation between them," he claimed, "was founded not, on compromise, but on attraction and repulsion, on a kind of interesting warfare." Even in discussing their idyllic honeymoon, Hutchins uses sexual imagery in referring to their conflicts:

> The sensuous April quarrels, the life-giving rain of them, the hot and liquid reconciliations, the melting joy of it.[48]

Throughout their marriage Hutchins continued to eroticize their struggles. In a 1916 letter to Neith, we see how infidelity augmented his sexual attraction to her:

> I am longing to hold you in my arms tonight. . . . I'd like to forget worries in a passionate embrace. I am full of lust and love and desire to talk and hear you talk. I don't know how I can go to bed alone. Send me a gossipy letter. Tell me you love me and also tell me about the flirtations you are having. Have you been unfaithful? Have you sinned? Did you like it? Come and hug me and confess it all. Do you like me better than ever?. . . . Do you think I am a disturber? You wrote that I am turbulent? Are you sorry that I am? . . . I am naughty tonight. . . . Dear why are you not here? I'd try to give you a good time. Did I ever give you a good time? Did any other man ever do as well? Better? Do you love me? Will you always love me? Well, why don't you say so? Kiss me, hug me, closer, closer. Ah! Ah! Ah! I'm quite wild. I don't dare go to bed. This is like my early youth.

This erotic conflict maintained comfortable distance between the lovers. Sexualized warfare undermined the sexual merging that threatened the independence of them both.

"I Told You to Go Away, but if You Had Gone, I Should Have Been Much Disappointed"

Neith's ability to resist Hutchins's demands stemmed at least in part from her recognition that her relationship with him fulfilled some of her needs for intimacy without undermining the autonomy necessary for her work. The journalist and writer, Mary Heaton Vorse, a friend in their Greenwich Village circle, said in a review of *The Story of a Lover*: "One feels throughout his account, the ceaseless activity of his love, the restless and loving prying into the spirit."[49] Neith, too, in their play *Enemies* says: "You, on account of your love for me, have tyrannized over me, bothered me, badgered me, nagged me, for fifteen years. You have interfered with me, taken my time and strength, and prevented me from accomplishing great works for the good of humanity. You have crushed my soul, which longs for serenity and peace, with your perpetual complaining" (191). But Neith's ability to write these lines belies her claim that he had crushed her soul, as does her counterclaim in the same play: "To have lived together for fifteen years and never to have bored one another! To be still for one another the most interesting persons in the world! How many married people can say that?" (195).

Hutchins's active engagement was necessary to overcome the emotional withdrawal Neith had learned in her family. The conflict engendered by his constant attempts to make her more attentive to his emotional needs forced her to keep talking to him, sometimes about her pain, even when he didn't really want to hear it. She did not close him off emotionally or psychologically. Neither children, women friends, nor other men ever replaced his pivotal place in her life. Just as conflict was central to Hutchins's sexual involvement with her, conflict was a key to her intimate relationship with him.

Neith was never lonely with Hutchins. The clash between their personalities created a bond that would not have been possible with a man more like herself. Both *The Story of a Lover* and *The Bond* indicate that Neith's spiritual affairs were with men similar to her in personality—men serious about their work, "lonely and unsocial and graceless, remote and bad." Neith and Bentley, like her characters, Teresa and Crayven, spent hours together without talking. But such a meeting of lonely souls was neither sexually attractive nor conducive to a lasting relationship. As Teresa says of Crayven: "He was more sympathetic to her in many ways than Basil, she even liked him better, but she had no real emotion for him" (1908 ed., 350).

Hutchins's emotional openness created for Neith a possibility of sexualized intimacy that she did not find in other men. Through her detachment, her ability to sustain the fight with him, and her refusal to become the permanent nurturing mother, Neith achieved an imperfect, but sustaining, relationship combining sexual pleasure and psychological intimacy in a society and culture still structured by gender differentiation and hierarchy. Unfortunately, Neith's and Hutchins's conflicts about redefining housework and childcare responsibilities and about the importance of work beyond the home for a wife were much less clearly articulated and struggled over. If the couple's intimate warfare could have incorporated these issues, Neith might have felt that the marriage was more her construction rather than one in which she reacted to Hutch's sexist behavior.

"No Remarks about Fresh Eggs or Soups or Underwear with Holes in It"

As is clear from Neith's poem, she was responsible for managing their household. Hutchins's writing verifies that he criticized her lack of interest in housekeeping and tried to change her: "I dinned nervously into her my demands. I insisted on economy and regularity, an affability towards neighbors and friends."[50] Neith resisted such criticism but never demanded that Hutchins share the responsibility. Both Neith's ability to resist and her inability to envision a radical alternative to the domestic division of labor rested on the availability of household help paid for by a modest investment income and presents from Hutchins's father to supplement the erratic income from the couple's writings.

Most of Neith's novels are about upper-middle-class life where there are always servants in the background, and her autobiography mentions an Irish girl who worked for them when they were first married. Although Neith and Hutchins were always moving, they hired household help in each place and brought a nanny for the children back with them from Italy in 1908. When Hutchins's father bought them a large old house in Dobbs Ferry, they hired several Italian servants and an anarchist friend, Hippolyte Havel, as a cook. Havel would cook, serve, and then eat with Neith, Hutchins, and their guests, often criticizing those that were more bourgeois. He quit about once a month because he could not stand the regularity of family life.[51] Despite this bohemian character of their household, Neith escaped from most housework. Her daughter claims that Neith learned to cook only in 1925.[52]

Most early-twentieth-century feminists were likewise middle-class and hired less privileged women as household help. Even the most radical feminist critics in the early twentieth century, like Charlotte Perkins Gilman, did not envision men participating in housework. Parenting, however, created more conflicts for working and creative women. Hutchins reports in *The Story of a Lover* that Neith was unhappy at the discovery of her first pregnancy in the second year of their marriage, that she "hated the prattle and needs and noise of small children" (1919 ed., 93). Like Teresa in *The Bond*, however, Neith too became very attached to her child. With the children, especially her first son, Boyce, Neith felt an intimacy and peace that she never found with Hutchins. Teresa, speaking for Neith, says: "He (the husband) is one and I am another. . . . I am forever outside and he is a stranger to me, in spite of all. But this, this child of mine, is really mine. I shall understand it, it will comfort me, it will belong to me" (46).

The only autobiography Neith ever published was about her relationship with her son after his death of influenza at age seventeen. In an intimate and painful memoir, *Harry* (1923), Neith admitted that she, against Hutchins's wishes, supported Boyce's desire to gain independence by spending a summer on a western ranch.[53] When news came of his illness and death, Neith, again against Hutchins's wishes, determined that she would travel alone to the ranch to bring back the body. Boyce's death was the most devastating event in her life.

Neither in her poem nor in other writing does Neith recognize Hutchins's contribution to parenting. Neith's silence about shared parenting, in all probability, reflected her ambivalence about relinquishing any of the primary responsibilities of mothering. Although Hutchins exaggerates their role reversal, he participated more in parenting than most men. In *The Story of a Lover* he says: "I have been more of a mother, more of a housekeeper than the great majority of men. . . . And she has been more of a father than the great majority of women—she has gone out to the larger world in her thought, her imagination and her work. . . . We have worked out our common life as if there were no conventional career for either man or woman." (141). Their daughters confirmed that because of his personality, because he often worked at home, and because sometimes he didn't work, Hutchins participated in child rearing. Miriam DeWitt recalled that her father "talked to our teachers, took us to museums and the theater, held me in his arms when, for a time, I was having severe nightmares, and was always willing to talk over our problems."[54] Hutchins was especially responsible in emergencies, becoming the primary parent when Neith had a nervous breakdown and becoming a nurse and physical therapist when their second son, Charles, contracted polio.

On the other hand, there were extended periods when Hutchins left the family to experience the "low life" in the ghettos and slums, to habituate cafés and bars, and periodically to wander by himself in Europe. His behavior points to a more general cultural contradiction. Almost as prominent as the "family man" in twentieth-century U.S. culture is the wandering male who surfaces as an expatriate artist or writer in the 1920s, a radical organizer in the 1930s, a beat on the road in the 1950s, and a dropout in the 1960s and 1970s.

Yet, reading a quantity of Neith's and Hutchins's letters impressed me with their positive feelings and commitments as parents. This impression was reinforced by conversations in the mid-1980s with their living children, two daughters who were then in their seventies. At least in retrospect, the daughters, Miriam and Beatrix, view their upbringing and family life as rich and interesting. They loved the travel and their parents' many interesting friends. Miriam said: "We children grew up in conventional surroundings and were brought up in a rather conventional way, while being exposed to the unconventional ideas of our parents and their friends."[55] They liked their father's nurturing and were only occasionally resentful of their mother's devotion to work (for example, when they had inappropriate or ill-tended clothes for school). They knew nothing about their parents' unconventional sex life and the deeper conflicts in their relationship.[56]

The Silence about a Wife's Creative Work

After marriage Neith Boyce chose a career as a novelist rather than continue to be employed as a journalist. Such work was one of few acceptable choices for nineteenth-century middle-class women. "Scribbling women," as they were called by "serious" male authors, could write at home in odd hours between household duties, and their writing was not viewed as real work. Even as late as 1926 and 1927, when the *Nation* magazine invited seventeen accomplished women to explore the personal sources of their feminism, more than half were writers who worked at home and could arrange flexible schedules. "Either an independent single life—or childless marriages—and careers essentially independent of the office and time clock enabled most of the *Nation* women to pursue their goals."[57]

Neith's poem does not reveal that her resistance to housework and her dislike for the "prattle and noise of small children" was primarily the result of her need for time and solitude to write. Her daughters still remember the closed door behind which she resolutely shut herself off for part of each day to do her writing. But none of Neith's novels or short stories deal with the importance of creative work for women, nor do either of Hutchins's autobiographies say much about Neith's writing. Few of the couple's surviving letters focus on this topic, but those that do reveal a depth of emotional conflict. In response to a letter from Hutchins in 1907, for example, when she was pregnant with their third child, Neith said with defensive anger:

I work no more than one and a half hours a day, usually not that much and do not feel it a strain, but a great pleasure. As to Charles, you are mistaken when you ascribe his delicate health to my working. I did no work before his birth, except a very few days at Sienna on the "Provident Woman." If he suffers through me, it can only be through the shock of my father's death and the unhappiness of that winter at home. So when you say that on several occasions I have sacrificed the family welfare, I think you are unjust and unkind.

In *The Story of a Lover* Hutchins recognized that Neith's "personal work, her writing, had been the way in which she felt she was herself" (167). But this is the only line in the book on this topic, and Hutchins does not reveal that he feels any conflict about it. Yet in 1941 in a letter to a younger friend Hutchins complained about Neith's continuing commitment to her writing: "I don't want you to feel about your work the way she does about hers. I have known her many years and she was always the same—unless she was 'building' and visibly building, obviously building, she was if not always unhappy, at least discontented and disturbed. This is perhaps an important cause of her constant work of one kind or another."

Was Hutchins's criticism of Neith's dedication to work a reflection not only of conventional ideas about women but also of ambivalence about his own deviation from the nineteenth-century norm of male productivity—his dedication to life rather than work? *A Victorian in the Modern World* defended his "wonderful wasted life," but the use of the word *waste* is revealing. In September, 1908, while he was caring for the children, he revealed his ambivalence in a letter to Neith: "I have a good story for you to write: How a father loses his keenness for his male intellectual labors by being put in a position where he pays sympathetic attention to children, becomes feminized as it were. I feel a little tendency that way myself!" Intellectual labors were tied to "masculinity." To abandon achievement was to become "feminized."

While none of Neith's writing addressed the importance of her profession, *The Bond* expressed her criticism of Hutchins's disdain for work. Her character Teresa says: "I hate self-indulgent, sensual, self-satisfied men. I hate comfortable men. . . . I wish I knew one man who didn't care for physical pleasures. I wish I knew a good priest, or some man who was ascetic by choice, who lived hard and worked hard—who had something besides himself to think about. . . . If only I knew someone with a cause—some prophet or other" (1908 ed., 116–17). Neith seems to believe that if Hutchins had been more committed to work or a cause, he would have been less interested in extramarital sex. But he might have then been more threatened by her work and have had less time for parenting.

It might be argued that if Neith had been a less private person, a more politically active feminist (a member of Heterodoxy like her friends), she would have found communal and ideological support for dealing with her ambivalence about domesticity and for asserting the importance of her own work. Yet the professional and creative women in Heterodoxy, who met in Greenwich Village every other Saturday for lunch and discussion or a speaker, did not focus on women's conflicts about work and family. While these meetings prefigured consciousness-raising groups in that women took turns telling their life stories, there was little exploration of conflicts these new women might face. That their creative work might conflict with their own and others' expectations of them as wives, lovers or mothers was not addressed, despite one researcher's calculation that 33 percent of the members of Heterodoxy from 1912 to 1920 were divorced.[58]

One of the most politically active members of Heterodoxy, the lawyer Crystal Eastman, wrote in *Cosmopolitan* in 1923 that the only way a wife with children could prevent herself from being absorbed by marriage was to live separately from her husband: "Women, more than men, succumb to marriage. They sink so easily into that fatal habit of dependency on one person to rescue them from themselves. And this is the death of love. The two-roof plan encourages a wife to cultivate initiative in rescuing herself, to develop social courage, to look upon her life as an independent adventure and get interested in it."[59] Whether it took place under one roof or two, however, Eastman believed it was the mother's job to raise the children with her husband as only a "consulting partner."[60]

Clearly, if she had been a member of Heterodoxy, Neith would *not* have found political language or arguments that could have helped her struggle with herself and Hutch about the importance of her work, accept his more casual attitude toward achievement, and validate his participation in child rearing. Yet, another reason that neither Neith nor Heterodoxy could address these issues, was that the opening of non-domestic, creative, and professional careers for middle-class women at the beginning of the twentieth century coincided with cultural devaluation of work for its own sake and stress on the need to work for money for consumption and leisure. Cultural images of the new woman moved away from that of "spinster" to the Gibson girl, the bachelor girl, and the flapper. All of these "girls" were urban, young, temporarily single, and increasingly sensual. The real women behind these images worked for a living, but the popular media defined them only by their new uses of leisure time. Bachelor girls in particular were single, working women, but the media presented their life as one of gaiety, freedom and romance because of where they could go and what they could do *after* work.[61]

Thus, neither in radical nor popular culture were there the resources to begin a dialogue between women and men over how to combine sex, intimacy, and work within a long-term marriage or relationship. Was the cultural focus—within Greenwich Village and beyond—on individual, psychological development responsible? Were Neith, Hutchins, and their friends excessively self-involved? Did their intimate conflict indicate a withdrawal from political struggle, or a breakdown of community, family, or morality?

After studying early twentieth-century U.S. intellectuals—including some of Neith's and Hutchins's friends—cultural historians Christopher Lasch and his student T. J. Jackson Lears argue such a negative view.[62] Lasch and Lears see the origins of a modern "culture of narcissism" seeking to justify a desperate preoccupation with the self arising from a breakdown in ethical standards, community relations and male authority in the family. Hutchins's and Neith's preoccupation with their relationship—the amount of time they spent in talking about their conflicts—would be seen as "undermining larger spiritual and ethical frameworks so that the preoccupation with intense experience often devalued political action and focused discontent on exclusively personal issues."[63]

As a feminist, I cannot agree with Lasch's and Lears's assumption that the personal is not political. Women will only become an authentic part of political life when the personal issues that primarily define their lives become important subjects for public struggle. Sociologist Richard Flacks makes an even more sweeping claim for the political salience of private life. He argues that the Left in the United States has only attracted a popular following in those periods—1908–15, for example, and the 1960s—when it has developed a politics about changing and improving private, daily life—when the Left has provided a community and a place for personal growth in addition to addressing other issues of justice and liberation.[64]

Sometimes when I think of the pain Neith endured in her relationship with Hutchins, I think she would have been better off leaving him, especially since there was so little cultural support for her struggle. But I never think that their conflict indicates narcissism or the breakdown of the family. Rather, I would conceptualize the problem very differently: the level of intensity and struggle in the Boyce-Hapgood attempt to forge an intimate and equitable marriage is not one that most couples could sustain. Hence, modern marriage from its inception had an inherent instability: either intimacy and equality were sacrificed, or the relationship was likely to split. From this perspective Hutch's and Neith's marriage was exceptional. The "warfare" between them was a creative struggle for the possibility of a more fulfilling personal life out of cultural, familial, and psychological resources that were both rich and problematic. As they suggest in the titles of the plays they wrote together, *Dialogue* and *Enemies*, Neith and Hutch were enemies—a man and woman engaged in warfare, but a kind of warfare that involved an exceedingly intimate dialogue. This contradiction—of a dialogue between enemies, a warfare that was intimate and nondestructive—embodies their cultural and personal creativity, despite limitations.

Notes

1. A few examples of this negative perspective include: ABC-TV documentaries: "The American Family: An Endangered Species," Fall 1978; "The Crisis in American Education," Fall 1984; "After the Sexual Revolution," August, 1986. Other examples are: Gwenda Blair, "Warm Ties Weren't Enough . . . I Found More," *Mother Jones*, (May 31, 1983); Ellen Willis, "Handle with Care: We Need a Child-rearing Movement," *Village Voice* (July 15, 1986); "Feminism's Identity Crisis," *Newsweek* (March 31, 1986); "Too Late for Prince Charming," *Newsweek* (June 2, 1986).

2. Joseph Freeman, *An American Testament* (London: Victor Glancz, 1938), 251-252.

3. May 15, 1898, letter from Hutchins Hapgood to his mother, in the Hapgood collection, Collection of American Literature, Beinecke Rare Book and Manuscript Library, Yale University. This and all subsequent letters of Hutchins Hapgood and Neith Boyce are reprinted with the library's permission and that of Beatrix Faust, the surviving daughter of Neith Boyce and Hutchins Hapgood.

4. Neith Boyce, "Autobiography," in the Hapgood collection, Collection of American Literature, Beinecke Rare Book and Manuscript Library, Yale University. Excerpts from it are reprinted with the library's permission.

5. Hutchins Hapgood, *A Victorian in the Modern World* (1939; reprint, Seattle: University of Washington Press, 1972), 16.

6. Neith Boyce Hapgood, *Story of an American Family: Letter and Commentary on the Hapgood Family, 1648–1917* (Chicopee, Mass.: Brown-Murphy, 1953).

7. Boyce, "Autobiography," 75.

8. Robert Allen Skotheim, Introduction to *A Victorian in the Modern World*.

9. Selections from Hutchins Hapgood's *The Story of a Lover* (New York: Boni and Liveright, 1919) and Neith Boyce's *The Bond* (New York: Duffield, 1908) are reprinted in this volume. Unless otherwise indicated, page numbers of these works are from the Feminist Press edition.

10. Warren Susman, " 'Personality' and the Making of Twentieth-century Culture," in *New Directions in American Intellectual History*, ed. John Higham and Paul Conklin, 213–17 (Baltimore: Johns Hopkins University Press, 1979).

11. Linda Gordon, *Woman's Body, Woman's Right: A Social History of Birth Control in America*. (New York: Penguin, 1977).

12. For a good discussion of these developments during the nineteenth century, see John D'Emilio and Estelle Freedman, *Intimate Matters: A History of Sexuality in America* (New York: Harper and Row, 1988), pt. 2.

13. D'Emilio and Freeman, *Intimate Matters*, 84. In Amherst, Massachusetts, for example, Mabel Todd and Austin Dickinson (brother of Emily Dickinson) carried on an extramarital sexual love affair for more than a decade in the 1880s and early 1890s. They justified their affair in such highly idealized and spiritual terms. See *Austin and Mabel: The Amherst Affair and Love Letters of Austin Dickinson and Mabel Loomis Todd*, ed. Polly Longsworth (New York: Farrar, Strauss and Giroux, 1984).

14. John Gillis, *For Better, For Worse: British Marriages, 1600 to the Present* (New York: Oxford University Press, 1985), 233.

15. See Niklas Luhmann, *Love as Passion: The Codification of Intimacy* (Cambridge, England: Polity Press, 1986).

16. More than one hundred women were members of Heterodoxy between 1912 and 1917. There is no record that Neith Boyce was a member, but some of her close associates were. Mabel Dodge, Mary Heaton Vorse, Susan Glaspell, Crystal Eastman, and Ida Rauh (the first wife of Max Eastman) were all members. See Judith Schwarz, *Radical Feminists of Heterodoxy: Greenwich Village, 1912-1940*, 2nd ed. (Norwich, Vt.: New Victoria Publishers, 1986.)

17. Nancy Cott, *The Grounding of Modern Feminism* (New Haven Conn.: Yale University Press, 1987) 42, 45.

18. For examples, see: Mary Austin, *No. 26 Jayne Street* (Boston: Houghton Mifflin, 1920); Mabel Dodge Luhan, *Movers and Shakers*, vol. 3 of *Intimate Memories* (1936, reprint, Albuquerque: University of New Mexico Press, 1985); Ellen Kay Trimberger, "Feminism, Men, and Modern Love: Greenwich Village, 1900-1925," in *Powers of Desire: The Politics of Sexuality*, ed. Ann Snitow, Christine Stansell, and Sharon Thompson, 131–52 (New York: Monthly Review Press, 1983).

19. Ellen Key, *Love and Marriage* (New York: G. P. Putnam's Sons, 1911), 20, 23.

20. Cott, *Grounding of Modern Feminism*, 49.

21. Quoted in Sheila Rowbotham and Jeffrey Weeks, *Socialism and the New Life: The Personal and Sexual Politics of Edward Carpenter and Havelock Ellis* (London: Pluto Press, 1977), 170.

22. Rowbotham and Weeks, *Socialism and the New Life*, 169.

23. Rowbotham and Weeks, *Socialism and the New Life*, 112.

24. Key, *Love and Marriage*, 217, 228.

25. Quoted in Rowbotham and Weeks, *Socialism and the New Life*, 171.

26. Floyd Dell, *Women as World Builders* (Chicago: Robes, 1913).

27. See Ellen DuBois and Linda Gordon, "Seeking Ecstasy on the Battlefield: Danger and Pleasure in Nineteenth-century Feminist Sexual Thought," *Feminist Studies* 9, no. 1 (Spring 1983); Caroll Smith Rosenberg, "The New Woman as Androgyne: Social Disorder and Gender Crisis, 1870–1936," *Disorderly Conduct* (New York: Oxford University Press, 1985). My earlier article, "Feminism, Men, and Modern Love," also took this position.

28. For accounts of some of these relationships, see the following: Blanche Wiesen Cook, *Crystal Eastman: On Women and Revolution* (New York: Oxford University Press, 1978); Augusta Fink, *I-Mary: A Biography of Mary Austin* (Tucson: University of Arizona Press, 1983); Dee Garrison, ed., *Rebel Pen: The Writings of Mary Heaton Vorse* (New York: Monthly Review Press, 1985); Justin Kaplan, *Lincoln Steffens: A Biography* (New York: Simon and Schuster, 1974); Robert Rosenstone, *Romantic Revolutionary: A Biography of John Reed* (New York: Vintage, 1975); Lois Rudnick, *Mabel Dodge Luhan: New Woman, New Worlds* (Albuquerque: University of New Mexico Press, 1984); Alice Wexler, *Emma Goldman: An Intimate Life* (New York: Pantheon, 1984).

29. This poem is in the Hapgood collection, Collection of American Literature, Beinecke Rare Book and Manuscript Library, Yale University. It is printed here with the permission of the library and Beatrix Faust.

30. Boyce, "Autobiography," 159.

31. Eleven percent of women born in the United States between 1860 and 1880 never married, the highest percentage in American history until perhaps the 1970s and 1980s. Ellen Rothman, *Hands and Heart: A History of Courtship in America* (New York: Basic Books, 1984), 249.

32. Neith's and Hutchins's families were in different ways dominated by the mother. This pattern was far from unique. Several studies of the Greenwich Village circle before World War I find a dominant pattern among the families from which these rebels came. One study of eighty-eight Villagers (including Neith and Hutchins) found that two-thirds of them were raised in households considered female-dominated. According to the study, "that domination was not the saccharine consequence of 'sentimental veneration of women'; it flowed, rather, from the personal force of the mothers and from the absence or

startling weakness of the fathers." See Kenneth Lynn, "The Rebels of Greenwich Village," *Perspectives in American History*, 8 (1974): 366.

33. Boyce, "Autobiography," 51.

34. See Nancy Chodorow, *The Reproduction of Mothering* (Berkeley: University of California Press, 1978.

35. Luhan, *Movers and Shakers*, 47.

36. Hapgood, *A Victorian in the Modern World*, 349.

37. Page numbers of quotations from *Dialogue* and *Enemies* are from the Feminist Press edition of the plays, reprinted in this volume.

38. *The Story of a Lover*, 161.

39. Letter to Mary Berenson (March 6, 1909) in the Berenson collection, Collection of American Literature Beinecke Rare Book and Manuscript Library, Yale University. It is reprinted here with the library's permission.

40. This letter, written in December, 1915, is in the Mabel Dodge Luhan collection in the Beinecke Rare Book and Manuscript Library, Yale University. It is excerpted here with the library's permission.

41. Letter to Neith Boyce (1913), Hapgood collection.

42. For further discussion of Mabel's and Neith's struggles with infidelity, see my essay, "The New Woman and the New Sexuality: Conflict and Contradiction in the Writings and Lives of Mabel Dodge and Neith Boyce," in *The Cultural Moment: 1915*, ed. Lois Rudnick and Adele Heller (New Brunswick, N.J.: Rutgers University Press, 1991).

43. Unpublished manuscript in Hapgood collection, Collection of American Literature, Beinecke Rare Book and Manuscript Library, Yale University. Excerpted here with the permission of the library and Beatrix Faust.

44. Hapgood, *Story of a Lover*, 167.

45. Hapgood, *A Victorian in the Modern World*, 418.

46. Hapgood, *Story of a Lover*, 1919 ed., 52. For a theoretical discussion of the relationship between female mothering and the construction of male and female sexuality, see: Chodorow, *Reproduction of Mothering*, pt. 3; Dorothy Dinnerstein, *The Mermaid and the Minotaur: Sexual Arrangements and Human Malaise* (New York: Harper and Row, 1976), chap. 4.

47. Hapgood, *Story of a Lover*, 155.

48. Hapgood, *Story of a Lover*, 1919 ed., 33.

49. *New York Sun: Books and Book World* (September 28, 1919): 1.

50. Hapgood, *Story of a Lover*, 1919 ed., 95.

51. Hapgood, *A Victorian in the Modern World*, 329.

52. Letter from Miriam DeWitt to Ellen Kay Trimberger, 1989.

53. Neith Boyce, *Harry* (New York: Thomas Seltzer, 1923).

54. Letter to Ellen Kay Trimberger, 1989.

55. Letter to Ellen Kay Trimberger, 1989.

56. Personal interview with Miriam DeWitt and Beatrix Faust, Provincetown, Massachusetts, June, 1983.

57. Elaine Showalter, ed., *These Modern Women: Autobiographical Essays from the Twenties* (New York: The Feminist Press, 1978), 17.

58. Schwarz, *Radical Feminists of Heterodoxy*, 60.

59. Blanche Wiesen Cook, ed., *Crystal Eastman on Women and Revolution* (New York: Oxford University Press, 1978), 80.

60. Cook, *Crystal Eastman*, 78.

61. Carolyn Forrey, "The New Woman Revisited," *Women's Studies* 2 (1974): 45.

62. T. J. Jackson Lears, *No Place of Grace: Antimodernism and the Transformation of American Culture, 1880–1926* (New York: Pantheon, 1981); Christopher Lasch, *The New Radicalism in America, 1889–1963* (New York: Vintage, 1967).

63. Lears, *No Place of Grace*, 160.

64. Richard Flacks, *Making History: The American Left and the American Mind* (New York: Columbia University Press, 1988).

SELECTIONS FROM
THE BOND

IN 1908 NEITH BOYCE PUBLISHED her novel *The Bond*, which probed the marital conflicts of a young married couple, Basil and Teresa, both artists of the upper-middle class. Within their marriage there is a separation that is still Victorian and quite distinct from the late-twentieth-century norms for couples. Husband and wife have separate bedrooms and some independent social and work activities. They are seated apart at dinner parties. Among these artists, however, it is now acceptable for the wife to socialize with other men friends. The husband, likewise, can have women friends.

What is new about Teresa's and Basil's relationship is the attempt to forge a deep psychological intimacy in their marriage. They talk constantly about their feelings, positive and negative, about each other; they talk about their attractions to others; they show each other love letters from admirers; and they are open about their jealousies. Sexual passion between them is less openly expressed in the novel, but it is an indirect theme. This intensity in marriages even when it causes conflict, is portrayed as essential to fulfillment in life.

Even more modern in Teresa's concern with maintaining personal autonomy despite her commitments as wife and mother. Autonomy and the ability to maintain power vis-à-vis Basil is a prerequisite for the continuation of their sexual and intimate bond. Teresa creates the possibility of an affair for herself to counter Basil's flirtation with another woman. Only by thus balancing the account could she renew their relationship.

That such themes were ahead of her time is seen from the contemporary reviews of *The Bond*. Short reviews in the *New York Times*, the *Nation* and the *Dial* were hostile. None of the reviewers were sympathetic to the wife's search for autonomy; none saw the conflicts between husband and wife as positive or progressive.

The *New York Times* said the book was about the marriage of two young artists who "bicker, quarrel, jar and nag."[1] An anonymous reviewer in the *Nation* characterized the book as a little drama of matrimony between two with artistic temperaments. He asked: "Is it a sign of the feminization of our popular literature that it should give such earnest attention to the intellectual fribbles and emotional 'hoboes' who may be observed in any great city hanging picturesquely upon the skirts of Art?"[2] The most negative was by William Morton Payne in the *Dial*:

The Bond has four parts. Parts 2 and 4 will be reprinted here in their entirety. The novel was originally published by Duffield and Company, New York, in 1908.

We are getting a little tired of the neurotic young woman who makes unreasonable demands upon life, and is unhappy because it turns out to be less exciting than she would like to find it. A typical example of this sort of woman, who worries over her own emotions until her whole moral fiber is weakened, is found in the heroine of *The Bond*. . . . The young woman in this particular case has health, a devoted husband, and an artistic gift of her own as a refuge from vagrant thoughts. She is, in fact, so happy when first introduced to us that she is quite sure that it cannot last, and deliberately sets out to make herself miserable by brooding over an imaginary future of misery. This morbid type of character occurs, of course, as a by-product of the life which we moderns lead at such high pressure, and the novelist has a right to describe it; but she can hardly expect it to appeal to the sympathy of sane and balanced minds. The heroine's destiny is worked out, after a fashion, without external disaster, and she comes to a sort of broken-spirited acceptance of life as it is. We could wish that the author's delicate talent had been employed upon a worthier theme, or a theme bearing a closer relation to normal existence.[3]

None of the reviewers mentions the couple's open and mutual experiments in infidelity and their attempts to negotiate the jealousy it aroused. In 1908 it was not yet acceptable, even in intellectual and artistic circles, for a woman to combat the double standard.

The novel begins when Basil and Teresa Ransome have been married one year. Basil is an attractive, personable man of thirty, gay and interested in life and people. He is a serious, but not great, painter. He does portraits, both for the money and for the artistic challenge of trying to capture the psychological core of his subject. Basil also draws ethnic and working-class street life. Teresa is a few years younger, also very attractive and witty, but she is moody and emotional. She molds small, decorative bronze statues and makes jewelry. Her career and artistic commitments are clearly secondary to Basil's, but she is not a subordinated wife. Teresa rebuffs Basil's complaints about her lack of domesticity and tries to protect her independence.

The opening scenes of the book focus *not* on Teresa and Basil's relationship but on a flirtation between Basil and Mrs. Perry, a wealthy, slightly older, unhappily married woman. Soon we are introduced as well to Crayven, a visiting English governor of an Arab province, who is attracted to Teresa. Basil and Teresa are engaged by the "difference" of these two. Mrs.

Perry is world-weary, spiritual, and mysterious. Crayven is quiet and remote and represents for Teresa "a simpler, less nervous life, more primitive with harsher externals, more space and freedom" (1908 ed., 105).

Teresa and Basil are part of a bohemian community that includes political activists (Teresa's feminist Aunt Sophy and a Russian anarchist) and nonconformists (Gerald Dallas, an alcoholic friend, and Erhart, an unsuccessful sculptor). Yet the Ransomes have rich friends, too, and are invited to dinner parties in mansions. They live in a small apartment but have a live-in housekeeper/cook and money for expensive clothes and vacations.

Two themes dominate part 1: the possibilities of adultery and divorce; and the conflict between Teresa's rational ideal of a marriage where both partners are free and independent and her emotional experience of increasing dependency on Basil.

Teresa had initially resisted marriage to Basil, but during their first year of marriage she has fallen more deeply in love with him. She tries to hold on to her ideals to counter Aunt Sophy's critique of marriage as a hideous state of bondage. For Teresa, "marriage was very simple. You married a person you adored, and even if he lost his temper sometimes over a beef steak or a missing shirt, he was still the most charming person in the world" (1908 ed., 90–91). But awareness of her emotional dependency makes Teresa anxious and jealous. As she and Basil are enjoying a beautiful day in the country to celebrate their anniversary, Teresa becomes preoccupied with the thought that other women will fall in love with him. She blurts out, "You're always wanting something new, always being interested in new people. Some day you'll be tired of me" (1908 ed., 95).

Teresa is also upset by how Basil looks at women on the street and how they respond to him: "She hated the interested, appraising look that betrayed a whole past of fleeting encounters, of fugitive souvenirs" (1908 ed., 30). To counter her dependency Teresa takes a perverse pleasure in getting angry and disturbing Basil: "It was necessary to make Basil a little miserable before making him happy" (1908 ed., 29).

Neith contrasts the personal liberation sought by the artistic, sensual, and nondomestic Teresa to the outdated politics of Aunt Sophy. Sophy demonstrates, gives speeches, and is a political organizer for women's rights, but she is portrayed as a slightly absurd woman, rigid and staid, with no psychological insight. Teresa dismisses Sophy's criticism of men, telling Sophy that men are more interesting than women. Yet fifty pages later we hear Teresa say, "Sometimes I hate all men. . . . I hate self-indulgent, sensual, self-satisfied men. I wish I knew one man who didn't care for physical pleasures. . . . I wish I knew a good priest or some man who was ascetic by choice, who lived hard, and worked hard – who had something besides himself to think about" (1908 ed., 116).

Part 1 concludes with Teresa's dismay at an unplanned pregnancy. She says to Basil, "I hate babies. . . . We'll both be slaves" (1908 ed., 132–33).

Notes

1. *New York Times*, June 13, 1908, 335.
2. *Nation*, May 7, 1908, 427.
3. *Dial*, August 16, 1908, 91.

Part II

I

With the first cold days of autumn, the Ransomes were settled again in town. Teresa brought back from a long lazy summer in the country blooming health and content. Peace of soul and body had wrapped her round. A calm like that of summer nature itself had grown upon her, after the troubled and passionate spring. She was conscious of withdrawing herself from all that could disturb her, of retreating within herself, gathering her forces, mental and physical, for her solitary ordeal.

One day soon after her return Alice Blackley came to see her, fresh from the sea and a summer at St. Moritz, elaborately dressed, and ready to condole.

"You're looking well, though – really well," she said. "How do you manage it? Most women look such frights. And that dress is clever. Why, actually you look – perfectly presentable!"

And she examined curiously Teresa's long sweeping dress of dark violet crêpe, pleated in innumerable narrow folds, flowing out from the square-cut neck to the hem. Teresa smiled.

"I should never dare, myself," said Alice.

"Why not?"

"Oh, a thousand reasons. First, I might lose my figure. Then think of the frightful bother of it all – babies do upset a house so. Then, I should be afraid—terribly afraid. To think what women go through! I don't see how they can do it, unless they want a child most awfully, and I know some do. But I don't. Aren't you afraid, Teresa?"

"I don't think about it," said Teresa dreamily.

"But how can you help it? And you know you can't get away from it, and it comes nearer every day—"

"The sooner it will be over. It's all in the day's work."

"But one *needn't*, you know, unless one likes. And I could never make up my mind to it. Think of the responsibility! To call another human being into this world by our own will, perhaps to suffer—"

Teresa looked at Alice's pretty, empty face and large, inquisitive, stupid eyes.

"Perhaps it isn't by our own will—perhaps it's something bigger," she said, as though to herself.

"Oh, Teresa, you are not religious—!"

"No, but—the world is vast and—mysterious. It has been going on such a long time, think, and always in the same way! Who is any one of us, after all, to set herself against the current of things? It's easier to go with the tide—to let one's self go—"

Teresa stretched out her arms with a vague, sensuous gesture and sighed.

"I can't understand it," said Alice. "Is Basil pleased?"

"I believe he is."

"Of course. There's more paternal instinct than maternal, I think, and no wonder, as they've none of the bother of it. I believe Horace would like to have fifty children, if he'd married somebody else. But he knows I won't. . . . What shall you do all this winter to amuse yourself, Teresa? Shan't you be awfully bored?"

"Perhaps. People will come and see me, I suppose. And I shall do some work—little things. I began a bust of Basil, but that must wait, now, till afterwards."

"Well, I'm glad to see you so happy about it. I shall send you something pretty for the baby. And you'll come and dine with us soon, won't you—just ourselves? Give my love to Basil. Has he been working?"

"Oh, yes. He's doing some panels now for a bungalow that Mrs. Perry's building down on her Long Island place."

Alice looked suddenly interested.

"Bungalow? But I thought she was building a big house in stone."

"Yes, but the bungalow is a bachelors' house near the main one. She has big crowds staying with her always."

"And what is it like—the bungalow?"

"Decorations all American Indian—Navajo blankets, pottery, baskets, what not—and half a dozen panels, landscapes, old Indian hunting grounds."

"Have you seen her place?"

"Yes, we've been there two or three times for a few days."

"Oh, you know her, too? Do you like her? I thought she was Basil's flame."

"I like her. Basil does, too, I imagine."

"And she likes him? Aren't you jealous? They say she's fascinating. I've just barely met her."

Teresa smiled. "I couldn't be jealous any more," she said. "All that seems so foolish, now."

"Then you were jealous? . . . I wonder what it's like! I couldn't possibly be jealous of Horace, could I? But, of course, Basil's different. I don't think I should want a handsome man for a husband. Husbands ought to be useful. What's *hers* like?"

"Mrs. Perry's husband? Oh, he's useful, I suppose. He's a peevish man, with nervous prostration. He travels nearly all the time. He seems to be interested in nothing but his symptoms and archaeology. He's writing a book on the Hittites. I believe he's a good banker, too."

"Well, I don't see what she has to complain of. I hear she's rather too gay. I should look after Basil, if I were you."

"No, you wouldn't," smiled Teresa.

This, too, Alice could not understand, and she went away, convinced that Teresa did not want the baby, and that she was profoundly jealous of Mrs. Perry, but dissembled out of pride.

When she had gone, Teresa began to walk up and down the room, sighing a little wearily. She moved with the pathetic clumsiness of a naturally graceful woman, slowly, the sombre dress rippling about her and hiding the lines of her body. Her head drooped as though owning the weight of her burden, yet its poise on the long throat had a touching dignity. She sighed, for she was beginning to feel the cramping conditions of the city, after her free and quiet summer. She did not like now to go out into the streets. She drove up every day to the Park, and walked there in quiet byways; but she missed her physical freedom, the exhilaration of quick motion, and the irresponsible gaiety of her former life. A touch of mysticism, new to her, helped her to feel that this experience must compensate for itself; and, in resigning her own clear individual preferences, in bowing to a necessity which seemed to lie in the life of love she had chosen, she felt the breath of a wider, vaguer horizon. The world was greater to her, more terrible, but more inspiring, because of this force that compelled her, to which her will submitted. But joy had always lain for her in the free expression of her will and the sense of her own power; her submission could not be joyous. Her face was that of a pensive Madonna. Its outline was fuller, and the narrow eyes had lost their gaiety, their hint of wildness. She did not think much about the child to come. It had not begun to seem an entity to her until, lately, she had made some clothes for it. A queer feeling of tenderness for it woke in her as she sewed real lace about the necks of its tiny dresses, and mysterious tears fell on the muslin.

She was thinking now about a night, just before their return to town, when another feeling about the child had come to her. It was a bright moonlight night, and she was walking on the verandah of their cottage, facing a little inlet of the Sound that glittered restlessly as the tide came in and rocked the sailboat anchored some way from the land. Charles Page, the young architect, had come down to dine and spend the night, and he and Basil were in the living room, smoking—Teresa now could not bear the smell of tobacco—and talking lazily, but interestedly. She glanced in now and then at them in the lamplight; they had forgotten her. They were stretched out in two long chairs, the whisky decanter and a box of cigars near by. It was late; Teresa was supposed to have gone to bed; they were too busy talking to observe her silent passing outside. Now and then she heard a fragment of their talk—they were globe-trotting, and their reminiscences of youth and many lands were familiar echoes. Basil showed Page a Japanese pipe, a light dainty thing, such as the women smoke, and Teresa could see the words form on his lips, and the smile, and she could see the picture—the little pale woman, formal and soft, waking in the night, emptying the pipe with a few breaths, and laying it down—.

And all at once the feeling had come to her: "He is one and I am another—I am forever outside, and he is a stranger to me, in spite of all. But *this*, this child of mine, is really mine. I shall understand it, it will comfort me, it will belong to me. I shall not need him so much." And the feeling had brought her a new peace, and the power to look at Basil more impersonally, to be grateful for his deep and real love of her, to think of him with almost maternal tenderness. The child, too, in time, would have needs that she could not satisfy, and live its life away from her—and yet it, too, she thought, would always love her.

But between her and Basil something had happened—the first weakening of the physical bond that unites two who are necessary and sufficient to one another. She did not altogether realize it herself. She thought no more about it than she could help, but it saddened her, and touched the cup of physical suffering that she must drink with a strange bitterness. The cost of love was after all, perhaps, in proportion to its sweetness; but one paid, not for love, but for the awful physical force that moved the human world, for its blind, impersonal hunger, for its primeval riot—

So the world was made—so it must go on—and the tyranny of that necessity drove men like sheep. The will to live, of life conscious and unconscious, the physical instinct, cruel, wasteful, and careless—at times it seemed to her to make of human beings mere foolish puppets, without will or dignity. If this *was* the world, who would suffer to carry it on? Except that one must—

Was it possible that she, too, had been caught in the mesh spread for all, and that love, that had seemed all joy and lightness, was only a cynical bait, set to entangle one?

When such thoughts beset her, she wished that she were religious, that she might see spirit and meaning governing the world, instead of brute force; but she could not see it. Happily, her dark moods were rather rare.

Basil came in now before the shadow had fairly settled upon her, and his caressing look and touch made her cheerful again. It was a point of pride with her that he should not feel her a burden, now that she was not going out. She liked him to go, and to come back and entertain her with accounts of his doings; and Basil readily adopted her own theory, that she was never bored with her own society. Now, as he dressed for dinner, she lay on his bed and talked to him; dictated what waistcoat he should wear, and tied his white tie. She told him of Alice's visit.

"Alice is an idiot," he said warmly. "She ought to have a baby herself. It's what she needs, only she doesn't know it, and I've told her so."

"You have a panacea for all feminine ills, haven't you?" said Teresa, with quiet sarcasm. "Marriage for those who aren't married, and babies for those who haven't babies—"

'That's right—that's what they all want, if they haven't got 'em."

"Then women are divided into two classes—those who have worries, and those who want them."

"Yes, and the last state is worse than the first."

"I wonder," said Teresa, stretching her arms wearily. "For me—I've always had more than I wanted."

"You're a lucky girl—don't put your arms up that way, dearest. You know—"

"Oh, be quiet, Basil! I'm so tired of having to think all the time about *it!*"

"Never mind, dearest, it won't be long, now." He came over to kiss her tenderly.

"Long? Ah, yet it will be—four months, and then *that* at the end—"

"Dearest, dearest, I wish I could do it for you."

"Yes, you do, you old silly!"

"I do, honestly. I'd like to be a woman for a while—it must be a tremendous experience."

"I'm not sure that all brands of experience are desirable."

"Well, *you* are all the better for all you've had—more interesting, sweeter, more beautiful. You were always pretty, but now you're beautiful."

She smiled pensively.

"And now I must go on, or I shall be late. Good-night, my love. I wish you were going, too."

"Good-night. Don't make love to Mrs. Perry."

She held him close for a moment, kissed his eyelids gently, and let him go with a smile.

II

The winter passed pleasantly enough for her. Plenty of people came to the house, and there were many of the little dinners she enjoyed, where two, three, or more men came in informally and talked of their own affairs, or those of the nation, with varying degrees of effectiveness.

Nearly all these men were of the sort that, as she said, "lived by their wits." They were civilised, sophisticated, a little hard, living the rapid life of the city; and few of them had reached the age of forty, at which the pace would begin to tell against them. She liked their free speech, and the reflection of their intense and interested lives. Erhart came often, and rather bored here by his large and massive egotism; he did not fit in well with the others. He was, Basil said, too purely the artist type. Gerald Dallas came back, looking much older, quieter than ever, with more than his old devotion. Teresa was for him, she felt, not merely an attractive woman engaged in the laudable but disabling work of child-bearing; she was an individuality which, once for all, had taken its place among the great facts of his life. His feeling for her was above any accident of her own life, or his. He never spoke of it, but in every other way he showed how important she was to him. The quiet hours they spent together were consoling to Teresa. Gerald's deep melancholy was like the effect of an autumn evening, of rainy woods, dark gliding streams, and the dull sunset gleam of defeat. He was a beaten man, but in many moods his sadness was more congenial to Teresa than Basil's buoyant optimism. Deep within her was a conviction that life, if it must be taken seriously, was a desperate business. Gerald seemed to her to fail not ignobly, for he at least had vision. He was one of the few people whom she could imagine existing after death. The world had obviously no use for him, but if there could conceivably be a better world, she thought Gerald suited to inhabit it. As a frivolous expression of this idea she modelled one day a little statuette of him, with wings, a halo round his bald forehead and a harp in his hand, which made him merry, for the first time since his illness.

· · · · ·

On an evening when February was melting into March in a wild storm of snow, sleet, and wind, Basil came in just before dinner and found Teresa standing by the window. She turned a ghostly face upon him.

"The baby is going to be born to-night," she said, "I've sent for the doctor and the nurse."

Basil turned as white as she and looked much more terrified.

"When did you telephone?—perhaps you're mistaken?—what time did it begin?—why doesn't he come?" he cried. "I'll telephone again."

He did so, but the specialist was out, and wouldn't be in for an hour. Basil paced the flat in an agony of nervous helplessness. Theresa stood silently by the window, leaning against the frame, looking out on the whirl of sleet that dashed against the glass. Now and then she moved slightly, but made no sound.

The nurse arrived, and Basil dashed out, got a cab, and drove off in pursuit of the doctor; ran him down, and haled him post-haste to the flat; where he pronounced that he would not be needed for many hours to come, and to Basil's dismay went off again. Two figures flickered before Basil's eyes: the nurse, calm and smiling, in her white uniform, moving swiftly about in Teresa's room; and Teresa, in her trailing black dress, walking slowly up and down the drawing room, and perfectly silent. She did not reply to Basil's anxious questions, and hardly looked at him. He wandered about in a lost way. Dinner stood untasted in the dining-room. He looked into Teresa's room. It was flooded with electric light. All the orange shades, and his wife's other little vanities, had been taken away. The bed stood out bleak and chill, with tightly drawn white sheets. The air smelt of drugs. This was no more the chamber of love, but a torture-chamber. Basil forgot what he had meant to ask the nurse, and went away with tears in his eyes.

It was a long night. No one thought of sleep. Toward morning the doctor came to stay. Teresa, exhausted, dozed for moments at a time, sitting on the couch in the drawing-room, holding Basil's hand; but after a few instants of semi-consciousness her eyes would start upon, her pale face flush red, and Basil lifted her up, while she leaned her weight upon him and gasped, her lips tight closed. This went on for hours. . . . Seeing her exhaustion, Basil once poured out a glass of champagne and begged her to drink it. But Teresa, as the agony seized her again, blazed up for a moment, snatched the glass and flung the champagne in Basil's face and the goblet across the room, where it shivered to pieces.

"Dearest!" he murmured humbly.

Teresa looked at him murderously, then suddenly caught hold of him, and sobbed under her breath. . . .

The livid dawn brought in a grey morning of storm. They took Teresa away, into the room. Basil was sent out two or three times on hasty errands. He swallowed a cup of coffee, standing in the dining-room. Mary the cook sat there with her apron to her eyes, mumbling a prayer. He looked at her with terrified eyes.

"You don't think she's going to die, do you?" he said angrily.

"Oh, no, Heaven forbid, but it do be so long," gasped the girl.

He went back and waited outside the door. He heard the doctor's voice, now quick and brusque, as he gave an order; now curiously gentle, as though he spoke to a child. . . .

All night she had not make a sound of pain. And, now, when the chloroform had put her will to sleep, and the voice began, Basil thought at first it was some animal crying in the street. It was with a horrible leap of the heart that he realised it—*that* was Teresa's voice. It sounded to him as though it came from far away—a wail from some cruel dark world of woe and anguish. And it went on and on. . . .

Then came a shrill scream that seemed to tear the heart out of his breast—another—and another. Then silence. . . . He leaned against the door, faint with terror.

The nurse came out to him after a time and said smiling, "You have a fine boy." He seized both her hands and began to weep hysterically. . . . Later, they let him in to see Teresa. She lay with her eyes closed. His tears fell on her hands. She murmured: "The jaws of death – the jaws of death – I'm all ground and chewed to atoms, Basil. I feel as if I had died –"

He could say nothing. The baby, about which he had not thought at all, began to cry. The nurse was bathing it, and she held it out for Basil to see – a red, angry creature, with bristles of black hair and pale-blue eyes. It shrieked lustily with wide-open mouth.

"Let me see him," said Teresa faintly.

The nurse brought the baby; and after one curious look of inspection, the young mother remarked: "How very hideous he is. Take him away."

· · · · ·

A week later Teresa confided to Basil, tearfully, that she did not like the baby, and that she was sure he was going to be a frightful nuisance and spoil their life together. She complained viciously, too, of her continued physical sufferings and weakness and her disturbed nights. She had braced herself with all her strength for the great ordeal of giving birth; and the minor discomforts and annoyances which followed she resented as something not taken into the bargain.

Basil groaned, and buried his face in the pillow beside her. He had caught a fearful cold on the night of the baby's birth, and he had had no rest or peace since. His household was disorganised, he was nervously anxious about the baby, which encountered the usual difficulties in adapting itself to a new environment, and signaled its displeasure by fairly continuous screaming; and Teresa's rebellion was the final straw.

"You see I was right," Teresa said weakly, "and you were wrong. You're always so cocksure with your theories! You were sure I should love the baby, and I don't believe you even like it yourself."

"I wish you'd keep quiet," growled Basil. "I think you're very silly. Why don't you make the best of things?"

"I won't. I never will make the best of things. It's a horrid confession of weakness. I insist on seeing them as they are. You're afraid to. You know we were perfectly happy before –"

She stopped, and two tears grew in her eyes and wandered down her cheeks. In spite of her physical uneasiness, she had the strange new beauty that women buy with the birth-pangs. Her white skin glowed with freshness, her lips were fuller and redder, and the two thick dark braids of hair lying across her shoulders framed an oval of cheeks and chin, exquisitely youthful and tender.

The baby, which was being carried about in the next room, a pathetic bundle of flannel over the nurse's brawny arm, now lifted up its voice again, and Teresa cried: "For heaven's sake, Basil, shut the doors! If that creature cries any more, I shall go mad!"

But it was time for the baby to be fed, and the nurse remorselessly brought it in. Teresa sulkily turned on her side and stretched out her arm to receive it. But when the baby, with whimpering eagerness and frantic clutches of its fingers, had settled to the breast, she looked down on it and smiled half unwillingly.

"How cuddly it is! So soft and warm! If only it wouldn't howl so—I wouldn't mind so much if it were always like this."

At the change in her voice Basil raised his head.

"Poor little thing, it's because it's hungry, or has the colic—I should think you'd be sorry for it," he said reproachfully.

Teresa lifted the baby's wrinkled red hands and listened to the small sound of sensuous content which it made in feeding.

"He sings just like a kettle—or an asthmatic kitten," she said, looking amused.

Basil's tired face, showing deep lines of nervous and physical strain, changed, too, as he looked at the picture of Teresa and the baby—her profile, with the long braid across the cheek, her ivory-white gleaming shoulders and breast, her dark lashes drooping a she gazed at the child with a quizzical smile in which emotion stirred—physical pleasure and perhaps a spiritual tenderness.

"You don't know how beautiful you are," said Basil, in a low, rapt tone.

She looked up at him softly, put up her free arm, and drew his head down on her full breast.

"If I'm more beautiful for you, I don't mind it all," she said. "All the babies in the world aren't worth you."

III

Teresa, however, took the baby seriously, and by dint of this conscientious care began to be fond of him. She resigned herself to the task of nursing him, supervised minutely the details of his daily life, and carried out Basil's theory that the baby must be saved all nervous excitement. He was named Ronald Grange, after her father. In the course of a few weeks he lost his black bristles and began to acquire a fuzz of soft brown hair; his eyes, after wavering in colour, decided to be brown, like Basil's; his complexion from brick-red became first a curious yellow, and then approached fairness. Teresa began to feel that he might ultimately be presentable. He was a strong child with a determined will to live. Major Ransome pronounced him a beauty, and in his grandfatherly delight called on the baby three of four times a week. Grandparents, however, were peculiarly obnoxious to Basil's theory; the poor Major was not allowed to hold Ronald Grange, or to prod any portion of his anatomy with a doting finger, or to chirrup to him. Basil considered that even looking at the baby as he lay in his crib was self-indulgence on the part of the elders which might involve some nervous strain for Ronald Grange. Basil was about the house pretty constantly for some time after the baby's birth, informing Teresa that he couldn't yet settle down to work. He kept a sharp eye on the nurse, and if Teresa fed the baby too early or too late he knew it. He kept many visitors away from Ronald Grange, and Teresa's Aunt Sophy went away in a passion because, after three visits, she had not yet succeeded in seeing the baby. Teresa, however, took advantage of Basil's occasional absences. She herself was not allowed to hold the baby any longer than was strictly necessary. But several times when Basil was well away she actually played with Ronald Grange, tickled the soles of his feet, kissed the back of his neck, and once, the Major arriving in the midst of such an orgy, she took pity on the poor old man and let him have his share. That day Ronald Grange was trotted on the Major's knee, chucked under the chin, poked in the ribs, and whistled to. Teresa felt guilty, and watched Ronald for some days for signs of nervous prostration. But there was now a bond of crime between her and the Major, and they continued at intervals to furnish the baby with contraband amusement.

Mrs. Perry had been in Florida for February and March. When she returned to town she came at once to see Teresa. Basil was not at home, and Teresa allowed the baby to be brought in, at Mrs. Perry's demand.

"I've brought some things for him," said the lady. "Oh, what a darling!"

Teresa looked sceptically at the baby's mottled face, and at her visitor; but Mrs. Perry's expression, as she took the baby and tucked it up against her shoulder, and touched its fuzzy head with her cheek, silenced the sceptic. Teresa watched curiously. Mrs. Perry walked up and down the room with the baby, and then sat down, holding him as though he were made of delicate crystal.

"How warm and soft they are!" she breathed, her full-lidded dark eyes closing slowly. "I like that smell of warm flannel. They're just like little birds, all soft down! What a darling!"

Teresa said nothing. She was thoroughly surprised. When the nurse came to take the baby, Mrs. Perry produced her gift—two little dresses beautifully sewed by hand. "I made them every stitch myself for him," she said. Teresa was oddly touched by this. Alice had sent the baby an ivory with gold bells. Many other gifts had been sent to him, but no one else she knew had actually made anything for him. Mrs. Perry asked to see his bed and his wardrobe, and she turned over his tiny garments with caressing fingers. When she went away Teresa thought Mrs. Perry was going to offer to kiss her, but to her relief it did not happen. She would not have liked to kiss Mrs. Perry, though she liked her.

She liked her with the calm and civilised part of her intelligence, and at the same time obscurely hated her. She appreciated Mrs. Perry's good qualities, liked the way she treated herself, but would not have been sorry to hear that some calamity had befallen that lady—for example, the loss of her good looks. Teresa knew that an intimacy existed between Mrs. Perry and Basil, and she did not know the extent of it. Basil had assured her that it was not an emotional relation, except in so far as Mrs. Perry had an emotional need for a friend to whom she could talk freely and profoundly, and look for sympathy. But Teresa believed that Basil would lie in such a case, though probably in no other. With her he had proceeded on a general plan of extreme frankness. Recognising the impersonal and almost masculine element in her intelligence, and allowing it, perhaps, more weight than it really possessed in her total makeup, Basil had laid bare to her all his ideas and feelings, and most of his doings. For the first year of their marriage he had had nothing to conceal, and his natural disposition to frankness, rather brutal sometimes and partaking a little of the crystalline hardness of his nature, had had full sway.

A cardinal point of his doctrine was that only emotional infidelity counted, and he passionately assured Teresa that this was quite out of the range of possibility for him. She tried to believe him.

But there were so many other things besides love, in this essential sense! And Basil's interest in the sex was as wide as the world. He had an inexhaustible curiosity, which he called psychological, and which Teresa called puerile; a keen, almost romantic, sense of the drama of life; a need of all sorts of free and indefinite human relations. His theories were in favour of absolute freedom among civilised beings in a generation which was profoundly anarchic. Teresa distrusted all theories. At the same time, intellectually, she approved of Basil; but this fact, as she pointed out to him, might not prevent her from hating him, and some time doing him an injury.

"I cannot get rid of the sense of possession," she said. "I regard you as my property, and your interest in other women as stolen from me. I know it's absurd, but you can't account for feelings, or get rid of them, either."

"So I am your property," said Basil. "But you don't want to lock me up, do you? You wouldn't care a snap for me if I was interested in nothing but you. It's because I know a lot of others that I know how much nicer you are."

"That's all very well, but I wish I didn't *care*. Sometimes I wish you hadn't told me things. Scenes come up to me—pictures—all sorts of things. Then I hate you."

"Oh, I forget sometimes that you're a woman," said Basil, with a humorous sigh. "I talk to you as I would to a man. And you like it."

"Oh, I like it well enough. But—perhaps it isn't awfully clever of you."

"Why not? Why? What do you mean?"

She smiled and wouldn't answer. When he pressed her to speak, she shook her head enigmatically. Basil took her by the throat and threatened to choke her if she didn't explain; whereat she laughed, and said gaily: "Never mind. We're good friends, anyway. I think we always shall be, and like each other best of all. It doesn't matter if we amuse ourselves a little by the way. There—that's the point of view I'm striving to reach."

"You are? Well, I thought you'd always had that point of view."

"In a purely abstract way, but I want to *feel* it—I want to put it into practice. I hate mere theories."

"That's all right—but a good many theories ain't practicable," said Basil, after a pause. "There's a difference, you know."

"A difference where?"

"Between you and me, for example."

"Oh, I'm sure of it. Many of your amusements wouldn't appeal to me at all. But I understand all you say about the claims of the temperament, and, do you know, I believe I have got a temperament, too! I'm certain I'm dying to be amused. And, then, if I am amused, I shan't mind if you are. You may investigate life as much as you choose, and make all the psychological experiments you please. And I won't be a bit jealous. I've made up my mind to get rid of that mean, sneaking feeling, and I *will*. And this is the way to do it."

"What is? You've always had your friends, if that's all. There's Page, and Alvord—and Dallas spends hours alone with you every week."

"Gerald! Dear old Gerald! . . . No, I'm not talking about him!"

"Well, who then, you little wretch?"

Basil laughed heartily and contemplated his wife with easy admiration. But she cast a glance at him from under her lashes, smiled slightly, and began to talk about something else.

• • • • •

She spent the summer with the baby at a dull resort on the Maine coast; and this rounded out an entire year devoted to Ronald Grange. Ronald was weaned, and throve, and began certainly to pay for himself. He was a vigorous and beautiful little creature; and Teresa, who bathed him herself and mixed his food and watched his sleep on the sands, now learned the intimate sweetness of his small, definite personality, felt the soft charm of his unfolding intelligence and expressiveness, was infinitely touched by his dependence on her, and his consciousness of it. She came to love him with part of the emotion that hitherto had been given only to Basil.

Except for the baby, Teresa was bored; she lived a perfectly hygienic life, and saw that she grew more beautiful. Basil's warm recognition of this fact, during the month that he spent with her, lent a new interest to life. Their separation, the first since their marriage, was due to money necessities. Basil had found that an income which sufficed for two self-indulgent people was not enough for two and a baby; and he had been painting pot-boilers for Mrs. Perry, who had a scheme for decorating her library with views of the natural beauties of America. He had been bored, too, as his daily letters showed Teresa; he had longed for her, restless in the loss of their companionship and the domestic atmosphere which satisfied some deep need of his nature; and when he finally came it was like an ardent burst of the south wind—a storm of happiness. He wanted to spend his whole day beside Teresa, to talk to her half the night; he was even jealous of the baby. It was a new honeymoon, more passionate than the first, and Teresa now first began to feel the full power of her beauty. Basil's aesthetic appreciation of her had grown steadily; she pleased him now more deeply than ever; and she rejoiced, for some instinct told her that, holding Basil by this feeling and by his domestic side, she held the real man.

IV

He was a man rather difficult to tie; and he had just escaped from a determined effort to entangle him, on the part of Isabel Perry. Isabel's choice seemed to lie between him and a convent. For some time past she had been studying the Catholic doctrine. A strong impulse of her passionate nature forced her toward that faith; but as yet she had only a desire to be convinced, not a conviction. In his last interview with her, at her country-house, Basil had found her much moved by a long visit that morning from a Catholic priest, in whom she thought she had found a sort of Pascal. The master of the house was away, for Isabel's advances to the faith were much more surreptitious than her love affairs. Basil was to lunch with her. He found her in tears, torn between the effect of the priest's talk and a violent revulsion.

"Let us go out," she had said at once on seeing him, and she had led the way out of the library that opened on a broad stretch of turf, into the wood. Walking there, she told him, in a depressed, nervous tone, of her difficulties.

"If I could only be *sure*," she said, clasping her hands over the breast of her white dress. "It seems to me that my religious feelings are only a result of my disappointment with life. I want to leave the world, not because I believe, *really* believe, that the religious life is the right one, but because I can't bear the life I lead. I would rather have absolute negation than the desire for something that doesn't exist. It's the *life* that attracts me. I couldn't become a Catholic and stay in the world. I wish to be shut out from it, to live in some narrow place, in a strict rule, to feel as mortal sin what I now want without really believing in it—and, *then*, I believe, I really *should* believe—I should see good and evil where now I see neither. I should feel that I have sinned, as I did when I talked to Father Damon just now—but now I don't feel it—"

She turned suddenly and took Basil's arm.

"With *you*," she said, "I always feel the other thing, the other appeal.

Just the thought that I was to see you to-day—and it kept coming up all the time Father Damon was talking—made me feel my inability to accept what he represents. To me just now, Basil, *you* are the world—not the world I want to get away from, my world—but the other, that I want without believing in it. I mean your point of view, your acceptance of life, the ease with which you take it—it seems to jar nothing in you, to leave nothing unsatisfied—you seem to me, in short, so happy—"

She stopped in her rapid talk, her rapid pace along the grassy walk under the trees, and looked up at him, pale and agitated. "You don't understand my unhappiness, do you? You can't help me?" she asked.

Her hand, clinging to his arm, her whole attitude of appeal, moved Basil, but he felt, more than emotion, a sense of constraint. Her eyes were appealing, but her mouth was imperious, eager.

"No one can help you," he said slowly. "We can't help one another—except by giving enjoyment now and then—that's my creed. I can't give you my enjoyment of life. I enjoy it because I am made to enjoy it. It floats me. It depresses you. You ask of life more than it can give. Perhaps that's the nobler attitude—I don't know. I'm sure it's the more romantic one. I'm not romantic, Isabel. Your alternatives of ecstatic happiness or the cloister both seem to me impossible. I can't understand wanting to be ecstatic, in or out of religion—but I see that you do want to be."

"But, surely, you believe, at least in moments of happiness, in a feeling of joy that might lift one out of the maddening groove of life—you believe in love, Basil?"

"Not as you do, Isabel," he said gravely. "Not as anything supernatural, mystic. I believe in it as a sweet, everyday food of life—good and wholesome and necessary, like bread and butter. But you think it must be nectar and ambrosia, sent down expressly from heaven! . . ."

He smiled at her—their eyes were on a level.

"Ah, you see, I've never had it," she sighed.

She looked away, down a bright vista of sunny grass crossed by tree shadows.

"You mention bread and butter, and lunch must be ready," she said. "Forgive me for boring you with my stupid troubles. I wish I could be happy in a commonplace way, like you."

Basil laughed gaily.

"I wish you could! Commonplace isn't half so bad as you think," he said. "Do resign yourself to it, Isabel, and don't talk any more to Father Damon! Fancy you in a nun's dress—your beautiful hair cut short—no, you mustn't do it!"

"How frivolous you are," she murmured, but she smiled and blushed suddenly. She was leaning against a great oak trunk, and she looked up at him. . . . Basil did not kiss her. He was conscious that it was expected, and in his mind there was a clear perception: It would be fatal. Isabel's emotional demand frightened him. The situation between them had been growing more and more definite and difficult. It was with a marked feeling of relief that Basil, after lunch, said good-bye to her for a month.

• • • • •

That month Teresa finished modelling Basil's bust. It was the first ambitious thing she had done since her marriage. She was in love with his beauty as she did it—the clear essentially sculptural character of his finely-modelled head, the free, dominant poise of it.

"That's you, Basil—*all* of you," she said, the day it was finished, after gazing long at it.

"It's a good-looking piece of work," Basil admitted.

And Erhart, who came up for a week to give his opinion on it, pronounced that it had bone.

"Of course one sees that it's a woman's work," he added patronisingly.

"Of course," said Teresa mockingly, "but one is astonished that the dog should dance so well, considering that it was meant to go on all fours—isn't that it?"

"Something of that sort. Do I hear your Aunt Sophy talking?"

"You will, sooner or later. I am coming round to her point of view."

"You a *feministe*! There are no young and pretty ones, remember that. Wait till you're thirty, at least."

"Oh, two years of being married to Basil are a liberal education in feminism. I'm at least forty in experience."

"Oh, nonsense. You adore Basil."

"Of course I adore him. His altars smoke with sacrifice. But all the same I think I shall raise one to the Unknown God."

"On which no one will be allowed to sacrifice but yourself, eh?" said Erhart. "You want a monopoly."

"Oh, there's no god sufficiently unknown for that!" Teresa laughed. "There's such a superfluity of adoration in this world. No wonder our deities are overfed. I think I shall put Basil on a meagre diet."

"Don't do anything to Basil, he's good enough. He's the most married man I know."

"He? He's the aboriginal wild man, roaming the happy hunting-grounds—in Mrs. Perry's automobile. And I keep the wigwam neat and clean, and look after the papoose."

"You couldn't do a better job," said Erhart aggressively.

Erhart came up to stay a week, but he stayed a month, in fact till the Ransomes returned to town, and occupied himself in making a bas-relief of Teresa's head. At first his attitude toward them both was what it had always been—friendly and frank. But soon he began to show some irritation against Basil. He devoted himself obviously to Teresa, tried to get her off on long walks alone, and was moody and bored when Basil was of the party. When he was alone with Teresa, he spent most of his time in criticising Basil. He declared that Basil was volatile, lazy; that he only amused himself with work and life; that he did not take even his wife seriously enough.

"He suits me," Teresa said calmly, a good deal amused. "He's a charming companion, and always interesting. And I can assure you that he takes me and the baby with the utmost seriousness."

"But he leaves you alone here all summer."

"He had to make some money, poor dear. You've no idea how expensive Ronald is. If you think he wasn't glad to get here—!"

"Oh, I suppose he was. He's fond of you, I think, in his way."

Teresa smiled.

"He's an awfully good fellow," Erhart proceeded. "It's too bad his habits are so irregular—bad for his work and everything, I should think. He's got some talent, and if he'd only pitch in and *work*—"

"Once for all, Basil isn't a grub. He knows he'll never be a great painter, and he's too much humour to take himself with awful serious-ness. He knows perfectly well the measure of his ability, he can do good work and he knows it, but what he cares most about is living."

"Living?" grumbled Erhart. "I really don't think Basil's way of living is admirable. I wish he didn't drink at all. It's no wonder he's nervous and irritable, and his temper bad."

"I thought you liked Basil," said Teresa demurely.

"I do like him—very much, in some ways. And that's why I hate to see him wasting himself so. It would be a lot better for you if he worked more regularly and successfully. I don't think he does as much as he might for you. You're the sort of woman that luxury suits, you need it. I should think it would be a pleasure to give it to you."

Teresa put a shade of melancholy into her faraway gaze. "My tastes are very simple," she said.

"Oh, that's because you're really very sweet and kind, and you never worry people; I've noticed that. But all beautiful women need a setting, and they all want it, too, if they haven't got it. When a man's lucky enough to be married to a woman like you, he ought to live up to it. Basil's a good fellow, an interesting fellow, but I don't think he deserves you, really."

Teresa's amusement in this conversation was so great that she repeated it word for word to Basil. Basil was not at all amused.

"I'd like to know what the devil he means by that sort of talk," he said. "I don't call it very friendly, abusing me like that to you. He's making love to you, that's what it is. I've noticed lately that he doesn't want me around. I like his nerve!"

"Don't quarrel with him," said Teresa, laughing.

"Quarrel! Of course not. Only I must say I don't like it. It's all right for him to admire you—I like men to admire you—but I don't see why he should turn against *me*. It's confoundedly unpleasant—but I never did like the fellow much anyway."

"He isn't the most subtle or the best-mannered person I know," murmured Teresa. "But he means no harm."

"Doesn't he? He doesn't mean any good, either, so far as I can see."

"Oh, yes—he wants to reform your habits, and make you ambitious, and me rich."

"The devil he does. He wants to make you discontented with me."

"Well, he can't. So you needn't worry. Don't take him seriously, or I'll never tell you another thing."

"Yes, you will! You'll tell me everything, or I'll choke the life out of you!" And Basil playfully clasped his hands about her throat.

Teresa laughed.

"It's pure self-indulgence for me to tell you everything, though at times I think its unwise. In this case, for instance. You don't like Erhart as much as you did before. I've done a wrong to him in telling you. But I like so much to feel that you know everything, and that everything is clear between us, at least on my side, that I don't care. I am immoral in my honesty. Only you mustn't show that I've told you, you know. That would be immoral of *you*."

"Oh, I won't, of course. Only don't let Erhart make love to you."

"*Erhart!* I should say not. You're—unpleasant, Basil."

"No, I'm not jealous," he said, laughing. "Only, if any man makes love to you, I'd like it to be some fellow I like, you know—some really good man. And that doesn't mean you're to encourage him—at least not much. Otherwise I don't mind at all."

"How generous of you!" said Teresa, with sarcasm.

There was now often a tinge of sharpness in her tone toward Basil. She knew that he had his reserves. He had been as diplomatic as possible on the subject of Mrs. Perry; but his practical wisdom had not quite deceived Teresa's instinct. She knew there was something he had not told her—but she felt also that, whatever it might be, it was not very important. She could not be deceived in Basil's feeling for herself; and she was learning to fight against her disposition to take seriously everything relating to him. In spite of his essential simplicity, in spite of his love for her, there was, she felt dimly, too much in him, in life with him, that might give her pain. She tried, therefore, to attain something of his own case of that quality which would have been lightness if his essential force, his reality, his will, had been less; but which now seemed to her more an enviable buoyancy and power of resistance to the ills of life.

V

One night in the early winter a party of people started out, after dining at the Ransome's flat, on a slumming expedition. The affair had been arranged for Alice Blackley's benefit; Alice was more eager than ever to see life, and she thought she would like to see it in undress. She had confided to Teresa lately that she was tired of artists (except Basil, of course), and that she did not believe they were any more interesting, when you knew them, than other people. However, Erhart was of the present party, which contained besides only Basil and Teresa, for Erhart was anxious to please Mrs. Blackley, having an eye always to the commercial side of his profession; and Basil had amiably brought the two together.

It was late when they started, the two women in quiet, dark dresses, appropriate for a pure tour of inspection. They went first into the Tenderloin, to two or three music-halls, and a place where coffee and cigarettes and Turkish furnishings competed with the inevitable whisky.

The music-halls were noisy, glaring with electric light, and filled with a crowd of men and girls, sitting or moving about the little tables, whose gaiety seemed as hard and thin as the light's blue flare. The tough faces of the waiters, the careless or determined cheerfulness of the women, the bored or excited look of the men of widely varying types, the perpetual drinking, all mixed together in a mirage of which pleasure was the least discoverable element. Some of the girls were very pretty, many of them were young, most of them well-dressed; and all tried to diffuse about themselves an atmosphere of reckless life, zest, enjoyment. But seen in the mass, all these various attempts resulted in one great effect of sham.

Alice's large eyes studied the scene intently. She was so much interested that it was difficult to get her away; yet she had a blank look, too.

"I thought it would have been more exciting," she said. "Don't they dance, or anything?"

The Turkish coffee place, with its dimmer lights and languid couples, she thought more interesting; but still her deer-like eyes looked vainly about for something she did not see; still she seemed perplexed. "Is this really life?" she seemed to ask. "*Are* these the haunts of vice? Are these people really the horrid people we've come out to see? And if so, why are they not more spectacular?"

From the Tenderloin they crossed to the Bowery, and walked slowly down the broad street, howling with the noise of the cars, bright with electricity, crowded with undistinguished people. From innumerable saloons and ten-cent shows came the tinkling strains of mechanical music. All the small shops which catered to the needs of the undistinguished were open, to meet their customers' leisure hours, and so the broad, dirty sidewalk lay in one continuous glare of light.

They went into one music-hall—a bare, untidy room, with a few men sitting over their beer, and on the platform a stout, middle-aged woman, in short skirts, rouge, and a picture hat, singing a sentimental song to the accompaniment of a cracked piano. Several girls walked about, talking to the sallow, stolid men. One stood alone near the piano. She was conspicuous in her solitude; and also because, for all the loose coat that hid her figure, it could be seen that she was about to bear a child. One of the men pointed a thumb at her over his shoulder, and said something to his companion; they both laughed. The girl smiled, with a piteous attempt at bravado.

Teresa hurried her party out of the place. Basil took them next to a saloon where he expected to find an acquaintance of his, an ex-prize-fighter, whose reputation for wit extended up and down and even beyond the Bowery. The saloon was crowded and noisy, and a blast of foul language met them as they entered. Basil hastily extracted his man, who saluted him with a "Hello, bloke!" Then the five went to have a "chop suey" at a Chinese restaurant to which the ex-prize-fighter led them with the air of a man who knew his world, and was quite indifferent to any other.

He was a small, wiry man, collarless, rather drunk, with a sallow face, hard as steel, in which smouldered two half-extinct black eyes. Scarcely a muscle of his face moved when he spoke. He slid his words out of the corner of his thin immobile lips, and they rapped with an emphasis like that of metal on metal. His eyes were perfectly expressionless as he observed the various members of the party. He had seen innumerable slumming parties, and while he was quite willing to talk to any of them for the sake of a supper, drink, and a few dollars at the end of the evening, their world did not interest him. He patronised them as easily as he did the Chinese waiters in the small room up a dirty flight of stairs, where he selected the best table, and issued his curt orders. The two Chinese, in loose linen coats and flapping slippers, brought rice, tea, and the curious mixture of veal, bamboo-shoots, and unknown condiments which figured on the sign outside. The prize-fighter addressed to them a few words in their own tongue, and a shade which might have been a smile passed over their faces, immovable as his own.

Then he took the big bowl of rice and a pair of chop-sticks, put the chop-sticks first into his mouth, then into the rice, and passed the bowl round the table. Rice was generally declined, but the party tried eating the chop suey with their bamboo sticks. The prize-fighter managed his deftly, and endeavoured to instruct the others.

"You've got 'em by the wrong end, see? Hold 'em so," he said to Alice.

She persisted in her own way, however, and he said with indifference: "All right, Sis, what you don't know won't hurt you."

Then, on Erhart's lead, he began to talk about a recent prize-fight. Erhart described to the rest of them, with aesthetic enthusiasm, the marvellous effect of the pink bodies of the men, seen through a cloud of dust; and the ex-professional listened cynically.

"I'm going to model Young, the light-weight," exclaimed Erhart. "I got him to promise to pose for me. I can do a bully thing of the fighter!"

"What's the good of that?" demanded the other. "If you want to make a statoo, you'd ought to take the champion. You make a good likeness of *him*, and I tell you, young feller, every saloon in the country'd take a copy. You don't know your own business.

Basil changed the topic and asked after the prize-fighter's wife.

"About the same," he answered. "A doc told her she had consumption, and she'd ought to go to the country. But she won't go and leave me for fear I'd get drunk too much."

"Why don't you go with her, then?" enquired Alice.

"Me in the country? What in hell would I do in the country?" he replied contemptuously. "There ain't no better air than there is right here on the Bowery—it's as good as Fifth Av-noo air any day, mind that, Sis."

Alice looked at Basil and giggled. Basil smiled wearily. He had been very silent all the evening, and when he was not talking his face looked gloomy. Teresa, too, seemed oppressed. She felt as though she were at the bottom of some vast slough, where unpleasant creatures of all sorts swarmed, living their pathetic lives. The perfect content of the prize-fighter with his particular spot in the slough was illuminating, yet it did not lighten the impression of the whole. The man interested her. She studied his face, but did not try to talk to him. The gulf between their worlds was too wide, and she knew that she was as intolerant of his as he of hers.

He began presently to talk about politics to the two men, and gave a racy outline of the Bowery's sentiments concerning a recent municipal election. In the midst of this, on a hint from Basil, the party moved on, the prize-fighter leading the way. They walked through Chinatown— quaint, dingy, mysterious shadow of the East thrown athwart the old houses of the Knickerbockers—and then they came out on the Bowery again, and went into another drinking-place. This was full of sailors, half or quite drunk. There were a number of young girls, shabbily dressed; and among them were two slight, pretty creatures, who looked not older than sixteen. As soon as they had taken a table, and, as a matter of form, ordered beer, a drunken sailor came up to their party, and leaning over the table and fixing a pair of child-like, sad eyes on Teresa, began a long story of his sufferings and wrongs on board his ship. His voice was so pathetic, his incoherent unhappiness so convincing, that the two women listened, quite fascinated; but he repeated himself, and finally lost himself in a maze of words, lurching heavily to this side and that; when Basil rose, took him by the arm, and led him away to another table, gave him a drink, and left him murmuring to himself.

Teresa looked about the room as though in a dream. The close air, the smell of beer, the throng of brutal faces, the drunken, lascivious eyes, the rough words caught here and there, made up an impression of naked sordidness so complete as to pass reality. The movements of the one waiter fascinated her. He was a young man, slim and powerfully built, with a face almost handsome, which had the same absolute hard-ness and immobility that marked the prize-fighter's. He moved quickly amongst the crowd, with a business-like, lordly air, his eyes everywhere at once. He swept off half-filled beer glasses, and brought full ones without being asked, balancing a tray in each hand. And twice in fifteen minutes he put down his trays, took an obstreperous sailor by the collar and jerked him through the door of the place into the street without moving a muscle of his face, or losing for an instant his business-like calm.

"That's the bouncer," explained Erhart to Alice. She wanted to know all about the bouncer, whom Basil was sketching on the back of a letter; but she was even more interested in the two young girls, and at her request Erhart asked them to come up to the table, and gave them some beer. They were not at all shy. The prettiest at once began to talk to Teresa with easy frankness; told her that she and her friend lived in a room together, and had done so for two years; that she was a morphine-fiend; and she showed, with a certain pride, her arm, covered with punctures. Her face was round and delicately coloured, without a touch of powder or paint. She had large, blue eyes, and curling brown hair. The other girl was paler, more nervous, but almost as pretty. Neither was over seventeen. The nervous girl slipped away in a few moments, and sat down at a table with a sailor. Teresa was still talking with the other, when at the far end of the room a disturbance began. The bouncer leaped to the fray, and ejected two individuals; but in a moment the room was in an uproar. The crowd surged down toward the door, overturning tables and chairs; every second man drew a knife or pistol. Basil, Erhart, and the prize-fighter pushed the three women toward the wall, and made a buffer between them and the crowd; but in spite of their efforts they were caught in the jam and forced under a hail of broken glass, toward the one narrow entrance. Basil stretched out his arms on either side of Teresa, and with vicious digs of his elbows and fists tried to protect her. Gleaming eyes turned toward him, and one man lifted a knife. Teresa, half-suffocated, almost lost consciousness, but fear for Basil sustained her. In a final, fierce stampede they were pushed through the door.

When they found themselves in the street, and succeeded in reaching the other three, it was discovered that Erhart had a deep knife-cut in the arm, and by common consent the expedition broke up. The Ransomes took Alice home. She was pleased by the evening; talked a good deal about the two young girls, and the possibility of reforming them, or at least of giving them some good clothes, so that they would have a better chance.

Teresa could not get to sleep that night. When she closed her eyes the room was peopled by the dreadful faces she had seen. The drunken sailor, the "bouncer," the girl at whom those men had laughed, the pretty young girl with the spotted arm, stood out on a background of sodden, diseased, malevolent human wrecks. This was worse than the sham mirth of the Tenderloin; perhaps it was the reality behind the sham. The figures all whirled round as though in a drunken dance, and behind them she seemed to see uncounted myriads of other figures, all driven on blindly, all mad, broken, blighted.

Basil had given her his sketch of the "bouncer" as they came home. She had seen in his eyes that night not only gloom and weariness, but also the impersonal interest in the scene before him that meant a stirring of his impulse to expression. He would put them all down on paper—those pathetic girls, those brutal or stupid men—all that complex of misery, all that waste of life. And it would mean to him just fact—just what *is*, what must be.

In her present mood she revolted, as she often did, against his acceptance of the world, involving even, it seemed to her, a certain pleasure in its hardness, its inequalities. Perhaps this was the artistic interest, the dramatic interest; but to Teresa now it seemed cruel to enjoy the sight of such a world, to use it as material for art. The impersonal side of Basil presented itself to her as a cool, observing eye, a firm noting hand; apart from his own human interests, he was not moved—the mass of misery did not move him. He dissociated himself from it completely. His attitude was: "I did not make this world—I'm not responsible for it—I can't help it. I can only observe it, recognise it for what it is—and make my own particular life out of it, a satisfaction to myself." Basil was selfish, egotistic, hard—but he loved her, and she loved him. A sudden need to be near him came upon her. She got up and went into his room.

The winter dawn was faintly beginning. He was asleep. His relaxed face looked sad, but sleep gave it also a curiously young expression, a strange beauty. She crept into the bed beside him; half waking, he put his arm about her, and murmured something softly. They had quarrelled bitterly the day before. But now, comforted to the soul by his nearness, and the word of endearment that had come unconsciously from the deep feeling that united them, from the depths below all surface storms, Teresa, too, could sleep.

VI

Difficulties had thickened upon them this winter. They had a larger flat, in a more salubrious (and expensive) neighborhood, and three servants. The baby had made this difference, with the result that they felt poor. Teresa, with a pang, had given up her bachelor rooms, for the work she was now able to do did not justify her in keeping them. But the rent of Basil's studio was high, and he had not sold anything lately, except the work he had done for Mrs. Perry. His book of drawings had been published, with a definite, but not a money success. The publishers had wanted to call it "The City Toilers," and by including mainly types of honest misery, to give it a sentimental air of pity. But Basil called it "City Types" and put into it what he considered his best work, irrespective of subject. The result could not please the sentimental public, but it pleased Basil, and also Teresa, who desired that his artistic ability should be recognised. But it did not bring in much money. For the first time in his life Basil felt the pressure of money needs. The demands of his household seemed to grow steadily, and his income was comparatively a fixed quantity. He had never counted on making money, but now he was obliged to speculate on his work, and this brought him face to face with his own practical limitations. It was a standing grievance that Teresa was not economical. But Teresa, though she honestly tried, could not be—at least not more than a few days at a time. Then she forgot about it. She was no extravagant, but the daily worry of overseeing cheating tradesmen and servants, as well as watching the baby and the nurse, and seeing that Basil's clothes were in repair, and his meals on time, was sure to overpass at some point the limits of her domestic capacity.

They were gayer, too, this winter than ever. Teresa, after her year of the baby, had a craving for people, a quite new delight in going out, the more so since she was more beautiful and more admired. And gaiety meant expense—clothes, dinners, cabs—and less work. It meant, also, more or less emotional disturbance. Basil's theory that he was not of a jealous temperament had had a good test, and had been found not to hold water.

Among the people that they saw most of, domestic happiness was regarded as an amusing or pathetic myth, as you happened to take it. It was a mirage, and the traveller in the desert, if he could not help pursuing it, always recognised his mistake. He did not reach the mirage; but he might find a pleasant oasis or two by the way. An apparently complete frankness about their domestic relations was also the rule in this society. People talked about their wives or husbands as amusingly as they could, and quite without sentiment. The pose of the successful ones was that they were simple good friends, and didn't interfere with one another. Behind this mask, which Basil and Teresa assumed also, went on, no doubt, many a drama like their own; and many a secret believer in the myth struggled and strove to reach what he considered to be real waters, spreading cool and peaceful, and real protection from the glaring, grinding world. Peace was, perhaps, not to be hoped for in the relation of two civilised and youthful people who had the ideal of freedom and enjoyment. The world was too much with them for any real seclusion of spirit to be possible. But they had the ever-present sense of life, an unfailing interest in one another. They might quarrel, but they were never dull, and neither had as yet a need for any other one person. They had days of perfect, simple happiness, when material difficulties were ignored, and their real relation seemed the only thing that mattered; days of frank, wordly companionship, when they talked frivolously of serious things, and a light way of taking the world made it all gay and amusing. And they had their black days, when all went wrong, when they barely spoke to one another or communicated by means of notes; when they accused one another of self-indulgence, selfishness, egotism; when Teresa bitingly recalled Basil's sensual weaknesses, and Basil openly regretted his bachelor freedom, and assured Teresa that she was never meant for a wife. These discords were frequent, but they never lasted long; neither could stand the strain. Basil could not work under it, and it blackened the entire firmament for Teresa. It ended usually in a passionate reconciliation, wherein Basil ardently told Teresa that he could not live without her, nor with any other woman; and she promised to be domestic; and then the sky was blue, and the sunlight golden, and a heavenly breath descended upon them, and life, youth, and love seemed divine.

Their latest quarrel had been ostensibly about household affairs. The monthly bills had come in, and seemed to Basil enormous. And the nurse had been discovered feeding Ronald Grange at an undue hour. All Teresa's faults as a housewife were once more gone over, and Basil, with his usual vigour, had asserted that she cared nothing for the household, for the baby, or for him, but only for her own amusement. The real reason for the explosion was that Teresa, on the previous day, had gone out with her most devoted admirer in his automobile, and lunched with him in the country. He was a Southerner named Fairfax; he had made a fortune in lumber; he was good-looking and had the caressing manner of his kind toward women; and for several months now he had been coming constantly to see Teresa. His time was about equally divided between the South and New York; and when he was away he wrote to her. She always showed the letters to Basil; they were friendly, gay, and interested. She admitted that she liked Fairfax very much; that she found him amusing and charming. Basil said that he liked her friendship with Fairfax; it was in line with all his ideas. He said once: "It's more exciting to drive a restive team than a quiet one; only you must look out they don't get away." His own interest in his wife seemed to increase. It had lost the quiet of the first year; it was more like the perpetual unrest of courtship. Her successes, her gaiety, intensified the appeal of her beauty to him. He seemed, too, to be less sure of her, and this pleased Teresa, and added to the light excitement of their life.

On the morning after their slumming expedition they took their coffee together amicably; Basil was gentle, but gloomy. Teresa questioned him keenly; he resisted; but at last his real feeling came out, and he confessed to a torturing jealousy.

"I didn't know I had it in me," he said savagely—angry, not with her, but with himself. "And I can't stand it. It makes me feel weak—mentally and physically. It turns me sick. I think I'm wrong, but I can't help it. I believe the thing is stronger than I am. You're the only person in the world, Teresa, that can really make me suffer. And I believe you could half-kill me!"

His anger and resentment of his own irrationality touched Teresa, his emotion pleased her, but the practical consequences thereof rather vexed her.

"I've only done what you told me to do," she said plaintively. "You said you wanted me to have my friends among men, just as you have among women. I didn't make scenes for you—at least not serious ones—when you were so much with Mrs. Perry. And yet I had more reason to, for she was making love to you, and Jack doesn't make love to me—not seriously."

"Seriously! There it is, then—he does make love to you. I knew it. His whole manner to you shows it."

"Oh, he's Southern, you know, and they have that gallant way. My father had it—it's a tradition. He *does* like me, I'm sure—perhaps he's a little bit *épris*—but you always said you liked men to be fond of me, so long as—"

"Yes, but you like *him*! You wouldn't want to spend hours alone with him if you didn't."

"Of course I like him, silly old thing! He's charming."

Basil groaned. "Woman have a terrific advantage to us," he said viciously. "Nothing I can do can affect you very deeply, unless I should fall in love with another woman, and I can't do that. But you could very easily nearly kill *me*."

"Then it's your own fault if we *have* that advantage," said Teresa calmly. "First you carry on yourselves in such a fashion that, as you say, we can't take your lapses seriously. And then you put such terrific emphasis on the slightest lapse on our part. Why do you put the weapon into our hands and then provoke us, if you don't want to get hurt?"

"Provocation, as you call it, oughtn't to count. A woman ought to be strong enough to stand for herself, for what she really deeply wants, without being influenced by another person's acts."

Two people can't live together intimately without influencing one another, and deeply. And especially a woman, for her character isn't formed till she's married. Of course, I can see how the other person would like to feel that what he does counts for nothing, for so he gets rid of all responsibility—only it doesn't work that way."

"The Orientals manage these things better," said Basil gloomily. "A Mohammedan can take as many women into his house as he can support, and they're all protected and cared for, and respectable. And if they're unfaithful, he can bowstring them. That's the right method. Monogamy is a foolish idea, and we waste an enormous amount of life in trying to live up to it. The Japanese are infinitely more sane than we are about the whole business. Sex ought to be divorced from emotion. They don't belong together. We've sentimentalised the thing till we don't know where we stand. It's all the fault of feminism. Women naturally sentimentalise it, and we've let them set the tone for our whole society, till we can't call our souls or bodies our own. It's weakness, and gets paid out as weakness always does. We belong to you now, you own us, and you make us feel it."

"Poor slaves!" mocked Teresa. "Why don't you rise and assert your rights? Put us back in the harem, and then go on with your great work of civilising the world in peace. I daresay we should be just as well off."

"I think you would. You can't be men, anyway, you know, and in our society you're bound to try to be, more or less. It's all wrong. The line ought to stand where it was drawn for all time, sharp and clear. Trying to rub it away is folly."

"*I* don't try to be a man," murmured Teresa. "I wouldn't be one for any amount. Poor, foolish creatures."

"Yes, you do try. You want the same freedom—"

"I thought we agreed the ideal was equal freedom."

"So it would be if women were capable of it, if they were like men, capable of dissociating ideas that don't really belong together. But they're not. They emotionalise everything."

"Even an automobile drive and a sedate luncheon? Really, you're silly, Basil."

"Perhaps I am," he admitted darkly. "But I can't help it."

"I don't think, really, that it's a tremendous compliment to me—your jealousy," said Teresa coldly.

"No, it isn't. But it isn't the other thing either. You're so much alive, Teresa! And you're beautiful, and you love admiration. And really I feel that you might sometime care too much for someone else."

"It's no use arguing with a feeling," said Teresa. "I won't go out again with Fairfax."

Basil took her in his arms, in a wave of repentant emotion.

"No, I don't mean that. You shall do just as you want to do. I won't deprive you of any pleasure, if I can help it. I believe you do care a little for me!"

Teresa smiled tenderly, but with a shade of melancholy. She did not like the interruption of her friendship with Fairfax, which she felt was probably inevitable. It seemed, too, like a confession of defeat in the course they had meant their marriage to take. If they could not trust one another freely, if they had to take serious account of small things, and manage and humour one another, what became of her ideal of freedom and frankness? Teresa did not want to give up her ideas or her amusements—but neither did she want really to hurt or disturb Basil. The talk left her troubled and melancholy.

VII

Basil himself saved the situation. That night they were going out to dinner, and in the carriage on the way he explicitly denied what he had said, pronounced it only a mood, and assured Teresa that he wanted her to be perfectly free, and not to give up the least of her amusements because of an unreasonable feeling on his part. He admitted emotionally that it was unreasonable, and stated his entire trust in her so convincingly that Teresa's spirits rose with a leap.

"That's all right, then—now we're ourselves again!" she said gaily. "I didn't quite recognise you in the role of Bluebeard! You give me carte blanche, and I promise I shan't want to look into the forbidden cupboard!"

"No, don't promise anything—except that you'll always like me better than anyone else."

"I needn't promise that—I can't help it. Life is so amusing with you, Basil! I feel so gay and young to-night—all the worries seem little things. The baby was so dear to-day—he's the most intelligent little thing, and so strong and alive! I'm going to model a little profile of him. Yes, he really *has* got a profile. And to think I didn't want him—what a fool I was! . . . But there's a good side to not wanting things you haven't got, and idealising them, and thinking if you only had *them*, how happy you'd be. I've never done that. It always seems to me that if I can't be happy with what I've got, I can't anyway. And I do really think I've got all there is to get in life—all there is for me. . . . I might like a little more money—but nothing else!"

Basil held her hand clasped in his, and listened.

"You like excitement," he said.

"Oh, a little, now and then—a new dress, an interesting talk—But I don't need much, do I, now?"

"I don't know. You wouldn't like to have anything cut off."

"Well, would you?"

"No—and I like you to be full of life, as you are. You wouldn't interest me half as much if you were different! You fascinate me, and always have. Only be good—as good as you can!"

Teresa did not protest when he rumpled her hair in a quick embrace. She laughed gaily.

"Life is good," she said contentedly.

The dinner was gay, and too large for general talk. Basil was near one end of the table, and Teresa near the other, with Fairfax beside her—a provision of the hostess. Teresa thoroughly enjoyed her tête-à-tête, for it was almost that. She knew that she was looking wonderfully well in her white dress, but Fairfax's praise was nonetheless welcome. He was one of the men enamored of women's luxury, and she was aware that he would have liked to see her each time in a new dress, and arrayed with more coquetry even than she cared to use. She laughed at this trait in him—it went with much else in his character that she

thought amusing, but rather despicable. But she liked his more masculine side – his energy, ability, and clear-headedness. He talked about men
and affairs with incisive force and had a lightly cynical attitude toward
life in general which went rather oddly with his devotional attitude
toward women.

He was, at bottom, thoroughly conventional; and part of Teresa's
pleasure lay in shocking him. He had from the first been amused and
interested by the freedom of her talk; then he had taken to combating
lightly her ideas; but as he knew her better, he became more vehement
in his protest. He thought her idea of marriage totally wrong; and he
had been horrified at learning the extent of her information about life in
general, and Basil's responsibility therein. He, as Teresa pointed out to
him, thoroughly agreed with her Aunt Sophy, that women should be
protected as much as possible from knowledge – outside their sphere.

"Only Aunt Sophy thinks our sphere is politics, while you think it's
domesticity," said Teresa.

"Of course I think it is. Her home and society – what more does any
woman want?"

"Ah, society! When you take in society, you let in the serpent, and
its wisdom! Unless you mean just an occasional tea-drinking, or a dove
luncheon. Do you think if one's to have any relations with men and
women one doesn't need all the knowledge possible?"

"You have your instinct – that can't go wrong," said the bachelor.

"Oh, can't it! You'd reduce us to the rudiments, wouldn't you? Why
shouldn't we have the amusement of contemplating the world and
people as they really are? It's the most instructive spectacle possible. I can
never be thankful enough that I married a man who isn't afraid of
reality, for me any more than for himself. *You* would shut your wife up in
a toy paradise, with everything upholstered in rose-colour."

"There are a whole lot of things I know that my wife would never
know, you may depend on that," Fairfax responded with emphasis.
"What nonsense, imagining that a man's view of life and a woman's can
ever be the same!"

"And can't one be supposed capable of taking to some degree an
impersonal view of life? Can't one forget occasionally that one is a
woman, and be simply an intelligence?"

"I should say not! What do you make of hundreds of generations of
inherited prejudices and ways of feeling, that colour your thought
unconsciously? You can't get rid of that heritage for an instant. . . . You
couldn't understand a man if you tried for a thousand years."

" 'Wonderful son, that can so astonish a mother'! Do you think I shan't understand my son when he grows up?"

"No, you won't, and if you're wise you won't try. We like women best that don't pretend to understand us."

" 'We'? Speak for yourself, Jack. There are plenty of men that don't believe in the doll's house. I shall see that Ronald Grange, when he grows up, has more modern ideas than you have!" And Teresa warbled frivolously:

" 'Woman is the chosen
      Ornament of home—
Man is what the beer is,
      Woman is the foam.' "

When they talked ideas, they were always combative; and in his sentimental moods as well, Fairfax showed his conviction that Teresa was a charming creature, married to the wrong sort of man, and in danger of being spoiled. Fairfax and Basil had never been more than mere acquaintances, and neither liked the other. Teresa understood that a mentally conventional man could never like Basil; and she was entertained by the attempt which Fairfax, like most of the men who had admired her, made to manufacture domestic infelicity for her. They were so sure that she *could* not be happy with a man like Basil!

Fairfax on this evening was full of regrets for his impending departure. He would have to be away from New York for two weeks on business, he said, with a melancholy look. He was in a mood, half of pique with her, half of more liking than he had ever shown. Teresa often glanced down the table at Basil during their talk, but could never discover that he looked at her. She thought he was looking tired and excited; and he seemed absorbed in his neighbour, a very pretty young woman whom Teresa did not know. Teresa had repeated to Fairfax Basil's comment on some remark of his own, and his pique was due to this.

"Do you tell your husband every earthly thing?" he enquired.

"Everything!" said Teresa joyously.

"And he reads your letters, too, I suppose."

"All of 'em. And I read his."

"You think you do, you mean?"

"Yes, I mean I think I do!"

"What childishness! As though two people could really keep up that sort of thing."

"Ah, but they can. And I assure you, it's most interesting."

"It must be. But do people never tell either of you things that are not meant for another person? Or don't you consider confidences binding? Aren't you two individuals at all, but only a corporation?"

"Something like that, I think . . . And you know real confidences are rare—at least to me. I don't care about them."

"Then can neither of you have a friend whose confidences *would* be real, and whose friendship would be for you as an individual, not for you as a corporation?"

Teresa reflected.

"Isn't it conceivable that a person might care for you, and mightn't care for your husband? And that he mightn't care to be served up for that enviable person's further enjoyment? Wouldn't you have any loyalty to a feeling like that?"

"It's a difficult question!" sighed Teresa. "Why bother about such things now? I came in such a gay mood, feeling quite happy and frivolous! Don't spoil all my pleasure."

"I wish I felt happy and frivolous. Then I suppose I might add to it instead of spoiling it."

"Yes, you might. What *is* the good of being serious at dinner? And such a good dinner, too—but not better than our lunch the other day. I did enjoy that."

"Did you?" Fairfax looked a shade more cheerful. "I'm glad. Perhaps we can have another when I come back. And I'll be as frivolous as I can. I need to be frivolous if I'm going to amuse two people."

He came back to that again and again. He assured Teresa that her idea of marriage was totally wrong—unsocial.

"Marriage is an institution—a part of the state, of the organisation of society. Two people marry really for the purpose of helping one another socially, I mean in a broad sense; of bringing up children. The mere personal relation is a very small part of it. The feeling with which they marry, if they're in love with each other, doesn't last, can't last. It's bound to change. They ought to adapt themselves to that change, and make a broader relation on the basis of it—to take the family as the unit of their interest, not one another."

"I don't agree with you."

"Well, you will, some day. You'll find out that it doesn't work. Why marry at all, from your point of view?"

"Because it's more practical, and because common interests, and children, and common social relations help the original relation – they're in the line of its natural growth."

"You want to take all you can get out of society, then, and not give in return?"

"I do give – I give children, for example. But my private affairs are no concern of society's. Conventions are only made to be broken. Why shouldn't I have my own way of breaking them?"

"If you hadn't this particular convention, then, you admit you'd be more a social being."

"Yes, but I shouldn't be so happy."

"You risk being very unhappy sometime. That's what it is to put too much stress on one special relation."

Teresa shrugged her shoulders.

"If Allah wills it," she said, and her brilliant eyes seemed gaily to defy fate.

VIII

Teresa, in a spirit of contradiction, and the heat of argument, had chosen often to exaggerate the completeness with which she and Basil carried out that idea of frankness. She was aware of Basil's silences; and she herself was not as absolutely frank and unreserved as she sometimes assumed to be; but this arose not from her wish, but from the impossibility of translating everything into terms of speech. It would have been impossible, for example, to repeat all of her talks with Fairfax, and as these became more frequent in the course of the winter, the impossibility of telling all led her to tell little or nothing. It was not, however, because she had anything definite to conceal; but that her interest in him – and he did interest her, as a type not very familiar to her – was to a certain extent counter to her interest in Basil. The extent was slight, and did not touch her real feeling; but it absorbed a good deal of her attention. Basil was working hard that winter; they went out a good deal; and they spent less time together than ever before. Teresa was less jealous of his time. She was a little more worldly. Insensibly some sort of a veil had come between them – impalpable, not yet recognised by either of them, but the natural result of interests superficially divided. They lunched and dined frequently apart. Teresa ceased to question Basil, and, though, of his own accord, he generally gave an account of himself, he made one important reservation. He was seeing Mrs. Perry often, and saying nothing to Teresa about that lady. Harold Perry, who played so small a part in his wife's drama, was away all that winter, looking up Aztec remains. Isabel, therefore, was free to investigate religion. But that interest was temporarily in the background. Basil had taken its place.

· · · · ·

One day he went to lunch with her, as he was expected to do several times a week. He had broken a dinner engagement with her two days before, at the last moment, in order to dine alone with Teresa; and the excuse which he gave did not satisfy Isabel. She was in the mood, increasingly frequent with her, of dissatisfaction.

"Well, you know," he said frankly, at last, "your friends bore me, Isabel. I'm older than I used to be, and I prefer my own sort of people. And you must remember that I'm working pretty hard, and that I'm often tired. When I'm tired I don't want to talk inanities."

"Inanities? Do you call Father Damon's talk inanity—or Madame Blaise's—or—"

"No, but those people don't come to dinner with you. I've enjoyed *them*, of course, but your crowd on Tuesday was quite a different thing—wasn't it now? You only wanted me to fill up a gap, to amuse one of the young women."

"I always want you," said Isabel. "But you aren't willing to come just to please me."

"I can't really please you by boring myself. You must remember that the time I can spend with you is limited. Why should we waste it in things we can't really enjoy, or in discussions like this? If you could be content to let me come just when I'm in the best mood, it would be better for both of us."

"I'm afraid I should see you very little then," said Isabel, with subdued bitterness.

"It must be little, comparatively, in any case. But there's no reason why that little shouldn't be pleasant. Really I can amuse you much better if you let me choose my own times and seasons."

"Amuse! I don't want to be amused!"

"Oh, yes, you do, Isabel," said Basil, laughing. "That's exactly what you want."

She was silent, and a look of deep melancholy shadowed her face. Basil saw it with discomfort, which he did not allow to appear. He began to talk about her plans for the winter, about a book which he was encouraging her to write. She had in mind publishing anonymously a *Journal of a Woman of Thirty* and had showed him some loose pages of it which had rather surprised him by a certain gift of hectic expression. She had also gone seriously into charity work, had joined several societies, had set aside a tenth of her income for such contributions, and was looking about for some special work to do for the poor children of the city.

In all these efforts to fill the essential void of her life, Basil lent what aid he could. Her real suffering touched him, though her passionate expression of it often irritated and repelled him. There was no deep sympathy in him for people like Isabel, ill-adjusted to life, with inordinate claims, with demands that seemed to him essentially unreasonable. The quality in himself which had attracted Isabel, his ability to be essentially content, what she called his happiness, was exactly what limited his sympathy, and his real liking for her. She was beginning to see that limitation in him, to feel that there was no place for her in his life. Passionately, all of a sudden, breaking in upon his talk about her work, she accused him of lack of spirituality, of essential materialism.

"*You* aren't interested in these things, in trying to make the world a little more tolerable!" she cried. "You don't believe in anything I'm trying to do. You take it only as another way of amusing me! I cannot imagine, Basil, why I ever liked you!"

"Neither can I," he said readily. "Perhaps you don't."

"No, I don't, I don't like you! It is only another instance of my making a mess of everything. Everything I touch turns wrong. There are some people who are meant to be unhappy in the world, and I am one of them. I've never seen anything clearly in my life except that. It is not meant that I should try to live in the world."

"Perhaps it is not," said Basil slowly.

She lifted her eyes, full of a mystic questioning.

"You think so, too, now, don't you, Basil? You know you have always argued against that feeling of mine, and it was for that, I believe, that I loved you. I was seeking for something to strengthen me against that feeling, and I seemed to find it in you. I believe that's how it was. But *you* have only shown me how wrong I was in fighting against it. . . ."

She was silent, and Basil, too. This was the first definite reappearance of her old mood for some months, and Basil felt no energy within himself to combat it. His interest in Isabel had at all times been only a pale reflection of her feeling for him, apart from the impersonal interest which she discouraged, and his relation with her had brought him more discomfort than anything else.

. . . . .

Basil was not happy during that winter. He regretted the emotional complication he had been drawn into, and found the inevitable process of getting out of it difficult and unpleasant. The only cheerful thing about the situation was that Teresa apparently did not suspect it. And even this had a tinge of bitterness, for he thought that if she had not been absorbed herself, she would have suspected.

Teresa was absorbed—but not in any one person—only in amusing herself. She had never before been so gay. She saw many people, and gaiety mad her more popular; she basked in the sense of being liked. She perceived that Basil was unusually moody, but now she did not always try to get to the bottom of his moods. He said that work and money were bothering him, and was no less affectionate to her, but rather more so.

Isabel Perry's demands ended by wearying him profoundly and he came to Teresa for peace and comfort. But he had a grievance against Teresa, too, and this was that she now made so few demands on him. By way of attaining peace with her, he accused her of being more interested in someone else. The jealously of Fairfax, which he had resolutely stifled all winter long, appeared clearly. Teresa, with a shock, realised his unhappiness, and not knowing all the reasons, put it down solely to her own account. The complete story of her friendship with Fairfax made it clear to Basil that he was only an element in Teresa's enjoyment. Teresa tenderly admitted that her winter had been frivolous, and that she had neglected Basil; Basil protested that she had been quite right to have as good a time as she could. Then came peace between them, and a return of their old gaiety together. Teresa once more became accustomed to hearing how much more charming, how much more beautiful she was than other women. She took the other women as nameless abstractions, and smiled at the praise.

In the spring she knew that she was to have another child, and this one she welcomed. She wanted a companion for Ronald, and she now loved Ronald's baby graces so intimately that all possible babies appeared beautiful to her. Once more, and all at once, the world of frivolity fell away from her. For the time it absolutely ceased to interest her. Once more the special atmosphere, cloistral quiet of spirit, serious-ness, and peace of mind, closed round her. She showed a quiet, dreamy happiness, for which Basil adored her.

They took for the summer a cottage in a quiet place by the sea, not far from New York, for Basil was to do some work in the city. He was now doing real pot-boilers—illustrations for two books, and some magazine-stories. Teresa assured him that if they could only tide over thus the baby's birth—for they were in debt—next year they might live more simply, keep within their income, and then he needn't do that sort of work, which he detested.

They began the summer very happily together, Basil going up to town two or three days a week, for his drawings had to be realistic pictures of some aspects of the city. They thought they might keep the little cottage till near time for the baby's arrival in December. June passed sweetly and calmly. But at the beginning of July Teresa had a great shock. Gerald Dallas shot himself; and she read the news, a brief, bald report, in her morning paper.

She had not seen him for months, their lives had been completely separated; but her affection for him still lived, and revived suddenly under the sting of pity and self-reproach. Basil that morning had gone to town very early. Trembling and faint, Teresa dressed, took the next train, and went to the studio. She did not find Basil. A telegram from Isabel that morning had summoned him to meet her. She was in town for the day. Accordingly he was lunching at a restaurant with her, and being called to account for his various deficiencies, when Teresa came to the studio. She hesitated a few moments, then scribbled a note and dropped it through the letter-slit, went down and found a cab, and gave the address of Gerald's lodging, taken from the newspaper account. The place was a cheap boarding-house, near one of the small squares in the lower part of the city. It was a broiling day, and the odours of poverty assailed Teresa's senses as she got out at the door and after some argument was admitted. In one of Gerald's two rooms she found a chattering group of women. One of them, red-eyed and flushed, a tall, robust girl, who had answered her knock, seemed to be the mistress of the place. To her, Teresa, half dazed, said she was Gerald's friend, gave her name, and was ushered into the room, where the other women, silent now, stared at her curiously. The tall girl began to pour out a flood of self-pitying explanations, mixed with tears.

It had happened the day before. He had taken the time when she, Annette, was away at rehearsal. He had written her a letter, which the police had taken, telling her what he meant to do, giving directions about his funeral, and saying that she was to take whatever possessions he left. The letter had been brought to her by a messenger, and she had come back and found him dead. He had shot himself through the heart, lying on the bed. He had been ill for several weeks, and she had had a terrible time of it.

Teresa went into the other room, which was darkened and hot. Annette opened a blind, and drew down the sheet from Gerald's face. Teresa felt suddenly calm and glad. She lingered for some moments, feeling tremulously the happiness of his peace, his escape from pain; then she kissed him on the forehead and went away, saying to Annette that she would come next day to the funeral.

At the studio this time she found Basil, that moment returned, and frantic with anxiety because of her note. She stammered out a few words in his arms, and fainted.

The summer was darkened for her by this event and by the physical weakness caused by the shock. Basil's devotion to her was complete, yet her prevailingly sad mood came to irritate him, since he felt she might shake it off by a sufficient effort. His remonstrances had no effect. Her melancholy and ill-health continued up to the time of the baby's birth, and were beyond the reach of her will. She was further depressed by fears for the effect of her state on the coming child. She felt, as she contemplated what was before her, that her strength would not carry her through, and she thought she might die, and feared it on Ronald's account. She thought much about Gerald. She was sure that if he had known her condition he would not have dealt her this blow. But he must have known in any case, that it would be a blow to her; and all life took a darker colour because of his inability to bear it.

In December Teresa was very ill. She went to a hospital, and there the baby was born, and lived but two days. It was a boy; and at her first sight of him Teresa thought she saw an epitome of all the sorrows of man. He was totally unlike her first child. His tiny face, with heavy, mournful eyelids, with strange, deep lines about the mouth, made him seem a creature as old as the world. To Teresa all the sad experience of humanity seemed foreshadowed or summed up in him.

He died; and Teresa's grief was passionate beyond the comprehension perhaps of any man. Basil, though sad himself, and full of sympathy for her suffering, could not understand its full extent. To him the child had never really lived; it was hardly more than an abstract expression of the terrible will to live of the unborn universe; an atom of the ever-pulsing energy which forced its way into the world, causing suffering and woe—all for a life of two days. But to Teresa the baby was a complete being, and she sorrowed for him as though she had wronged him herself of his life. And she sorrowed for herself, for the joy, comfort, recompense, she had lost. She passionately wanted the physical presence of the baby, wanted to forget everything in such a half-animal, half-spiritual peace as its small, clinging life would have brought to her. She revolted against the uselessness of her suffering. She desired to die, and for weeks thought she might.

For a time she was indifferent to Basil, and even to Ronald, now nearly two years old. But she was cared for in spite of herself, strength began to come back to her, and soon she could go to the apartment they had taken for the rest of the winter. In the spring they meant to go abroad, Teresa and the baby first, Basil following as soon as he could get through some necessary work. He had still another book to illustrate—a book made up of magazine articles on the foreign quarters of New York. Basil despised the sentimentality of the letter-press, and promised himself some recompense in making his drawings as biting and brutal as possible. Teresa's illness had been expensive, and Basil had recently had to pay a note for a thousand dollars, endorsed by Major Ransome for a friend. Need of money drove him finally to agree to a demand which he had fought off for some time. Isabel Perry wanted another portrait of herself. She wanted it, Basil knew, simply in order to secure his presence at definite times. At first he had refused flatly, and kept to his refusal for several months. But at last, in a moment partly of feeling for her, and partly of harassing consciousness of debt, he promised to do it—and when he had left her he cordially hated their whole embroglio.

IX

The portrait was begun; and Isabel, having carried her point, became for a time extraordinarily sweet and docile. Three sittings a week having been conceded, she made no other demands on Basil's time, which he wished to devote, outside of work, to his wife. He made great efforts to divert Teresa, to induce her to go out, to make her take care of her health, which was re-established very slowly. She recognised his care of her gratefully, though almost dumbly, and tried at times to meet his wish, but an overwhelming lassitude of mind and body left her no energy of will. She wanted nothing except absolute peace and quiet, and Basil's keen desire that she should begin to live again interfered with her recovery. She began to feel that she should not get strong till she got away by herself, and at last expressed a wish to go at once to Europe. This was in March; but the dangers of the winter crossing for herself and Ronald, and her own physical weakness resulted in a joint veto of Basil and the doctor; and Teresa yielded passively. She lived on, therefore, in the apartment, seeing as few people as she could manage, not going out unless she was forced; disarming Basil's impatience at her persistent negation by her extreme gentleness. She ceased to talk about the dead baby to him, because she saw he thought her morbid. Sometimes she thought that Gerald Dallas would have understood her, but there was no one else. Everyone else tried to amuse her. Fairfax came a few times to see her, but the great change in her, and her evident lack of interest in him, discouraged his visits. There was only Major Ransome whom she was really willing to see. The Major's whole-souled acceptance of woman, as a weak creature who must be coddled and indulged in her unreasonableness—rather amusing, in view of the two strong-willed women who had married him—somewhat comforted Teresa. But after all the Major bored her. She did not want him or anyone else, not even for the tiny Ronald, whose extreme vitality made him a too exact copy of Basil. Basil was not too cheerful at this time, but he tried to be. His intensely positive nature made him unwilling to accept grief as Teresa did. He wanted to forget their misfortune, to find again their joy in life, and to supply it meantime by interests which seemed to Teresa factitious and feverish. He was working hard himself, and as a last resort he tried to get Teresa to think of her work again. But her first essay with the clay discouraged him. She modelled in secret, only showing it to him when it was done, a little statuette of the dead baby, as he lived in her thoughts: a tiny naked creature lying with relaxed limbs, its heavy-eyed, deep-lined face expressing all the pathos of life manqué. At Basil's almost weeping protest Teresa silently put away the little image, and did not touch her clay again.

• • • • •

Isabel, in the second portrait, instinctively wanted to have expressed her charm as a woman—the thing by which she had tried to attach Basil, and, as she knew, failed. She had chosen a dress of black velvet, which in the evening brought out wonderfully the intensity of her hair and eyes, and subdued her Spanish skin to ivory. But the harsh light of the studio denied her all charm of mystery and suggestion; even as the keen reality of Basil's nature had stripped their relation of the romance, the sentimentality, which she had striven to give it, and brought out its essential commonplace. After four sittings under the painter's cool gaze, it became apparent that the portrait would have nothing of what she wanted. With her usual impetuosity Isabel expressed her dissatisfaction.

"Basil, you are making me out an old hag! I won't be painted like that, I'm not like that, I'm not ugly! You are doing it on purpose! . . ."

Basil shrugged his shoulders.

"I don't paint pretty pictures," he said indifferently. "If you want to be done all rose-colour and illusion, you ought to go to one of the lady-painters. You said the other picture was ugly, too, and yet you liked it—or said you did."

"It was different—it was not brutal like this!"

"Perhaps you can't judge it very well, at this stage."

"Yes, I can see what you mean to make it—something that I would never in the world exhibit, or even hang up anywhere. Perhaps it's because it's so big and—pretentious."

"I thought that dress demanded a big canvas," said Basil ironically.

He laid down his palette and brushes carefully, definitively, and said:

"We won't go on with it."

"I didn't mean that," said Isabel quickly.

She was standing near him, holding up the sweeping velvet train with both hands, on which the diamonds glittered coldly.

"No, but I mean it," said Basil.

She looked at him, dropped her train, and moved to put one hand on his arm.

"Don't be silly, Basil, or sulky. I daresay I'm wrong, and it will come out all right. I know I oughtn't to criticise—"

"No, it won't come right. I was a fool to undertake it. I didn't want to do it. I can't do a pot-boiler of that size!"

He smiled, took out his cigarette-case—and her hand slipped from his arm—and began to smoke with quick, nervous exhalations of relief.

"I'm punished," he said. "I started the thing to please you, Isabel, and, worse, still, for the money. I felt like a slave. I don't believe I could have finished it. You're perfectly right to dislike it. Good Lord, how glad I am you dislike it! Now, if you'll forgive me for being a bungler and wasting your time, we can forget it. Do forgive me, will you?"

"I really don't think I shall," said Isabel slowly, clasping and unclasping her nervous fingers. "I don't like to waste my time, as you say. And I think it's childish of you to be so piqued by a hasty word of mine—"

"It isn't that, dear Isabel—it really isn't that, but something deeper—

my conviction that I wasn't making a good thing of it, and couldn't. I haven't liked it from the start. I hadn't the mood for it. I couldn't *see* it. I didn't like that dress, for one thing—"

"Then why didn't you say so? You know I would have taken any other—"

"No, it was your choice, and I was trying to do this simply and solely for you, and that's the reason I've failed. I'm enough of an artist anyhow not to be able to do anything good except for myself. I shall know that another time."

There was a deep suppressed bitterness in his tone which indicated more than his feeling about the picture. Isabel was silent for some moments. In her thoughts, as well as his, perhaps, the picture symbolised a deeper failure. She moved restlessly, walked away from the easel, trailing her rich dress carelessly over a brush that had fallen on the floor; she flushed, bit her lips, and finally said sharply: "I shouldn't think you'd like to admit a failure like this without—without really trying to do as well as you can by it—and by me. I want you to go on—perhaps the mood will come—if not, I shan't reproach you—and I shall have got something out of it—some satisfaction—"

"I can't," said Basil gently. "It's useless, it's only wasting your time— and my own. I couldn't let you pay me for a picture I thought bad. If I'm to do pot-boilers, they must be for people who honestly want bad things. For that you're too intelligent. Let's say no more about it, please."

"You will not, then, do what I ask, if only to please me?"

"I can't."

"Then you're brutally unkind to me."

Basil's face flushed quickly. In a flash of his quick temper he caught up a brush from the table and splashed two blue streaks across the face and neck in the portrait.

Isabel burst into tears. She went waveringly toward the divan, sank down on it, and swept hysterically into a cushion. Basil, with his back to her, stood silent, passionately resentful; his fingers, clenched in the pocket of his coat, crushed a handful of cigarettes to fragments. When Isabel, finding that she was not to be consoled, stopped crying and summoned the remnants of her pride, it was still some time before she could speak. Basil was still immobile, and there was no sign of softening in his attitude. Isabel, as quickly as possible, took the course which her instinct pointed out as the necessary one. The silence had become terrible to her.

"I was wrong," she said dully. "I have been, I am, wrong. I cannot get what I have wanted. And it is not your fault. I was wrong when I said you had been unkind to me. Perhaps you might have been kinder—perhaps—but I think you have done your best. You aren't exactly a kind person. One must—just make up one's mind to the bitterness of it. One must see—one's own folly. I have seen it—oh, I have so tried not to see it. I couldn't bear to see it. Now I shan't try any more. I shall—accept it."

Her head sank. She smoothed the folds of her dress over her knees with a slow motion. Basil turned toward her a tired, tormented look.

"Let us not talk any more to-day," he begged. "On my word, I'm done—absolutely done—"

"Yes, I'm going now. . . . And I shall go away at once—south somewhere, Florida, I think."

"You'll let me come and see you before you go."

"Oh, yes, I should like to see you once more. But no more scenes, Basil—I promise. Just a quiet talk—and then good-bye."

Her tone was dull and exhausted. She sat still, looking musingly at the floor, and Basil was about to go toward her when a knock sounded at the door. Basil opened. It was Teresa.

In the instant of greeting her, while he stood inwardly hesitating and blocking the view of the studio, Mrs. Perry rose and went quickly into the dressing-room. It did not take Basil more than five seconds to decide that he must let Teresa in, and he did so, flattering himself that his hesitation had not been noticed.

"You're surprised to see me, aren't you?" she said smiling. "Are you busy? I thought, suddenly, I'd like to go out and dine to-night at one of our old haunts. Would you like it?"

"I would, of all things," he cried fervently. "Come in, Mrs. Perry's been posing. I'm free now, and we'll have a walk first, if you feel up to it. Are you strong enough? How's the weather?"

"Cold, but nice. I'd like a short walk anyway—I feel almost energetic!"

She came into the room, loosening her furs. She was dressed in black, which she had worn ever since the baby's death, and her face was rather thinner and paler than before, though the frosty air had given her an unusual tinge of colour.

In passing she glanced at the portrait on the easel and stopped in surprise.

"Why, what have you done?" she cried.

Basil wished he could have got the picture out of sight, but said cheerfully: "Spoilt it. Too bad, isn't it?"

Teresa studied the canvas.

"A fit of temper? Of course, I can't tell very well now, but perhaps you were too quick. Still, you can always take off that blue paint, can't you?"

"No. I was working on the face, and it's all gone. It was bad—the whole scheme of the thing. I felt from the beginning that it wouldn't do. Of course, I'm sorry to have muffed it. But it's a relief not to go on with it, when I see it's a failure."

He spoke volubly, moving about quickly, putting away his brushes and palette; and finally he took down the canvas and set it with its face to the wall. Teresa sat down on the divan, and they talked cursorily for some ten minutes. Mrs. Perry found some difficulty in dressing without a maid, and also wanted to get rid of the marks of tears. In this she was hardly successful. Unfortunately she had no veil. When she came out finally, Teresa's first glance at her face resulted in a second quick scrutiny. The two women met conventionally. It was their first meeting for nearly a year, and whatever feeling of intimacy there had been between them had long since disappeared.

"Would you mind calling a cab for me?" Mrs. Perry said to Basil, after the first greeting to Teresa.

In her tone was a certain hint of imperiousness. Basil went out, with a naive sense of escaping from an uncomfortable situation.

"Well, the picture has been judged a failure, you see," Mrs. Perry said rapidly, pulling on her gloves. "I'm so disappointed—I'd really set my heart on it. But I suppose there's no appeal. Artists have their ways of feeling about their work that ordinary mortals can't be expected to comprehend—isn't that true?"

"I suppose it is," Teresa said mechanically. "It's a pity. Have you wasted much time on it?"

"Four sittings—a good deal for a busy person like myself. But—I won't grumble any more."

"Basil will be sorrier than you, I'm sure. He hates to make failures."

"No—I don't believe he's very sorry. He wasn't interested in it. He'll never be a success as a portrait-painter, will he?"

Teresa smiled. "Not a worldly success, I fancy. But I don't believe he much wants to be."

"Oh, I daresay not. Only great painters were, weren't they? They all wanted to please a duke, or a king, or somebody. Of course, when a painter gets a big name, like Sargent or Whistler, he can have as many moods and whims as he likes; it only makes people run after him the more. I've heard so many stories about that Swedish man that painted everybody last year. He did about two portraits a week, and he said when he got back to Sweden that if he could have painted with his left hand he might have done two at once. He started pictures of all the De Morgan girls, and made love to one of them, and Papa de Morgan kicked him out of the house; but he insisted on being paid for all the pictures just the same, under threat of a lawsuit, and got the money. And they got him to paint the King of Sweden, and he painted him looking half asleep and quite idiotic, not at all regal. Then one of the princesses sat for him, and he came quite drunk and slapped off the portrait in no time. That's what it is to be the fashion!"

Mrs. Perry laughed nervously. Her voice had a harshness character-istic of her in emotion. Teresa listened gravely, turning her muff in her hands. Her narrow eyes were cooly observant.

Basil came and announced the cab, and Mrs. Perry nodded and said:

"Thank you. I'll send for my dress to-day. Don't bother to come down."

She advanced to shake hands with Teresa. "Good-bye—I haven't seen you for so long—I'm sorry—you're looking a little ill, aren't you? I'm awfully sorry. I shall be leaving directly for Florida, else I would come to see you. Good-bye—I hope we shall meet next fall, and you'll get strong and well meantime—"

"Thank you—good-bye," Teresa said indifferently. She had risen—their eyes met on a level. . . . Mrs. Perry turned quickly and went out.

X

Why was Mrs. Perry in such a rage?" asked Teresa calmly, as they walked up toward the Park.

She walked more easily, with more energy, than she had done for many months, and her face above the grey fur looked suddenly ani-mated, though by no means happy.

"In a rage, was she? Why, what did she say? She didn't like my spoiling the picture," Basil answered off-hand.

"Was that what she was crying about?"

"She wasn't crying—Teresa!"

"She had been, about five minutes before. She was in a thorough hysterical passion. I'm not exactly blind, Basil."

"You're fanciful, like all women," he said uncomfortably. "Now, don't—please, dearest!—don't fancy things. You don't know how happy I am to have you here with me, looking like your dear old self again—I'm so happy that you felt like coming out. We'll dine together as we used to do—oh, how I have missed you, these last months!"

His voice shook, and he took her hand and put it through his arm. It was dusk. The avenue was crowded with carriages, though the walk was comparatively free. In the clear frosty air the lights of the street sparkled and flashed gaily.

"Were you really glad to see me?" said Teresa slowly.

"Glad? If you knew how glad—"

"But you'd rather I'd have come a little later—after she'd gone? I'm sure *she* would."

Basil sighed impatiently.

"How long since you began the picture?" Teresa asked meditatively.

"Oh, only a week or so. I'd only worked on it four times. Thank heaven, I haven't got to touch it again! She's going away, and I hope I shall never see her again."

His involuntary expression was too unrestrained, too savagely convincing. Teresa was silent, and drew her hand away. He began to talk, too quickly, about other things. She answered in the right places, and he began to think the other question had dropped; but she came back to it abruptly.

"I see now what you meant by saying you had missed me these months. . . . I might have known that *your* life would not stop just because mine did. . . . I have been half dead, it's true, but you—you could not be. But I did not think it was *this*. . . ."

"You're utterly mistaken. Whatever interest I had in her stopped long before. These last months—for a long time—it's been nothing but—"

He stopped suddenly. He had meant vaguely to express his weariness of the whole affair, but saw too late how it was committing him. He was not a practiced liar.

"Long before," said Teresa slowly. "You mean—before the baby?"

"Yes, I mean—oh, I mean she did interest me somewhat, as you know, at one time—some time ago—"

"Ah, it was then," said Teresa in a far-off tone.

But it's nothing you need care about. I was never emotionally interested in her, if that's what you're driving at. I don't see why you question me. I tell you I don't care for her, and never did, except as a friend, a person that it was interesting to talk to occasionally. She *is* interesting, objectively—so much temperament and energy somehow gone to waste. But even in that way I'm not interested now."

"Why not?"

"Oh, because nothing interests me just now, except being quiet with you. I'm infernally tired. I'd like to get out of everything and go away somewhere and have nothing to think of but work—my *own* work, that I haven't been able to do at all this winter."

"I'm so sorry. But you're sure there was nothing else—nothing but friendship—nothing emotional between you?"

"Absolutely sure. Not that I think you've any right to question me like this, but I answer this once—there was nothing of what you seem to suspect."

"Basil, you lie badly," was her quiet comment.

"How dare you say I lie!" he burst out. "I won't say another word to you about it! First, you cross-question me as you've no right to do, and then you say I lie! I won't stand it."

Teresa walked on a few steps farther to a corner, and stopped.

"Will you get me a cab, please?" she said gently. "I'll go home."

"No, Teresa!" he cried wretchedly. "We can't separate like this. I can't quarrel with you now. Let us go and have our dinner—don't, don't quarrel with me, for heaven's sake!"

"I don't want to quarrel," she said in the same deadly quiet tone. "Let us go to dinner, then. But I'd like the cab—I'm cold."

In the carriage he felt her shivering beside him. She hid her face in her muff and replied by monosyllables to his anxious questions. Basil had given the address of a down-town restaurant where they had often dined together gaily, and they had rather a long drive. When they were seated at the table, Basil, worried by Teresa's deadly pallor, made her drink a little brandy. To his surmise that the walk was too much for her, she assented absently, and then said: "But it is time I made some effort. I see that myself now. Life does not stop for one. Life goes on. And one must live, too, while it lasts."

She spoke without emotion; in her neutral eyes, that rested everywhere except on Basil's face, there was a look of suffering.

"You need a change. I've felt it for some time, only you didn't seem strong enough—"

"If I don't get away now, I shall die," she said, in the same quiet way. "I shall start next week. I want to be away, alone, all summer."

"Alone? But you're not fit, Teresa—"

"Oh, you know I'm to be with Nina and her family—that's arranged.

We shall go to some quiet place, where I can be at peace, and get strong."

"Alone, then, means just that you don't want me."

Her assent was silence. She looked away, at the faces of the other people in the room, and her face was quiet as marble.

Basil's head dropped. Neither of them had made more than a pretence of tasting their food. He began to make lines on the tablecloth with a fork. After some moments she looked at him. She saw that his face was haggard, and pale under its brown tone. She recognised in its drawn look of nervous fatigue the accentuation of a change that had been coming about for some time, that she had noticed at intervals during the winter. At last he glanced up, and his eyes, that had always seemed to her so strangely young, now in their passionate misery sent a pang to her heart.

"Perhaps it is best for you," he said with some difficulty, looking down again. "Perhaps you will be better off, away from me. But it isn't best for me."

"For both of us, I think," she said gently.

"Not for me! I want you, I need you, and now more than ever. You could be a thousand times more to me now even than you have been. For this last year you've hardly been mine at all—you've been away in spirit—you haven't been conscious of me much of the time—"

"And, therefore, you took a mistress."

His fork dropped with a clatter on his plate.

"I did no such thing! But if I had tried to have—not a mistress, I couldn't—but some sort of active interest in my life, most people wouldn't blame me—"

"It was because I was so unhappy," Teresa said in her far-away voice. "Life seemed to have been taken out of me for the time. I *could* not be anything else, do anything but go on from day to day. . . ."

"I know, I'm not reproaching you—and you don't understand me, either. All these months you only have been in my thoughts—you have been my only real interest, though I tried to be interested in my work. I've wanted only to take care of you—if you remember, you know that's true."

"Yes, you have tried. I have been a great burden."

"Never to me have you been anything but the dearest part of myself, the dearest thing on earth. Never a burden. I've often been sad because of you, but if you think I've loved you less—"

He could not go on. He took up his glass with a shaking hand and drank.

"I can't understand," said Teresa, and her voice was a low cry of pain.

"I wish to God you could know every thought of my heart, every act of mine—then perhaps you would understand. You would know, at least, how I love you."

"But you can't tell me, can you?" You can't tell me the truth about—this."

Basil was silent now. Uppermost in his consciousness was a feeling of unbearable fatigue, confusing his mind. He thought vaguely that if he had not been so tired he would not have got into this intolerable predicament. How to get out of it he could not see. The impulse of confession was so strong in him that he had to fight it down consciously. He desired intensely to tell Teresa everything, to make her feel as nothing else now could, the real unimportance of his liaison, to himself and to her. But a feeling that he would be a cur if he told, miserably held him back. He had not yet admitted anything to her. He must deny it, not for his own sake, but for that of the other woman. Only he could not deny convincingly. His lies, he knew, must be half hearted. Each one put another barrier in the way of Teresa's understanding of him, given the moral certainty of the truth which, in some mysterious way, she seemed to to have acquired. How she had leaped to that certainty he could not see. In another woman her attitude might have been a ruse, but Teresa was not artful. She believed that he had been deceiving her, and was still trying to do so; she could not possibly know how essentially truthful, so far as their own real relation went, he had always been.

"You can't tell me—can you?" she repeated softly.

"I can't tell you more than I have already said. I've not been unfaithful to you, Teresa. This suspicion that you've got in your head is absolutely wrong."

"Will you swear it?" she asked with a faint mocking smile.

"Yes, if necessary. But you might be willing to take my word."

"No—don't swear—don't swear," she said musingly. Then she looked straight at him. "I'll ask you no more questions. It is finished. *That* leaf is turned down. One lives and learns—unfortunately. . . . Something is changed in me, Basil—this day has made a difference in our lives. I don't quite know what it is yet—I haven't got adjusted to it. It came on me so suddenly—like a physical blow."

"I don't know what you're talking about," said Basil violently. "But I know I've had as much as I can stand. Life hasn't been any too pleasant of late, and this caps the climax. I think it *is* better you should go away. Then, perhaps, I can feel like a free man again, and not like an infernal miserable slave!"

"Yes—poor Basil," said Teresa softly, mockingly.

"Have you had enough to eat?" he demanded, a flame of anger in his eyes.

"Oh, plenty, thanks. Pay the bill and we'll go. And give the waiter a good big fee. It's been such a pleasant dinner."

Basil did not look at her again till just as they were leaving the restaurant. He had sent for a cab, and now he said:

"You can go home alone, can't you?"

"Perfectly." Her eyes met his—wrath meeting wrath.

She drove away in the cab. Basil walked up the street, with wild desires to smash something seething in his mind. Brutal dissipation presented itself as a means of forgetting for a time the world and his tormented soul. He turned into a music-hall and sat alone at a table, and drank three strong whiskies, and looked at the spectacle about him with haggard, forbidding eyes. In half an hour he got up and went home.

He let himself in quietly, and paused at Teresa's closed door. He heard her sobbing—deep, racking, choking sounds of pain. He turned the handle of the door, called her name. The sobs were stifled then, but he heard them still. He called her again, imploringly, angrily, pleadingly, and shook the door, and threatened to break it down. But it remained locked.

PART 3 OPENS WITH TERESA in Paris, still melancholy about the loss of her baby six months earlier. In the Louvre she unexpectedly meets Crayven, three years after their brief meeting in New York. Teresa sees him several times in Paris and discovers he is spending the summer in Switzerland, close to where she and her son will vacation with Teresa's sister Nina and her large Italian family.

Before she left New York, Teresa had, in her words, "a partial and unsatisfactory reconciliation with Basil " (1908 ed., 262). His misery had broken down her resistance, but Teresa was still tormented by Basil's relationship with Isabel Perry. As a result, "something was gone—the old confidence, the old assurance. Joy was gone and trust; and love that remained was bitter, a torment" (1908 ed., 262). Basil wants them to spend the summer together near New York, but Teresa has to get away "and hide herself like wounded animal" (1908 ed., 263). She sails to Europe with her son.

In thinking about her relationship to Basil, Teresa articulates her view of love and marriage:

> Love, as she loved him, meant complete spiritual possession, complete confidence, or unhappiness. She would not resign herself to unhappiness. She would not live with endless suspicion, sordid quarrels, nagging. She would rather live by herself. . . . There was only one thing that would convince her [of his sincerity] and that was the truth about the other woman, and this Basil apparently would not tell. And it seemed to Teresa that if he would not tell, it must be because he had too much to conceal, even that spiritual infidelity which he had constantly denied. . . . It would have been much finer to have taken Basil at his word, to have risen superior to this whole episode, it would also have been more sensible and more worldly—only it would have been quite false. (1908 ed., 263–65)

The intense involvement and authenticity Teresa seeks in marriage is contrasted to the views of her sister. Nina is married to a handsome, charming, irresponsible Italian, who most certainly is unfaithful. Nina has five children and manages a complicated household. She says of marriage: "It's an affair of family, it isn't two people in love with one another. . . . You know how much Ernesto was in love with me. After the first year, when the children came, of course it had to be different. . . . You have to realize that your life is the family, and that the man has his life away from you" (1908 ed., 258–59).

Teresa will not accept Nina's views, but she begins to refocus her anger on Mrs. Perry and on herself:

> Basil had been right—she should not have gone away from him. She should have answered his appeal. She had been wrong toward him in many ways. She had never of her own will sacrificed anything to their love—had given nothing but what she wanted to give. She had yielded too much to her grief that last year; she had not thought enough of Basil. What he had done was only what all men did. Men were cursed with a perpetual need of action. They could not be quiet any more than vigorous children. The thing was to direct their insensate energizing

into the least harmful channels. She had never tried very much to direct Basil. She thought of him now as a small boy shut up in the house on a rainy day, and told to make no noise. Yes, that had been her attitude toward him all that last winter – and she had paid for it. She had given the other woman her chance. A sudden flood of rage against Isabel welled up in her and dried her tears. She considered ways and means of being revenged upon her. The blood beating in her temples told her how it was possible to stab, to poison, to choke a rival. Something wild rose in her, as a thousand times before, at the thought of their caresses, and all the softness of her mood was gone. The tender letter to Basil, like so many others she had imagined or even begun, was never written. (1908 ed., 285–86)

Teresa turns her attention to Crayven, at first without a conscious recognition of what she is doing. Crayven leaves his wife in the city to stay in a mountain village near Teresa. She is aware that he has come to see her and is grateful for the attention. They fall into an easy companionship, walking together in the afternoons and dining and playing cards with Nina's family and friends in the evenings. They talk very little about their personal lives, but an unspoken intimacy grows up between them. Despite her self-absorption, Teresa begins to see that their relationship could be interpreted as romantic. She accepts this: "Something was changed between Basil and herself. She no longer felt that they belonged absolutely to one another. The bond that was too strong to break, that had been too strait to bear, was in some way loosened. She no longer felt accountable to Basil for herself" (1908 ed., 297).

Crayven begins to be more open. He confesses that he was first attracted to Teresa because she looks so similar to a woman who rejected him ten years ago. Teresa is hurt and disappointed. "So this was the reason of his interest in her – a fancied resemblance to a boyish love! He had said she would not like – and she did not like – it. Her vanity was hurt, and she felt suddenly remote from him, bored, and thought of Basil" (1908 ed., 307). Teresa is also upset when Crayven takes her to meet his wife, a worldly and superficial woman, with whom he has nothing in common, and from whom he lives completely separately.

Teresa is caught off guard, however, when Crayven confesses that he has fallen in love with her. She recognizes that she had tried to attract him to hurt Basil, but she realizes that despite her ulterior motives she has become involved with Crayven:

The strange possibilities of life – the fact that all one's life might have been different – might even be different – rushed upon her in a dizzying flood. Her world seemed suddenly to become unreal, pale – she lost her grasp upon it, in the feeling that another choice had been possible. And something deep in her answered to Crayven's emotion – a deep correspondence of temperament, some sort of inevitable affinity. And a wild sense of the adventures of life, a desire to set back once more the boundaries of experience, to launch into the unfamiliar, stirred to her. "Strange – I could have loved you," she said wonderingly. "Then love me! Good God! If you only knew how lonely I am – how stale life seems to me! I want a little happiness before I die." (1908 ed., 337).

But when Crayven tries to kiss her, Teresa freezes:

Hard reality stared her in the face – the sense of her bondage. She was not free for a moment, she could never love Crayven nor anyone else. Something far deeper than convention, which she would willingly have thrown overboard, bound her, body and soul. She liked Crayven thoroughly, she felt affection for him, and in her rebellion she wished passionately that she could care more for him or could be deceived into thinking she cared – but she could not. All that pleasant shimmering illusion of possibility was gone. He was more sympathetic to her in many ways than Basil, she even liked him better, but she had no real emotion for him. Basil had taken it all – all! He had taken her whole self, her will, her imagination, her entire power of loving. She was drained of it all. There was nothing left. She was bound – bound! And she wept with anger as she realized how completely she was delivered into his hands, how vain had been her pretense that she could do without him, could "console" herself. He might be unfaithful, but she never could. How strange was that bond, deeper than the will, deeper than any sympathy of mind, taking no account of the many things in him that she deeply disliked, of the fact that she really disliked his character! It was infinitely more than a physical bond, it was a passion of the soul. How strange and how terrible! (1908 ed., 349–50)

Teresa and Crayven have an emotional, forgiving farewell. On the boat going home, Teresa realizes that she will not easily forget Crayven.

As she lay at night on deck, motionless for hours under her rugs, and watched the rush of the dark water into darkness, she thought of his long ride through the sands. She seemed to see him wrapped in the Arab cloak, his face rather tired but philosophically calm, as when she had seen it first. He was going back to his work—to danger, perhaps. The incident, for him, was over.

It was probable that she would never see him again. She breathed out an intense wish for his safety and well-being, into the vague night (1908 ed., 357).

PART IV

I

Basil was there on the pier, when, crippled by a mid-Atlantic storm, the ship crept in, a day late. A haze of summer heat hung over the bay and the city; a hot breath came from the land. In the crowd she caught sight of him, a head above his neighbours, his eyes eagerly lifted, searching the crowded deck. He saw her, and waved his straw hat. It was a smart Panama, and his light-grey coat looked new. But Basil was always smart. When they met, with a quick clasp of both hands, in the midst of the crowd, Teresa's glance devoured his face, noting its slight pallor, slight sallowness about the eyes.

"You're well?" she said breathlessly.

"Oh, all right. But it's beastly hot! Must get you and the boy straight out of town—"

Smiling, he caught Ronald up and kissed him, laughing with pleasure.

"How you've grown, old man! Forgotten me? Do you know who I am?"

"Papa," said Ronald, with his superior smile.

"Good for you—what a memory you've got! . . ."

He put Teresa, Ronald, and the nurse into a carriage and sent them to a hotel, staying himself to see the luggage through the Custom-house. It was nearly seven o'clock, and Ronald had been put to bed, when Basil came. Teresa was lying on her bed, her head still whirling from the effect of the voyage. Basil wanted first to see Ronald again. The child was in the next room, not yet asleep. He went in, and Teresa heard his voice—

pleasant-toned, fond, and joking—and heard Ronald laugh sleepily. At last Basil came back, shutting the door, and sat down beside Teresa.

"What a splendid fellow he is—what a beauty!" he said, with a little shake in his voice. "I'm fond of that boy, Teresa."

"Turn on the light—I want to see you," said Teresa lazily.

Basil turned on the light and took off his coat, showing a pale-blue silk shirt which fastened neatly about his strong throat with a blue tie and a gold pin; then he sat down again on the edge of the bed. Teresa lay looking at him. Her loose, dark hair swept across her forehead and cheek, and her lowered eyelids showed a narrow line of blue.

"How hot you look, poor dear," she said softly, looking at his forehead.

"Yes—beastly weather. Must have a bath before dinner. Are you too tired to go out somewhere? I'll find a cool place to eat."

"Tired—no. Only my head's queer yet. We had a rough voyage."

"I know—odd at this time of year."

She touched his sleeve caressingly.

"What a nice rig! Blue's your colour—mine too, oddly. Red suits Ronald best. He's looking well, isn't he?"

"Like a fighting-cock! You've taken good care of him. And you . . . you're looking very much stronger. . . ."

"You haven't said you're glad to see us back."

"And you . . . are *you* glad? . . ."

"If I'm glad!"

Basil bent to look into her eyes, gathered her up in her loose white dress, and her arms went round him in a clasp that seemed as if it could never loosen. They held one another, silent, for long, long moments, and to Teresa all bitterness, all chance of misunderstanding seemed to ebb away out of consciousness. Just to have him there, in her arms, was like bread to a gnawing hunger, like water to a biting thirst.

· · · · ·

They dined together at one of their old haunts, on a balcony overlooking a broad street. It was not a fashionable quarter. The restaurant and the street were full of foreign *bourgeois* people, less noisy because of the heat. Low thunderclouds hung over the city; it seemed to gasp for breath. Teresa wore the white dress and hat which she had put into her steamer-trunk with an idea of this occasion. Basil studied her face with keen attention.

"You look younger—you look awfully strong and well—it *has* done you a lot of good. It's too bad to pull you back into this heat—we must get out of town to-morrow. You haven't told me what made you decide so suddenly to come back," he said abruptly.

"Because I wanted to—I was bored there. Are you put out with me for coming so soon?"

"Am I? Did I want you to go? Did I, Teresa?"

"No. But you might have got used to my being away. You look at me as though I'd been gone a year."

"And it seems to me you have. You seem strange to me, Teresa."

"That's it! That's the very way you look at me—as though I were a stranger! You'd forgotten me."

"Forgotten you!"

"Yes, you were forgetting me—if I'd stayed a few months longer, you'd have forgotten how I look! It's true—you said so yourself."

"I didn't. I said you seem strange, and you do. It's as though you were a person that I must begin to know all over again. Don't you like that? Would you rather have me feel that I know you like a book, like an old hat? Drink some of that white wine."

"You were forgetting me," murmured Teresa, as she took up her glass. "Confess that you're surprised to find how nice I really am. Had you forgotten that I'm pretty? Could you tell the colour of my eyes? You've got no memory, Basil, and therefore no soul. All you have is a habit." She smiled at him. "You've a habit of me, or a habit of getting on without me. Oh, *I* see that you could get on without me, and I shall never give you the chance again!"

"Will you swear to that?"

"By sun and moon I swear!"

"Well, I'm content then. I get on damn badly without you, that's the truth."

"But you get on. And I can't get on at all without you—not at all. I've found that out."

"Then I'm glad you went away, if that's true."

"Yes, only I knew it before."

They looked at one another and drank a silent toast. To Teresa the world about her—the stifling night, the breathless air, the crowd of ordinary people—had taken on the colour and glow of the wine, a mysterious radiance. She was eating very little, but the food seemed good. The waiter in his musty black coat, with a tired napkin over his arm, seemed a pathetic and amiable human creature. She glanced at his grave face, as he awaited the order of the *entrée*, with sympathy. How dreary he must be of people choosing their *entrée*! But no—he was pleased to suggest that one of those queerly named dishes was better than the other—he looked interested. How amiable!

She smiled joyously at Basil. "And now tell me what you've been doing with your unchartered freedom—confess how you've enjoyed being a bachelor!"

"You can't be a bachelor when you've been married," said Basil with conviction. "It's living at *table d'hôtes* when you've had your own house—it ain't the cheese. I hate bumming round."

And he looked at her with deep content in his eyes.

"We'll get a little place in the country somewhere for the autumn, and I shall sit down and do some work. I haven't done anything decent since you went away."

"What *have* you done, then, you fraud?"

"Oh, I wrote you—those beastly illustrations—and another thing or two. But it's been hot, and every day or so I had to pick up and go out of town. I couldn't settle down to anything. I want my own place—and you in it."

"But, dear boy, you don't like my housekeeping!"

"Bother housekeeping! You do it as well as you can, that's all. I don't care much what I eat."

"Poor, dear Basil! But I *will* do it better this time—I really will. I want a settled place too, a place where we belong. I'm so tired, as you say, of bumming. I thought when I came home this time that I never wanted to see Europe again. It's the fourteenth time I've crossed that stupid ocean—and oh, I thought of all the years of wandering when I was a child, and how we never had a home. And I'm sick of it. And you and I, Basil, have never had a place of our own. We've lived like two sparrows, building our nest under somebody else'e eaves. And I want my own eaves! I want a house somewhere, I don't care if it's in a beastly suburb, or where—and a garden, and about ten acres of trees, and an asparagus-bed, and a cow!"

Basil laughed.

"We'll have it, then—by Jove, that would suit me! But where shall we get the money?"

"Why, we have thirty-five hundred a year, haven't we? We could pay for it in three or four years."

"Yes, but what should we live on, then?"

Teresa looked slightly dashed.

"Oh, we'll make enough to live on," she said, recovering herself. "I can make a good deal if I try—and I won't have any new clothes, and I'll buy all our food at the cheapest shops. I'm sure we can do it."

"Very well, we'll do it. I'll do anything you really want, Teresa."

"Will you?" she murmured.

She drank her wine absently and set the glass down, and looked at him with a strange, passionate expression of doubt.

"Who knows?"

"What do you mean?" asked Basil.

"Who knows what you would do for me? Who knows what I am to you?"

"*I* know, pretty well, I should think. Try me. I don't think there's much I wouldn't do for you."

"Would you—"

She stopped suddenly, made an impatient gesture, and said, "No— that's nothing. I won't say that."

"Won't say what? What is it? Say what you had in your mind."

She refused, but Basil pressed her eagerly. For some ten minutes she resisted, but at last she said: "Oh, I'll tell you, then. All that came into my mind—that thing about—Mrs. Perry." The name cost her a slight effort. "And I started to ask if you would tell me now all about it. But I don't really care—that's why I stopped. It would make it seem too impor- tant to me. I don't care what happened—only tell me this, you didn't care about her?"

"I *have* told you—not an atom."

"Then she was a fool."

"I suppose she was."

"Oh, well, that's all—keep the rest to yourself. As I should do, in a similar case."

"As you would? How do you mean, Teresa—in my place, you mean?"

"No, I mean in *my* place."

With her elbows leaning on the table and her chin in her palms, she smiled at him slightly. Basil studied her delicate, subtle face. It struck him suddenly that there was a new force about it. It might only have been the poise of recovered health and energy—but it seemed more. She looked somehow surer, more experienced, with more reserve. There was a suggestion of malice in her look. He considered her profoundly.

"I don't know what you mean, you little devil," he said caressingly, "but I know you're more charming than ever. It's about time you came back."

"Yes, said Teresa softly. "It was time – if I meant to come back. And, on the whole, I did."

"What do you mean? There's something in your mind – there's something you haven't told me."

"Is there? Is it possible?"

"Now come, Teresa! Don't grill a fellow, and on a night like this – and the first minute you get back, too! You don't hate me, do you? I'm so confoundedly happy to get you back – I've never been so happy in my life."

Basil's voice quavered, and he seized her hand across the table.

Teresa looked at him strangely, and was silent. She smiled as he filled her glass again with the topaz-coloured wine, and gazed out dreamily over the street. The black night, mysterious and ominous, with the roll of thunder coming nearer, seemed now to have left only a core of radiance about them. The low clouds, the flaring lightning, all threats, all uncertainties, pressed in upon the sensuous dream, and seemed to concentrate it into an infinite moment, inexpressibly sweet.

II

They found a house on Long Island, and Teresa took a perverse pleasure in the fact that it was within an easy distance of Mrs. Perry's big country-place. Basil had objected to this neighbourhood, but had been over-ruled. The house was exactly what they wanted – an old farmstead, which had been made habitable by a painter of their acquaintance. It had a big studio, a straggling old-fashioned garden, and an orchard where Ronald could play. There were glimpses of the sea. They put in some of their furniture, which had been stored, and Teresa announced that they were settled till December, by which time they might perhaps have found their permanent home. This, she said, must be in some place not infested by the rich; where, therefore, land needn't be bought by the square inch.

Meantime she devoted herself with great energy to the task of making their temporary abode comfortable. She became an active house-wife, and sang gaily as she went about with her sleeves rolled up, ordering the place. Basil had settled himself promptly into the studio, where he welcomed interruption. He announced that he was hard at work, but when Teresa passed the door or Ronald looked in at the window, he seized upon their society, and would come out to lounge about the house or the garden, smoking and cheerfully inspecting their activities. His tuneless whistle was frequently heard. He was very happy. Teresa too had recovered her old gaiety. The clouds of the past year seemed all to have disappeared.

Basil left all practical arrangements completely in Teresa's hands. She was to choose their home, and everything was to be exactly as she wished. He applauded the meals that she caused to be set before him, made light of any drawbacks, and proclaimed that he had never in his life been so comfortable. He was disinclined to stir from their domestic precincts even for half a day, and neither of them wanted to see any people. He took Ronald down to the beach every day, and taught him to swim. He wanted Teresa always within sight or hearing. He wanted, he said, to wallow in unbridled domesticity.

One morning Teresa, idly looking over the newspaper as she sat in a hammock, with Ronald, scantily clad, making mud-pies near by, saw on the first page an article, under portentous headlines, on the threatened war between England and Turkey. Turkey had marched troops into the Sinai Penninsula, on the pretext that it was not a part of Egypt. England had let it be understood that if the Turkish forces were not withdrawn she would bombard Constantinople. This was the gist of the despatches, eked out by comment and prophecy from various sources to make a startling column and a half.

Teresa read the article several times. It had come, then, the "trouble" that Crayven had foreseen, and that had called him back to his post. And what had come to him there, in his old fort in the desert, with his handful of soldiers? An emergency like this, she knew, had been always before him. Half civilian, half soldier, he was one of those many Englishmen on the outposts of the Empire, living and working obscurely, perhaps fighting and dying obscurely—it was all, as he had said, in the day's work.

She dropped the newspaper and lay back, thinking of him.

She was sure that he would meet his emergency well, with the quiet courage that gives a touch of the heroic to even the simplest human figure. He was steady of nerve and strong of will. He would be calm under fire, he would make the most of his resources. He would assuredly not give way. If there were any dispute about that old powder-magazine and that well—the only water to be had within three days' journey—she could quite see him declining to give it up to a Turkish army camped about him. He was the sort of man who would shut his eyes naturally to the odds against him – and even, out of pure obstinacy perhaps, put a match to the powder magazine.

Ronald came up to her, to exhibit a particularly fine pie, and she said to him:

"Do you remember the man – that gave you your stick, you know?"

"Yes," said Ronald thoughtfully. "Is he here?"

"No – he's far away, across the big ocean and the desert. And he's in a fort, with cannon, and there are a lot of soliders who want to shoot him and take the fort."

Ronald brought his two bare heels together and his hand to his forehead, in the military salute that Crayven had taught him.

"Salute, sir!" he said. "If he has cannons, why doesn't he shoot the soliders?"

"Perhaps he will, but there are such a lot of them."

Ronald looked very solemn, and dug his thumb into the mud-pie, destroying its symmetry.

"How many are there?" he asked after a pause.

"Oh, I don't know – thousands, perhaps – heaps of them."

"Will he fight with a sword, like granpa, or will he shoot their heads off with the cannons?"

"I don't know, dearest. Go and make another pie, will you? That one's quite spoilt."

"No, make me a fort, with cannons."

"No, I can't now, dearest, I'm going to write a letter."

She went into the house, meaning to write to Crayven. But Basil called her into the studio to show her a drawing he had just finished, and presently it was lunch-time. The letter was not written that day, nor the next. After all, why write to him? He had said that he didn't want letters.

But within the week there came a letter to her from Crayven. It had been sent to Switzerland, and forwarded by Nina. As it happened, Teresa was out when the rural postman brought that day's mail; and Basil, according to his frank custom, opened and read the letter. When Teresa came back from her walk with Ronald, Basil gave it to her, with a number of others, without comment. She sat down on the step and began to look them over. Basil, smoking rather nervously, was walking up and down the verandah. When she came to Crayven's letter and looked at the signature, she changed colour slightly and glanced up at Basil. He met her glance sombrely. She read the letter, which had been written a day or so after Crayven's arrival at his post, and which was rather too expressive. Then she folded it up carefully and glanced up again at Basil.

"I wish you would not open my letters," she said calmly.

"I daresay. I won't in the future. I didn't know it was a love-letter. Perhaps you'll tell me, if you don't mind, who the devil is 'Athelstan'?"

"Oh, a man you know—Crayven, that Englishman, you remember."

"And how does he happen to write to you like that? Where have you seen him?"

"He was in the Val d'Illiez this summer."

"You never mentioned him to me."

"No."

"Why didn't you?"

"I didn't choose to."

"Do you mean to tell me about this now?"

Teresa was silent, looking away through the slanting shadows of the orchard. Basil was looking at her, quite pale. She shook her head finally.

"Not on demand. You've no right to demand it. I shall tell you if I choose, when I choose."

"Very well, Teresa. I don't know what you've done, I don't know whether you know what you're doing now—I don't understand the thing. Do as you like, of course, about telling me."

He went into the house, and Teresa sat still, in one position, till tea was brought out, when she got up, her whole body aching from constraint. Basil sent out word that he didn't want any tea and that he was going to town for dinner. Ronald ran up for his bit of cake; and when Basil, with a curt "Good-bye," departed, trotted down to the gate with him. Basil called over his shoulder: "I may not be back to-night."

Teresa made no answer, but smiled faintly and scornfully.

It took no more than this, then, to break up the peace of their reunion! How absurd, to quarrel about Crayven! She was angry at Basil's ready distrust of her. The letter *was* over-expressive, but—

She read it again. Yes, it was a love-letter, but a melancholy one. It was by no means the letter of a happy or triumphant lover. It was not very long: and at the end Crayven said that his district had already been invaded, and that a force of three thousand Turks were camped at two days' journey from him.

"I may not write again," he ended. "But if I get out of this I will, just to let you know. Of course it's a chance whether this letter gets through—but if it does you'll know why I wrote it. I can't help it—I can't go out without a word to you. I was fool to say I didn't want letters—I do want them. But don't bother about me. Write if you like. But if anything happens to me—there's only one chance out of many that it will—don't let it trouble you. It doesn't matter very much to me, you know."

She sat down and wrote to him, and then walked to the post-office to mail her letter, taking Ronald with her. A way of getting news of him had occurred to her. She sent a cablegram to a friend of hers in London, asking him to find out for her Crayven's situation. She also bought an evening paper, but there was nothing in that except scarehead prophecies of the despatch of an English fleet to Constantinople. She threw the paper away and went slowly home along the quiet country road. A fresh wind was blowing from the sea. The September heats were coming to an end. The first hint of autumn was in the air.

So far, since she had read Crayven's letter, she had been thinking only of him. It was not at all like him, she thought, to alarm her for nothing. He must have believed himself in danger, and, as he was not a timorous nor an hysterical person, the danger must be real. She was touched that he should have thought of her and have wished to send her that message, which might be the last. After all, it had been a genuine feeling that he had had for her; she had been sure of it ever since that last day in the Swiss forest. And she felt affection for him, and a longing to know that he was safe.

She regretted nothing about the affair; not even the fact that his letter had made trouble for her with Basil. She did not regret her silence to Basil, nor that he now knew that she had concealed something from him. Of course he would be angry. He had believed always that she had no secrets from him; and in fact, till this, she had had none. It was Basil's doing, that she had kept this from him. If he had his secrets, she also had a right to hers. She had not deliberately resolved to practise any deception upon him; she had not deliberately engaged in a relation which she knew he would resent. She had been led into it instinctively by her feeling of partial estrangement from him, and for this he was responsible. He had made her feel that, after all, she was separate from him; he was one person and she was another. They loved one another, but each, after all, had a life outside that love. Basil had not sacrificed to her his caprice for Mrs. Perry, nor his loyalty to the consequences of that caprice. He had no right then to demand an account from her. He had taken the wrong tone. He had gone off in a rage. No doubt he could not help that—he had been taken by surprise and deeply disturbed. He would come back, perhaps, more reasonable—and then she might, or might not, explain. Meantime, she was not sorry that he was disturbed. It would not hurt Basil to suffer a little. He had made her suffer. And with her return she had forgiven him, she had given herself to him again completely, without the shadow of a reproach; less joyously than before, but more seriously, more passionately. She had loved him more because she had—from his point of view—offended against him, and because the account was balanced. She did not feel in the least sinful because of this, but she knew that he would think her so. This consciousness gave her an additional tenderness for him, and it freed her absolutely from her resentment of the affair with Isabel. It had enabled her to forgive Basil, and to put the thing entirely out of her mind.

Well, and now? She did not quite know what would happen now, but for the moment she was indifferent. Basil must come back sometime, and then they would see.

She dined alone; and afterward walked by the light of a half moon down to the sea. This was the side of the island which faced the open ocean, and great breakers rolled in to fling themselves on the shore. The wind was still rising. It blew her hair about as she sat on the sand, and whipped it into strings over her forehead, and left on her lips the salt taste of the sea. She sat there till the moon was near setting, feeling with deep pleasure the tumult of the night, and, with something that was not pain, the tumult, the exciting uncertainty of life.

III

Basil returned by the last train that night. Next morning he breakfasted in his room, and Teresa did not see him till near noon, when she went into the studio to get a half-finished clay model. They usually worked side by side some hours of the morning, but now Teresa gathered up her materials, with a cool "Good-morning," and went out again. Basil did not answer, but looked up from his drawing-board with a haggard, somber glance. She noticed that the sheet of paper before him was entirely blank.

Luncheon came and went in perfect silence, except for Teresa's conversation with Ronald, who had lately been promoted to take his dinner at the family board. After luncheon Teresa put Ronald to bed, and went into the studio. There was the blank sheet of paper, over which Basil had spent the morning. From the window she could see him walking up and down in the garden, and she saw the well-known nervous motion of his hands as he threw away a half-smoked cigarette, lit another, and presently threw that away too. The day was cool and clouding over. She lit the fire ready-laid in the big grate, and moved about the room, putting it in order, and clearing away the litter of pipes and cigarette ends and burnt matches which Basil had left. Then she looked out at him again, irresolute. Basil was capable, she knew, of sulking for a week straight on. It was not now as it had been in the first years of their marriage, when any constraint between them was more pain to him than to herself, when he was always the first to insist on an understanding. But—this was not an ordinary case of sulking. At luncheon he had eaten almost nothing and his eyes looked as though he had not slept. He was suffering.

After a little, she put a white scarf over her head and shoulders and went out to him. He looked at her with that same sombre expression, and when she slipped her hand through his arm he drew away.

"Basil, aren't you making too much of this?" she asked, walking on beside him.

"No," he said curtly.

"It seems to me you are putting on tragedy airs without much reason."

"Does it?"

"You are trying to bully me."

He made an impatient gesture.

"I'm not. You can do as you damn please. Apparently you have done so. Only if you think it's going to make no difference—"

"What difference?"

"Just this—that we won't live together anymore."

"Basil! . . ."

"Yes, I mean it. I shall go away."

"How absurd you are!"

"Perhaps so—but if you think I could endure to live like this—You simply don't realise what you've done. You seem to think it's nothing!"

"I'm not aware that I've done anything so frightfully serious."

"No? Well, you've shaken my whole idea of you, my belief in you—that's all. It never occurred to me not to trust you. It never occurred to me—but now—I wonder if you've lied to me all along."

"I've never lied to you—never."

"How can I know? How do I know what you are? I don't know you at all. I call that lying—to come back to me with a secret like that. I should never have known, except by accident, that you had had a lover."

"A lover? No."

"Yes! A man doesn't write that sort of letter unless—and a man that you barely knew—a stranger—My God, Teresa, what has come to you?"

He stopped short, clenching his fists, deathly pale, the muscles about his mouth twitching violently.

"And you refuse to tell me—"

"I haven't refused. I said you had no right to demand that I should tell you. You have your secrets—why shouldn't I have mine?"

"How you talk!" he burst out. "Like the silliest, shallowest sort of a new woman! 'Rights'! It isn't a question of rights—it's a question of necessity. Some things can be and others can't. Secrets! I've never had a secret from you that counted for anything. And you can't have this sort of a secret from me. You *can't*, if we're to go on at all. Understand?"

"Don't bully, Basil."

"Bully! . . . By the Lord, you *shall* tell me!"

He turned like a flash and his two hands, trembling, closed tight round her throat.

"Basil, . . ." she murmured, looking at him with half-shut eyes, almost smiling.

With as abrupt a movement he released her, flung himself down on the bench under the apple-tree and hid his face on his arms. Teresa stood still and looked at him.

"Basil . . . I can't understand why you behave in this way. You *don't* trust me, then, at all, really? There was nothing in that letter to cause all this."

He was silent.

"I've never loved anyone but you."

"All the worse!" He lifted his head and looked at her. "What was it, then, that made you do this? Vanity? I could forgive you if you loved someone else, but this! . . ."

"Vanity? Perhaps, and perhaps you had something to do with it, Basil."

"I had? What do you mean?"

"You know well enough. You know what happened before I went away. You know how I felt about it—or perhaps you don't know."

"What idiocy!" said Basil savagely. "Do you mean to say that because of *that* . . . I don't believe you."

"I'm lying, then?"

"I don't believe that made any real difference to you. How could it? You know well enough it didn't, to me."

"And this doesn't, to me."

"But it does to me! It makes all the difference to *me*! Don't tell me you don't care for that man—I know you do."

"Yes, in a way—I am—fond of him. It's true."

"Yes, it's true. And you've written to him."

"Yes. And I've sent a cable to London to find out whether he's dead or alive."

"Yes!"

Basil got up and walked a few steps down the path, and stood still. Teresa wrapped her scarf more closely about her and shivered slightly. A cold wind swept through the orchard; dry leaves came fluttering down from the apple-trees.

"We can't go on," said Basil, hollowly.

"What did you say?" she asked, moving toward him.

"I don't know . . . but I don't think we can go on. I can't stand this . . . I shall go away."

"Go away—where?"

"Anywhere. I shall go away from you."

"You mean you'll leave us—Ronald and me?"

"Ronald . . . yes."

"As you please, Basil."

She turned and went back to the house by another path. There she took her work and shut herself up in her own room. It was cold; the fire was not lit. She shivered, walking up and down the room, but it did not occur to her to light the fire. Her discomfort seemed part of a general past that had enveloped the world. And yet there was a core of warmth somewhere, a thought that caused her a certain exultation. It was absurd of Basil to take this thing so seriously, but she was glad he was absurd in that way—she was thoroughly glad that he cared so much! Only, if he did take it seriously, who knew? She had no intention of being humble about what she had done. Perhaps it had been foolish, but had Basil alone the right to be foolish? Where was his right to sit in judgment upon her? How angry he had been at that word—"right"! Possibly it was a foolish word—they could not theorise about this situation. It was a question of necessity, Basil had said—in other words, of his demand. And he had enforced that demand by a threat. . . . Yes, he might go away—and she could not let him go. Necessity . . .

She sat down and took up her damp clay, but her fingers were stiff from cold. She shivered, and all of a sudden tears came to her eyes. Why had she hurt Basil so? How had she been able to look at him, to see that he was suffering, and almost rejoice in it? What had come to her? "My God, what has come to you, Teresa?" he had cried. Yes, what? An instinct of cruelty, for one thing. Never before had she deliberately made any person suffer, as she had been conscious of doing just now. A feeling of recklessness, carelessness of herself . . . Crayven . . . that day in the forest . . .

She did not regret it. If Basil suffered for it, she must suffer for it, that was all. Of course she would not let him go. What he demanded she must yield. There was something behind his demand, something more than his own egotism. Necessity . . .

IV

The question of his right to know was then waived. That night she told him what there was to tell, with complete frankness. He would leave no detail to the imagination. He wanted to know all, all.

It seemed to Teresa that there was not very much to tell. It seemed to her that Basil's infinite questions wanted to wring more out of the facts than they contained, almost. It seemed to her that some part of his intelligence was trying to construct, quite impersonally, a drama, in which she figured merely as an actor. This was a momentary impression, swept away by the outbreak of his emotion.

He was moved as she had never seen him. Never before had she seen hate in his eyes, and she saw it now. It was as though an earthquake had convulsed the depths of an heretofore quiet sea, and all sorts of monsters came tossing to the surface—monstrous thoughts, blind words. She sat silent while the storm raged, her hands clenched on the arms of her chair, her eyes fixed on Basil's face, which for the first time looked ugly to her. All the strength and brightness of his aspect were gone, swamped in the nervous frenzy that shook him.

"It is his pride that is hurt," thought Teresa. "It is his vanity, his sense of possession. . . ." And she felt farther removed from him at that moment than ever before. It seemed possible to her that this might really mean a break between them. It was clearly in his mind, the idea of separation. And he threw out a fierce threat—he would take the child. At that, every atom of colour left her face. She sat, ashy-white, staring at him. She felt her heart beating with great dull throbs—she felt the life ebbing out of her body in anguish. He might ruin her life, then. It was an enemy that she saw before her, and one that she could not fight. He had not the right to take the child, but the thought of such a contest between them was impossible. If it came to that, she would kill herself.

There came a silence, at last. Basil had hurled at her everything he had to say, and he stood at the far end of the room, not looking at her. She had no impulse to defend herself—it would have been physically impossible for her to utter a word, to move even. At last he went abruptly out of the room, and a moment later she heard him leave the house. She sat where he had left her, while the fire died down into a bed of coals, and grey ashes gathered over it and killed the last red gleam, and the chill of the frosty night crept into the room . . .

When she heard him come back, hours later, she went shivering to her bed, but she did not sleep. He was there, under the same roof with her, but a freezing terror lay between them—the terror of the end of love, of ugliness where there had been beauty, of death where there had been life. Was it possible that such a failure could be theirs? Was this thing real, or was it a spectre, a shadow, that they might still escape from? She did not know . . .

Whose was the fault? *Hers* directly, she knew. How prodigal they had both been of the real treasure of their lives, how careless of the precious thing they held! But who could have guessed that it was fragile? How had it been possible to think that what held them together needed cherishing, needed care? Had either of them really conceived before that that bond could be broken? Had either of them imagined such bankruptcy?

And now it was facing them. She knew instinctively that this was the real test of their relation. She knew that Basil's fault could not have ruined the scheme of their life together; she knew that hers could. She saw herself as the key-stone of the structure; she saw suddenly that there was, that there must be a structure, and that it must depend upon her. All the laboriousness of life, the grey aspect of duty, the necessity of infinite, incessant exertion of the will, for self-control, for self-sacrifice— all the puritan conception of the world and the human soul—surged over her like a cold muddy sea. Was this, then, what one must live in? And to what end? To pass the endless struggle on to someone else?

For the first time, it seemed to her, in the long hours of that night, she saw the world as it really was. She saw it as a long combat, and she saw that no relation could escape this law of struggle and change, certainly not hers and Basil's. Between them, too, it must be a combat, a struggle to keep what they had conquered, a fight against those things in one another, in themselves, that tended to destroy, a long fight against decay and the death of what was precious.

She saw in a flash how she had injured a certain ideal of herself in Basil's mind; she saw all the power of that ideal to bind, to anchor him. She saw how he had set her apart, because of it, from all feminine lightness and weakness, too well known. And the violence of his reaction against the having to change his idea of her showed her how much it had meant to him. It was perhaps unreasonable, his ideal, his idea of her, but she acknowledged that he was right to want her to realise it. Now, perhaps, it would never be real to him again. She had broken one of the cords that bound him to her. She saw before her a battle to regain what she had lost, or to replace it by something else. She took up her courage in both hands and vowed herself to that battle. If she could not be to him, now, what he had thought her, she would make herself a new value to him. They might be fellow-sinners, but he should not, for all that, hold her for less.

· · · · ·

At dawn he came into her room, came and put his head down on her pillow, and said wearily that he could not sleep. At that she burst out crying wildly, sobbed out passionately her humility, her regret, her fear, her love. And they clung together like two waifs in a storm, feeling darkness and danger all about them . . .

All that day Basil spent moodily by himself, fitfully trying to work, or tramping about the place. In the afternoon a cablegram came for Teresa — her informant said that the danger was past, and Crayven safe — and the storm broke out afresh. Basil's resentment surged up furiously — Teresa replied bitterly.

"You treat me like a slave," she said at last, in deep humiliation. "I am an individual as much as you. You haven't the right to judge me."

"But I do judge you. Either you belong to me, or you don't. It's as simple as that, and you can choose. If you belong to me, you don't belong even by a thought to anyone else. That's all there is to it. If you're my wife, you'll have no lovers, by letter or any other way. You'll have no more letters from Crayven—"

"You issue your commands as though I had nothing to do but obey."

"It isn't a question of commands and obeying. It's a question of seeing a clear situation, recognising what it means to me and to you . . . and I'm not sure, even if you do recognise it, that I can ever trust you

again. I can't feel toward you as I did before. You'll always be different—
less mine than you were. . . . I can't understand how you could do this
. . ."

"And you? You keep the full right to do exactly as you choose,
yourself? You won't recognise any responsibility in what has happened
. . ."

"The question is entirely different for me and you—you know it
must be so. If I made a mistake I paid for it, long before this, and now
you have made me pay a thousand times over. But you'll have to pay
too, inevitably. If you were trying for revenge—!"

"No, it wasn't quite so crude as that! But perhaps it was inevitable,
too, that you should suffer for what you made me suffer—"

"You suffer? You didn't, you didn't really care deeply—"

"Oh, didn't I! Didn't I! Do you believe that, Basil? I had no idea of
making *you* pay, though. I had impulses to hurt you, I hated you sometimes, but I never deliberately meant to make you suffer—but perhaps
you ought to, for what you did to me. You made me worse than I was,
Basil."

"Don't say that—it isn't true!" he cried. "Haven't you given me
enough? . . . It isn't only for myself I feel this," he went on. "It's for you,
too. It's because I know in the end it's always the woman that pays. If
you injure our life together, you'll pay even more than I shall. If you,
being what you are, should have a lover, you'd have to pay for that—pay
in injury to your pride, in a thousand ways. A woman that gives herself
to a man who doesn't deeply love her—a woman who has anything to
lose—is a fool. The reaction takes him away from her, as sure as fate, and
even a man who isn't a brute can't help making her feel it. You've
nothing to gain in that game, Teresa, and everything to lose. And first
of all you lose me—if you care anything about me. For I tell you, I
couldn't stand it. If you did that sort of thing again, I believe I'd kill
you—at least I'd take myself off where you'd never see me again. . . . I've
had more than one impulse to do it, anyway."

"What—kill me?" said Teresa, with a wan smile.

"No, go away from you. I'm not sure that I shan't, as it is. I can never
believe now that you really care about me. You might find somebody
else, who'd make you happier. You've always disliked a lot about me,
anyway."

"And you—what would you do?"

"Oh, I'd knock about somehow and work. I've had enough of
women. There isn't one that I've any respect for now."

Basil's anger sank into a cool and biting mood, which lasted on from day to day. He talked less and less to Teresa, and finally became almost altogether silent. He shut himself up in the studio for the greater part of the day, and now he was really working. He was forcing himself to work, and Teresa saw the marks of this fierce effort of will in his face. And she saw in it a new hardness, forming like a mask – a jaded, an older look . . .

Basil was cutting himself off from her. They were very little together now. She felt that some change was impending. Something was going on in his mind, of which he would not speak. Whatever it was, it would have some practical effect. She felt that he was deciding something, and without her. Was he slipping away from her? . . . Was she to lose him, really, and for a thing so slight in itself as her relation with Crayven, whatever that relation might have indicated to Basil? She could not believe it possible. But she was proudly silent, too, while her very heart seemed turning to ice within her.

V

Silence came to be the atmosphere of the house – a silence with no peace in it. Basil was now working hard, at a picture for which he had made innumerable studies from models in town – a group of nude figures in a sylvan landscape, in astonishing tones of blue and yellow colour. He was absorbed, and he had no moments of relaxation. When he was not working he roamed moodily about by himself. When Teresa spoke of his picture he looked at her gloomily and answered shortly; and once when she pressed him with questions he said, "Don't talk about it. You're not interested in my work." She saw in him a desire to bury himself in that work, to shut her out. Yet he might have retreated to his studio in town, and he did not do so. He sought no other person. Apparently he wished to be near her and yet apart from her; and to make her feel daily, hourly, the cold pain of this separation of spirit.

After a week or more it grew intolerable to Teresa. She went into town, spent the day with Alice Blackley, looked up her Aunt Sophy, who had just come back from a lecture tour in the West, and finally telegraphed to Basil that she would dine and stay the night with Alice. The dinner was gay. Alice made up a little party on the spur of the moment. One of the men was Jack Fairfax. They went to a theatre and ended with supper at a restaurant, prolonged into the early hours of the morning. Teresa threw herself into the rather boisterous merriment of the occasion; her gaiety had a sharper, harder edge than of old. Fairfax talked to her and watched her with reawakened and growing interest. She talked to him as though she found him interesting; and before they parted it had been arranged that he was to motor out with Alice on the next day but one and lunch at Teresa's house.

That luncheon was also boisterous, owing, as Teresa now perceived, to Alice's new atmosphere. Alice had quite done being aesthetic. She was living now with smarter people, and she was conscientiously playing at being fast, as she had before played at being artistic. She drank two cocktails before luncheon, and during the meal alternately chaffed Basil and made eyes at him. Basil returned the chaff and the eyes with interest and rather brutally. Alice was beautifully dressed; Basil, with the frankness of a student of the human form, admired her figure, and received on the spot a request to paint her portrait.

"Only in town, you know," she said. "I can't come out to this dreary place. Why on earth do you stay here? Only a pair of turtledoves like you two could stand it."

"Hard up," said Basil laconically.

"Oh, nonsense—come to town and I'll get you heaps of people to paint. Or if you've got a few thousands by you, ask Horace for a tip. He can put you on to something good, he's been making pots of money."

Basil smiled—at Teresa, and she flushed hotly over all her face. It was the first smile for ten days! It meant, she knew, only an ironic comment on that "few thousands" of Alice's—they would have felt rich with a few thousands by them. At least they still had their poverty in common! Alice noticed her flush and stared curiously at her.

"Flirting across the table," she said. "I always say you are the most domestic people I know. By the way, do you know Isabel Perry's back? She's somewhere near you here, isn't she?"

"Half a mile away," said Teresa.

"No, really! I'm coming down to stay a weekend with her next month. How jolly! You'll be there, too, perhaps—you're great chums, aren't you?"

"I haven't seen her for nearly a year."

"Oh, but you *were* great chums? Or was it Basil? Yes, now I think of it, it was Basil," and Alice smiled wantonly. She was not ill-natured, but she was a little excited.

Basil looked at Teresa and she saw boredom and disgust in his quick glance. He became ceremoniously polite to his guests, which always meant, with Basil, that he wished them away. His finely-cut face, with the new look of austerity that the last fortnight had given it, with its new hardness, took on an expression of satiric patience. He paid Alice some outrageous compliments, and at last even her not very acute sensibilities were touched.

"What an old prig you're getting to be, Basil," she said carelessly, as they left the table. "You're so different from what you used to be—there isn't any more jollity about you now than there is about a town-pump. And you look as if butter wouldn't melt in your mouth. Really, you're a wet blanket. I'm going to take Teresa off with me in the motor. I'm sure *she* wants a little life, poor dear."

"By all means, give it to her," said Basil. "I'm quite aware that I'm dull company, as you say—I'm only a poor grub, plugging away. I don't pretend to compete with bright butterflies like you and Fairfax."

Teresa went off in the motor, which Alice insisted on driving herself at a flying speed, and which came to grief, descending a hill, at a sharp turn. A tire burst, and the machine was left with the chauffeur. Alice and Fairfax walked to a near-by station and took a train, and Teresa walked home—six miles along the silent country roads. It was dark when she reached the house, and Basil came out to meet her.

"An accident?" he said irritably. "I thought there would be one—it's lucky your neck isn't broken. I wish you wouldn't go out on that sort of a tear again."

"Oh, it's amusing," said Teresa coldly.

"Amusing! You find those people amusing! Or was it the chance of breaking your neck that amused you?"

"Both, I think. I like the sensation of something happening, even if it's only rushing along in a motor."

"Or swilling cocktails at lunch and flirting, I suppose?"

"*I* didn't swill any cocktails. Really, Basil, you're turning over a new leaf."

"I'm not the only one. I don't care much for this last leaf that you've turned over. Alice is getting too vulgar—"

"Anything is better than living in an ice-box, as I've been doing lately."

"Is it? All right, but if you want to bring that sort out here, I shall have to work in town."

He went into the studio, and Teresa looked after him despairingly. After a few moments she followed him. The room was dark, except for the firelight. He had thrown himself into a big chair before the fire, and was staring into it, his head bent in an attitude of weariness. She went over to him and put her arm about his shoulders. Brusquely he shook it off.

"Don't do that," he said sombrely.

"Bas . . ."

His name died on her lips. She stood for some moments, looking dumbly at his head, at the gleam of the fire-light on his hair and his averted cheek, then turned and went out of the room.

• • • • •

That week Basil's father came out to spend a day. He had been ill, at his suburban home, for a month or more. Twice Teresa had been out there to see him, in a little house full of half-grown children and the odours of liberal German cooking. The Major seemed much more himself, away from that atmosphere. Yet he was greatly changed, physically, by his illness. His smart clothes hung upon a wasted figure, his cheeks had fallen in, and the old scar near his eye showed more distinctly against his present pallor. He was changed mentally, too. He talked about himself and his ailments, and the old wounds he had received in the war, which were troubling him again. His voice was querulous, and he moved feebly.

But he had all his habitual fondness of Teresa, and showed it. Several times he called her "Daughter"—the name was sweet to her. He brightened up to talk to Ronald, but a half-hour with the child fatigued him. It tired him, too, to talk to Basil, and Teresa caught more than one troubled and puzzled glance as the old man began to feel some change in his son. It frightened him, she could see; and she saw, too, that he dreaded any fresh blow to his sapped strength; his own troubles were all he could bear. When Basil went away, saying he had work to do, and leaving them together, the Major was visibly relieved. He did not ask about Basil, but leaning over the fire he began to talk again about himself. He told Teresa in what battles he had been wounded, and strayed into detailed war-time reminiscences, and talked about his hero, Grant; and rambled and wandered on, while she half-listened, putting in a gentle word now and then, and looking at the fire.

She was thinking, first about the Major, and realising with a shock his physical breaking-up. Then she thought what a blow to him would be any trouble between herself and Basil, and how an open rupture would affect him. If it came to that—and she was thinking it might— they ought, if possible, to spare the Major the knowledge of it. They would not have very long to wait. . . . He was the only one of the family on either side who would keenly feel it. Her own parents were dead, her Aunt Sophy would rejoice at her freedom, and Nina—Nina would say she had deserved it, perhaps. A hot flush blazed up in her face at the thought of Nina—and she became aware suddenly that she had not been listening to the Major, and that he was talking in a new tone.

He was talking about Basil's mother. He seemed to-day to be living altogether in the past. He seemed now to be living over again vividly the love of his youth. Physical weakness had made him garrulous and he talked as though he were talking to himself. He murmured and crooned over old scenes of his wooing; her looks and words; her daring, her cleverness, her beauty.

"I've never seen a woman like her, my dear," he said. "I've lived thirty years in the world since she died, and I've never seen a woman fit to tie her shoes. *I* used to tie 'em, by Jove, and put 'em on for her. She'd never put on her own shoes and stockings in her life before she married me. She might have had many a more brilliant match than *I* was, but she took me, a poor young soldier. Good God, what was *I*, to deserve such a creature? The day she promised herself to me, it seemed to me as if a goddess had stooped down and kissed me. And she was proud! . . . You can't imagine how beautiful she was . . . when she took down her hair it covered her to her knees in a glory like copper and gold . . ."

Something like a sob broke the old man's voice.

"My happiness was brief," he whispered, and became silent; his lips moving now and then, without sound.

Teresa thought: He is dying, though perhaps he does not know it. He is thinking of *her* because she was the great emotion of his life, and he feels that he is going to find her again. Perhaps he will find her. But then what will become of poor Agatha, who has cooked for him these many years—and what will *she* do when she gets to heaven and looks for him? He is her husband, too. But he's forgotten her, and her children, and even Basil—and he remembers only the woman with the copper hair that he loved thirty years ago—and has loved ever since. But perhaps there will be different heavens. The Major and his lady with the copper hair will live in one full of bright armour and glorious warriors and champing steeds; and Agatha will have one full of the most wonderful things to cook—and I daresay that Major will drop into dinner with her occasionally, and fib to the beautiful lady about it . . .

She glanced up at him. His eyelids had dropped and she thought he was asleep. She sat perfectly quiet for fear of waking him, and her face was tender as she looked at him.

But all the same – she thought – there might have been some difficulties in living with Basil's mother. Perhaps the Major hadn't had time to find them out. But if he had ever offended her, he might have found his goddess a stern judge. . . . And she smiled with bitter melancholy.

The Major, when he came to go away, as she walked out with him to the carriage, took her hand and looked wistfully at her, and said: "You're not looking well, Teresa."

"Oh, I'm quite well," she said in surprise.

The Major shook his head.

"No, you're not," he said, and she caught again that look of troubled apprehension in his eyes.

Basil, who was going to take the Major home, looked at her too, a sudden quick scrutiny, but he said nothing.

Ronald came to kiss his grandfather good-bye, and Teresa, too, kissed him; and as she leaned over the gate and watched the carriage drive away down the darkening road, it seemed to her that all the world was sinking in decay: the old man there, the fading sunset that she saw through leafless trees, her own fading life. For the Major was quite right – the strain of the last weeks was beginning to show in her face. The colour and the life had died out of it, under the freezing pressure of pain and dread.

VI

Some days later Mrs. Perry came to see her – greeted her without affectation of cordiality, with a square, straight look in the eyes, and said: "I've just found out you were here. I live nearby, you know."

"Yes, I know," said Teresa, perfectly at her ease.

"I have a good many people coming down to see me. Perhaps you would both come to dine some night."

"I think so – with pleasure."

"Do you like it here? Shall you stay long?"

"I don't know how long. Basil finds he can work well here. I'm sorry he happens to be in town to-day."

"Perhaps you would come on Sunday to dinner? Eight o'clock. I don't know that it will be very amusing for you – it isn't for me."

And Isabel smiled listlessly. She had changed much in the year past.

She was much quieter. She sat quiet in her chair, and her long hands lay quiet in her lap. She was pale, and looked ten years older than when Teresa had seen her last. She was plainly dressed in black, had left off all her jewels, and all the restless, nervous animation of her former manner had gone, with the glitter of the diamonds of which she had been so fond.

Teresa watched her curiously, while they chatted about Alice Blackley and various people they knew in common. She was surprised to find that the sight of Isabel moved her so little. She thought of the emotions Isabel had cost her, almost with a smile. All that seemed far away – since then she had travelled far. She could look at the other woman quite calmly, and realise impersonally her interest. Isabel was a person, one could not deny that – and much more a person now than she had been a year before. Some experience that meant a good deal to her had intervened. Teresa found herself wondering what it was. She felt she might risk a question or two. Whatever Isabel might have been once, she now plainly had herself well in hand. She could carry off a rather difficult situation, like the present, without a fault of taste. There was no danger of any scene. They understood one another. Isabel was honest – she had made no attempt to put things on a false basis. Things, as they stood, were tacitly taken for granted, that was all. And, as they talked about indifferent matters, simply, without constraint, they were approaching one another: not sentimentally or with any impulse toward embarrassing confidences, but with the feeling of one definite personality for another, with a certain pleasure in this non-hostile contact.

"Have you been ill?" Teresa asked finally.

"Nervous prostration, I believe it was," Isabel answered sceptically. "I'm supposed to be still having it, whatever it is. It is rather pleasant now. It's simply a disinclination to do any mortal thing, and I like that. After nearly forty years of activity for its own sake, it's pleasant not to want to do anything, and to have a headache at the back of your neck if you try to do anything."

"But Alice said you were seeing a lot of people."

"Oh, just seeing them. One needn't talk, you know. They come and dine and gamble. Sometimes I don't even appear. If they didn't come I should be trying to read or something. As it is, I watch them, and enjoy my own decay. . . . Well, then you'll come on Sunday? I shall send a motor over for you. You can't drive in these country cabs – you'd freeze to death. May I see the boy?"

Ronald was brought in, and envisaged the lady with his cool but not unfriendly gaze. They entered upon the subject of automobiles, or "Wongs," as Ronald called them; and finding that the lady was the possessor of the splendid red Wong now waiting outside the gate, Ronald warmed up, asked for a ride, and departed cheerfully in company with the stranger.

· · · · ·

Basil, when informed of the dinner-engagement, looked blankly at Teresa.

"You said we'd go? You might have asked me first. I don't want to go, and I don't think I shall. What have we to do with that crowd?"

Teresa's reply was less cold because of the "we."

"I think perhaps we ought to go once. It would be rather awkward not to go at all, after her visit."

Basil was plainly disconcerted. He looked at Teresa with astonishment not quite sufficiently veiled by indifference.

"You can call on her if you like. I can't see why I should go."

"It would be mere politeness to do so, I should think."

"Should you? I'm not going in for mere politeness."

"Well, there's no need for going in for bearlike savagery. I should think you'd hibernated long enough."

"I suppose you're bored and want to see some men. But if we go there we shall lose a lot more money than we can afford, at bridge."

"We needn't go again. But I think she'd feel cut if we didn't, this once. She was rather nice to-day—I liked her."

Basil dropped the talk abruptly there, but Teresa felt that her wish would prevail, and it did. And this gave her a pleasure which seemed to herself pathetic and almost humiliating.

She dressed on the night of the dinner with extraordinary care. She had chosen a mauve dress with touches of silver, which brought out the colour of her eyes. It was a French dress, of rather an extreme fashion; and she followed out the same note of exaggeration in the way she did her hair, making its natural mass appear more strikingly, just as her slight and supple figure was shown to the greatest advantage. Usually she was content to leave her good points more or less to make their own effect, simply; but on this evening her appearance had the touch of obvious art. It would not have been more obvious if she had put rouge on her cheeks. She preferred to look pale; and her pallor was as intense and striking as the rouge would have been.

She came down from her room ready cloaked and hooded, and Basil did not see her otherwise till she entered Mrs. Perry's drawing-room, where a dozen people were assembled. Teresa was aware on her entry that she was frankly stared at, and that Basil was, for a moment, staring too. Among the guests were several that she knew—the Kerrs, Alice Blackley, and Fairfax. Isabel Perry made a simple and rather majestic figure in black velvet, which had seen several seasons, with her hair quite carelessly done. Simplicity was decidedly her note now, a perfectly genuine one, and there was a certain air of the great lady about her. As she had said to Teresa, she made no effort for her guests. They seemed to have been asked because they could amuse themselves.

Isabel's husband, as usual, was not present, and Teresa found herself at the table between Fairfax and a tall, blonde, very handsome youth of the smartest aspect. She saw that Basil sat at his hostess' left hand, and that Isabel talked impartially to him and to the dull Mr. Kerr on her right. Isabel's Spanish eyes looked sad, and seemed to explore remote horizons. Basil also looked remote, and Teresa noted that he drank steadily each wine in succession, even champagne, which he did not like.

There were more men than women in the party, and Teresa soon found that she had an audience of four and that she was talking with animation. She would not let Fairfax absorb her attention, and his frankly amorous manner interested her less than the ingenuous remarks of the blonde youth, who openly admired her also and told her why. He had evidently been drinking a little too much, but his exuberance amused her.

"I can't stand sly-looking women," he confided to her. "And I can't stand the bread-and-butter sort either. I like women who have a spice of the devil in them, you know, and yet look good, too. Women who've seen the world and all the kingdoms thereof. And they needn't be too young, either. I admire them most about your age. I don't mean you're not young. Why, you might be eighteen, hang it—I beg your pardon—but what I mean is, there's experience in your face. I like experience. I never care to talk to a young girl—they've got no ideas of their own. And I don't like women that pretend to know it all, either—like Mrs. Blackley. She's so awfully knowing. I don't like that dress she's got on—it's affected. I hate those Empire things—they're only suitable for teagowns—and I hate women wearing artificial flowers and things in their hair."

"You're rather hard to please, it seems to me," said Teresa.

"Well, I know what I like, and why shouldn't I? I like your dress—it's a lovely color, and that silver embroidery on the chiffon is beautiful. Do you live in New York?"

"No, I live out here in the country. My husband is a painter—there he is up at the end of the table. I have one child, and we live on four thousand a year."

"How—how clever of you," stammered the boy. Teresa smiled sweetly on him and turned back to the others. There was no talk that interested her, but under her boredom she was conscious of a kind of excitement. It was pleasant after all—to be among people again, to be admired, to have a certain feeling of lightness. She was frivolous in her talk with Fairfax, and sharp when he tried to be serious.

"I wish I knew what has happened to you," he murmured at last, exasperatedly. "We were friends once, you know. And you have changed completely—not only to me, but your very looks have changed. The lines of your face are sharper and harder—"

"Age, of course," interposed Teresa, "but it isn't gallant of you to point it out. And to-night, too, when I really tried hard to make myself presentable."

"You are beautiful to-night, and you know it. What I mean has nothing to do with that. It's a spiritual hardness and sharpness—it's as though your face had been worked over, remodelled—"

"Massage, perhaps? No, I don't go in for any of those beautifying processes."

Fairfax stifled an angry ejaculation.

"Well, so be it," he said, and his rather sensual face showed a dark flush. "I see you don't want to talk to me as you did once. I don't know that I've given you any reason to snub me, but if it amuses you—"

"No, it doesn't, Jack," said Teresa, with sudden feeling—partly regret at having hurt whatever feeling *he* had, partly fear lest something ugly in him should revenge that former friendship he spoke of. "I don't want to snub you. But I *am* changed, that's true. And the reason is, I'm unhappy. Now, for Heaven's sake, don't say another word."

"I beg your pardon," he said in a low voice. In his startled, grave look she saw this time genuine feeling. He was silent, while Teresa plunged back into chatter with her younger neighbours. At the end of the dinner, amid the brilliant disorder of the dessert, with the women leaning their bare elbows on the table and most of them talking loud, Fairfax leaned toward the laughing Teresa and said: "I say, if you ever want anything or anybody, you know, I'm at your service, and anything I've got."

She nodded, barely looking at him, as the women left the table. His words sent a cold shiver over her. That it could be supposed possible that she should need a service from Fairfax! What did he imagine? Why had she said that to him—that she was unhappy? Need the world know it, if she was? Were people to comment on her inmost life—was her soul to go in rags before them? Have you heard? The Ransomes have separated! I thought it couldn't last! He was rather gay, you know—and she—?" Her pride flamed up, and anger against herself, for that betrayal to Fairfax.

In the drawing-room Alice Blackley began to talk to her in a high key of frivolity, but to Teresa's relief a message was brought in by a servant: Would Mrs. Blackley go to the library for a few moments and see Mr. Perry? Alice swept out with a conscious smile. Teresa knew this little custom of the dyspeptic and semi-invisible host; he liked to chat occasionally with someone who amused him.

When the men came in, bridge began. Teresa's partner was the blonde youth, who played extremely well, and she won nearly forty dollars. She was watchful of herself now, self-possessed and coolly gay.

· · · · ·

Her high spirits left her suddenly when she and Basil got into the motor for their homeward ride. She was silent, muffled in her furs. Something of her old feeling about Isabel had come up again, and the fact that she was riding in Isabel's motor irritated her. A mere nothing had reillumined that feeling—she had seen Basil and Isabel look at one another, and in that look she seemed to see their past intimacy. It was nothing, for Basil could not very well altogether avoid looking at Isabel. There had been no ardour in that glance, certainly, but there had been, or so Teresa fancied, an equally unavoidable *recognition*. Now she passionately regretted having insisted on going.

"Did you enjoy it?" asked Basil coolly.

"No! . . . Why, did you?"

"Certainly not. I was bored to tears—but I expected to be. I thought you seemed to be amusing yourself."

"I wasn't, though."

"At any rate, you were amusing Fairfax and some of those college boys. And I haven't seen you look as gay for weeks. Why don't you admit that you enjoyed your flirtations?"

Basil had become aggressive and rather excited.

"Don't talk nonsense," said Teresa wearily.

"Nonsense, is it? Why, you were got up so that no man in the room could help looking at you. I never saw you dressed that way before. I thought it rather bad form."

"I daresay you prefer Mrs. Perry's form. I thought you looked at her appreciatively."

"You thought nothing of the sort. I don't know what you call the way Fairfax looked at you. It was indecent."

"Was it? How interesting. I didn't observe it."

"Then you were the only person in the room who didn't. You mean you liked it, I suppose. Of course, you can get plenty of that sort of thing, if you like it. You're beautiful, and you can have all sorts of men after you if you look and behave as you did to-night."

"Be quiet, Basil," said Teresa dully.

"Why should I be quiet? Why shouldn't I admire you, too? You *were* beautiful—you took my breath away when you came into the room . . ."

The automobile stopped. They were at home. Basil helped Teresa out, stopped to tip the chauffeur, and hurried into the house. He came into Teresa's room, where she stood in the middle of the floor, staring at the fire, which was almost out.

"Why don't you have them keep your room warmer?" he asked sharply. "You'll freeze here—why hasn't somebody stayed up to look after the fire? I'll ring."

"No, don't—they've gone to bed. It doesn't matter."

"Well, it does."

Basil threw off his coat and vigorously made up the fire. Teresa emerged from her furs and sat down before it.

"Keep your wraps on till the place gets warm, why don't you? You've got nothing on."

"I don't feel it," she said indifferently.

Basil looked at her, shivered slightly—looked away—looked at her again. He took her coat and put it about her.

"I wish you'd take some care of yourself—you look ill, and apparently you're trying to *be* ill."

"I thought you said I looked well," said Teresa, still staring at the mounting flames.

"I said you looked beautiful . . ."

He bent down and touched her arm, kissed it, and suddenly clasped her in a fierce embrace.

Teresa pushed him away and got up.

"Don't do that," she said under her breath.

She stood looking at him, her body tense, her eyes shining like steel under half-lowered lids.

"Don't you—don't you care for me any more?" he stammered.

"I hate you!"

He waited a moment, then turned toward the door.

But to see him go, like that, to feel that silence shut down upon her again! No—at any price, on any terms, not that! She called him, and her voice was almost a shriek. She ran to him and threw herself into his arms.

VII

Two days later came the first snowstorm of the winter. The house was cold and uncomfortable. Basil was alone in it all day, for Teresa had gone, early in the morning, to look up a real estate agent. Their plan of buying a house had lain dormant all this time, but now the idea had taken possession of her mind, and with all her energy she was bent on working it out. For one element of doubt, which had lately reduced all plans to chaos, was now removed. It was certain, at least, that she and Basil were not to separate. They would go on together; on what terms Teresa was not yet absolutely sure, but, she rather thought, on her terms.

She came back late for dinner, tired, chilled, unsuccessful in her first search, but cheerful, to find Basil hanging restlessly about the house, not having been able, he said, to work that day. Over their dinner she described gaily the outrageous defects of the houses she had seen, and praised their present domicile by comparison. Basil was gloomy, drank a great deal of whisky, listened absently to what she was saying, and finally said that he thought they would have to stay where they were for the winter; they couldn't afford anything better. Teresa disagreed instantly. She had her plan. "We are going into town for three months," she announced firmly. "At least, as soon as your picture is finished. And we shall do that every year. Neither of us can live absolutely buried as we are here, all the year round. We're too young—or not young enough—for that! You need people and I need them."

"I don't need anything but work—and peace," said Basil sombrely, "and we're in debt."

"No matter. You'll sell your picture, and I shall make something. And we'll make up next year. We shall take this house on a long lease, or buy it on the installment plan. We shall live here nine months of the year. We can live quietly and cheaply, and you can work. This studio suits you, and I can make a charming garden. After what I've seen to-day, I'm sure we can't do much better. By degrees we'll make the house over to suit us. It will be comfortable, except in the dead of winter, and then we shall take a little apartment in New York. There, Basil, that's my idea—do you like it?"

"Well enough. But I don't believe we can make it go."

I shall make it go," said Teresa. "To-morrow I shall look for a place in town—something over in the old Chelsea district—cheap and not too nasty. How did work go to-day?"

"Not so well. I'm still trying to pull those two figures together. It'll come, I think. But I couldn't work to-day. Everything seems so grey—all the colour gone out of the world. I feel terribly old."

"You've been working hard this month."

"It isn't that. But I'm sad. I've been sadder to-day than ever before in my life. I've been taking account of stock."

They had dined at a small table before the great log-fire in the studio. Now the table had been pushed away. Teresa was leaning back in a low chair, very tired and drowsy from the heat after her long drive. Basil got up and walked about the room, stopping before his picture, of which the glowing blue and yellow colour and the sharp lines made an almost violent effect, even in the subdued light.

"Yes, Basil?"

"An account of stock," he repeated. "I've done a lot of thinking to-day, because I couldn't work. And I couldn't work because you weren't in the house. I thought about you. And I was sad because I know now that I can never get away from you. For a while I thought I might—I wanted to. I wanted to have some new experience, new life, apart from you—something that wouldn't cost me so dear. I want it still—but I know I can't get it. I can't get away from you. You're in my blood . . ."

He turned and walked abruptly up and down. Teresa was silent, spreading her long fingers to the blaze of the fire.

"Always before," he went on, "I've had a feeling that there were any amount of things before me, in work, in life. It's still so—more than ever so—in my work. I'm at the beginning of something infernally interesting. If you've considered that thing I'm doing, you can see it. . . . But I don't care about work alone, if I can't live too . . . if I can't be happy or at peace . . ."

Still she was silent, and after a moment, standing before the picture but not looking at it, he said: "Here I am then—thirty-three years old, with a family, not enough money to live on comfortably, with an idea of painting which it will take me years to work out, and which probably won't bring in any money for some time to come, if it ever does. I believe in it. I could work with more interest, more intensity than ever before, if the other conditions of my life were right. But I'm not sure that I can work in spite of them."

"What conditions?"

"Well, money. I feel I ought to be making some, but if I do that, I can't do anything else."

"As to money, give my plan a trial for a year. Let me see what I can do. I've ideas for some work too—some models for little things in silver that I'm sure will sell. And we are not so far behind now. I'm sure by next year we shall have caught up. If necessary I'll borrow from Aunt Sophy. She'd be glad to lend me anything."

"Borrow? I can't see that that would make us better off."

"Only for the time. We've been extravagant this last year, and then my—my illness—"

Teresa's head drooped, and her eyes closed sadly. Basil looked at her for a moment, then came up and touched her hair.

"Poor Teresa," he said softly.

That note of tenderness had been missing these many weeks. Teresa sat motionless; two tears rolled from under her closed eyelids.

"Well . . . what else was it, besides money?" she asked, after a moment.

"Oh, I have been thinking about you—and how we are bound together."

"Yes."

"And yet you did a great deal to break that down. You made me want to break it. You've made me suffer—and I can't love you as I did before."

"Can't you."

"No, you don't belong to me as you did. You were such a beautiful thing to me. I care for you more in one way than I did, now that I realise all the strength of your hold on me. I couldn't work to-day because you weren't in the house. I want you with me, all the more perhaps because you're not really with me. But it isn't as it was once. The peace and sweetness of it is gone . . ."

He spoke almost dreamily, as though the whole thing were remote, objective, and he looked at Teresa as though she were miles away.

"We shall get it back," said Teresa.

"No . . . never . . ."

"Then we shall get something better. Peace and sweetness aren't all.
. . . What I see," she said, still with her eyes closed and the tears on her
cheeks, "is that what we have is the main thing, the best thing. I feel now
that it can't be destroyed, neither by what I do nor by what you do. . . .
You take me with my weaknesses, as I take you with yours. I don't say it
will be all peace and sweetness—we're too near one another for that. I
suppose you will often hurt or irritate me—perhaps I shall hurt or irritate
you. I don't want to do it—but I can't promise that I shan't—I promise,
though, to leave you as free as possible."

"But I can't promise to leave you free," said Basil darkly.

"No matter."

"No—you mean you'll take as much freedom as you want. But what
I can't endure is suspecting you."

With sudden violence he took up a letter that had been lying on his
desk and threw it into Teresa's lap. She saw Crayven's writing on the
envelope. Without hesitation she took it, bent forward, and dropped the
unopened letter into the hottest part of the fire.

"Why did you do that? Were you afraid I should want to read it?"
demanded Basil.

"No. I'm tired of all that."

"Of what? Not of his letters?"

"Yes—everything about it. It doesn't matter."

"But it does! . . ."

"I tell you it doesn't! What you do matters more, because you don't
love me as much as I do you."

"Love me? You're in love with Crayven!"

"You've let me nearly die this last month of your indifference. . . ." A
sob broke Teresa's voice. "I tell you I can't live in that way. If you didn't
love me—"

"Someone else would, I suppose."

"No, if *you* didn't, I should die. I have been dying this last month—
I've been really ill. Look at me—do you see how thin I am?"

She sprang up and went close to Basil.

"I see that you're beautiful," he said softly. "Ah, you have me! . . ."

"Then be good to me! We shan't live forever!"

"I feel that I've lived a hundred years or so."

She answered with Lady Macbeth's appeal: " 'We are but young'!"

And half-smiling, passionately, she drew him down in her arms, into the great chair, and curled against him. They were both silent for a time, cheek to cheek, looking into the fire. . . . Each of them was seeing, perhaps, their past together, and its many memories. Each of them was silent before the future.

SELECTIONS FROM *THE STORY* OF A *LOVER*

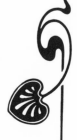

WRITTEN IMPULSIVELY IN 1914, Hutchins's *The Story of a Lover* was published anonymously in 1919. In this autobiographical work the forty-year-old Hutchins conducts a probing self-analysis of his deep attractions and even deeper conflicts during his fifteen-year marriage to Neith. He analyzes his affairs and his attempt to have Neith experiment with infidelity—although her contemplation of an affair provoked intense jealousy, which led in one case to physical violence. In a letter to his mother dated December 19, 1919, Hutchins explains his motivations in writing the book:

> Now I have something to tell you—partly a pleasure and partly a pain. I have a book out called *The Story of a Lover*. It was published about two months ago. I have been in doubt whether or not I ought to tell you about it. It is published anonymously. It is the finest thing I have written. But the reasons I have hesitated to show it to you is that I feared it might give you pain as it is based on certain episodes of my life with Neith—what you already know in general—but it is different, the book I mean. When I wrote the book several years ago, I did not intend to publish it. I was unhappy about Neith at the time, and this was a kind of relief, to express my feelings. I really wrote the book for her and for myself. And I can see now that I misrepresented myself because I took her point of view and misrepresented her because of my unbalanced feeling. I am not—and never have been—so invasive and irritating as I represent myself in the book—for Neith in some moods thought any attention invasive.[1]

In a similar letter to his mother, Neith gives her view of the book:

> A fact is a curious thing, and may look quite different to different people. My own feeling about the book is that it isn't at all true to *my* facts or feelings, that is, it represents a very different truth from *my* truth. Nevertheless, it is both true and beautiful. My merely personal feeling would have been against publishing it. But I believe it is a book that will outlive personal feelings, and be of permanent value. Hutch would not have published it as long as his father was here, but he felt

---

The Story of a Lover was originally published by Boni and Liveright, New York, in 1919. Reprinted with permission of Beatrix Hapgood Faust.

you would see it from a more impersonal point of view, as a work of art, which it certainly is.

Hutchins hoped that *The Story of a Lover* would become one of the best-sellers of that year. Soon after its release, however, the police seized all copies of the book and indicted the publisher on charges of obscenity. A judge dismissed the case, but the publicity did not help the book's sales. Hutchins wrote some years later: "The court incident conveyed to the public a wrong idea of what the book really was, and therefore alienated the reader who would have felt the real thing, just as it disappointed those who were looking for obscenity."[2]

There were some positive reviews of the book. The *Dial* reviewer called it "one of the extraordinary pieces of literature of recent years."[3] A friend and neighbor in Provincetown, Mary Heaton Vorse, said in the *New York Sun*: "This book is the greatest addition to that literature of personal record which we call human documents that this country has seen in this generation."[4]

Many more reviewers, however, attacked the "neurotic" character of the author in even more hostile terms than those leveled against Neith Boyce more than ten years earlier. The *New York Times* said the autobiography "narrates the history of the love life of a self-conscious neurasthenic."[5] Henry Marks, a reviewer for the *Chicago News*, wrote perhaps the most negative review:

I have read this book with amazement. That any educated person could be so naive is fairly incredible. It is not the story of a lover; it is the story of a sexual psychasthenic. . . . "Anonymous" is a constitutional neurotic. He is burdened by a persistent and harassing sexual tension which he is unable to relieve in his marriage. . . . The writing of this book, from every page of which oozes forth a passionate intensity and overemphasis, betrays his urgent suppressed and frustrated need. And for this reason, if for no other, I claim that the book is unhealthy, and that far from representing the universal, or even not very uncommon experience of lovers, it belongs in the class of the pathological.[6]

Liberal publications like the *Nation* also condemned the author's unconventionality in terms that we would now label sexist:

He sentimentalizes the object of his love throughout, and it is almost by accident that he gives us a glimpse of that by no means unknown kind of menage in which the husband sweeps the floors and nurses the children because he is too sentimental to insist on the performance of plain and obvious duties. One's final impression of him is that of a pathetic figure who has substituted endless self-torment and subtle, pain-shot revery for one virile act which might have liberated him with little pain to any one.[7]

Even Floyd Dell, another central figure in Greenwich Village intellectual life, objected to a book that focused on intimate personal life. Dell's review in the left-wing *Liberator* (the postwar successor to the *Masses*) used terms that implied it was unmanly to analyze sex and love: "It is not the story of a lover; it is the story of a pathetic philosopher. He is pathetic because he tries to think the things that can only be felt and to say the things that can only be done."[8]

Comparing *The Story of a Lover* to the best-selling autobiography of 1919, *The Education of Henry Adams*, highlights the degree to which Hutchins deviated from conventional expectations.[9] Henry Adams was thirty years older and from a more illustrious ancestry, but both men were the sons of businessmen, both had graduated from Harvard, and each had rejected a teaching position at that university in favor of free-lance journalism and writing. In the second decade of the twentieth century, both men wrote as anarchists critical of the industrial bourgeoisie. Both rejected conventional ideals of masculinity, were attracted to feminine values, and sought spiritual meaning outside of a religious context. Like Hutchins, Henry Adams sought "sensuous vitality, emotional dependence and innocent faith."[10] When their personal relations failed to meet these ideals, both men were subject to periods of pessimism and depression.

The Education of Henry Adams has become one of the most famous American autobiographies, assigned regularly in American history and literature courses in our universities. Although *The Education* presents a very personal account of Adams's experience in the public realm—especially his close association with several presidents and cabinet members—it makes only vague allusions to his personal life. Most striking, it omits twenty years of Adams's life—from age thirty-four to fifty-four, the years of his mature adulthood. These were the years of his marriage, ending in his wife's suicide. Despite Adams's avowals of the superiority of American women and the failings of American men, an autobiography that could not mention his wife's name nor discuss his marriage, let alone analyze its tragic ending, could not transcend the nineteenth-century separation of public and private worlds. Adams's autobiography contained no psychological introspection; it remained pre-Freudian, despite his positive references to psychology's discovery of the unconscious.

Hutchins Hapgood, in contrast, wrote about his own experiences of love, sexuality, and marriage, but his peers were not ready for such personal self-scrutiny from a man. And, while she applauded his introspection, Mary Heaton Vorse, for example, objected to his sexism. She said in her review:

> He gives the impression of a man traveling through a peaceful and beautiful unknown country, cherishing it, penetrating into its mystery, enhancing it through his understanding, planting within it things that were not there before, forever working it, working sometimes destructively, sometimes destroyed by its very perfection; himself always the active one; the country existing peacefully, being appreciated, being loved, being hated, being assailed, being enriched, but never active itself. Now, a person is not like a garden or a landscape. This remote lovely woman of whom he wrote was not passive like that. . . . That is what one feels throughout his account—the ceaseless activity of his love, the restless and loving prying into the spirit, the constant closeness would increase the remoteness of any human soul. Quiet would be the only response to such aggression—quiet and silence.[11]

A feminist today might also object to his failure to acknowledge any debt to the earlier novel by his wife. In a long discussion of the genesis of *The Story of a Lover* in his autobiography, Hutchins never mentions the influence of Neith's novel. Hutchins broke out of literature's separate spheres, but he did so by continuing a sexist tradition of ignoring while appropriating women's work.

The beginning chapters of the book contain philosophical and spiritual musings about the nature of love and marriage as well as a very specific, psychological analysis of Hutchins's own experiences. His first paragraph sets a central theme—that of Hutchins's love for Neith and his complaint that she has never equally loved and appreciated him: "I was thirty years old when I saw her for the first time. . . . I fell in love at first sight. She did not see me—and I sometimes think she has never seen me since, although we are married and have lived together for fifteen years" (1919 ed., 7). Several pages later he repeats this complaint: "I loved her for the essence of her being and she liked me warmly for what I was able to say and feel. . . . She felt aesthetically my qualities. She did not love Me. . . . She married me at last without being more than deeply pleased" (1919 ed., 16–17, 25).

Hutchins records how their differences attracted him:

> How different her nature and her past from mine! She had never struggled with herself. She did not need to, for herself did not disturb her. Imperturbable, she struggled only with her work, with what she was trying to form. She was an artist and singularly unconscious of herself. Keen to external beauty, she was not interested in the subjective nature of her Soul, or its need, or how it worked. In fact, her soul seemed to have no needs. . . . She was no self-conscious neurasthenic, as I was! She was cool, unconscious, poised—cold the ignorant would call her. And the Silence which breathed from her when I first saw her has been hers ever since. (1919 ed., 12–13)

From a late-twentieth-century perspective, Hutchins is oblique about his sexual relationship with Neith, but for his time he is quite open. He hints that he may have had sexual problems with her:

> A beautiful love relation is impossible without a delicate sexual adjustment. . . . And it is not an easy thing for a civilized man and woman to have an adequate sensual relation. . . . When I first met her, I was not at all conscious of any sensual desire. My relations with women had been casual, fragmentary and nervous, and I had not learned to associate physical intercourse with spiritual emotion. So that, at first, our relations were lyrical and light on the sensual side, playful and athletic, smiling, and to her a little foolish and unmeaning. . . . She did not feel the sad, colorful need of full self-and-sex expression and in her eyes was not the longing left by long nights of mutual giving-up. It was in large measure because I had not learned to be patient and quiet, to study her needs and to care more for her pleasure and emotion than for my own, not realizing that the two were inextricably dependent, one upon the other. It is probable that women instinctively know more than men of the art of love on the physical side. . . . The deep quiet woman with whom I lived unconsciously shaped my sex relation with her. She taught me the subtlety of the approach, the constancy and the continuation of it, and she herself continually grew in sensuous knowledge. (1919 ed., 66–67)

Emotional differences and perhaps sexual difficulties made Hutchins try to change Neith:

From the start I tried hard to disturb her. I felt that if I could disturb her, she would love me. . . . I said she had no soul. I said it repeatedly in all manner of ways. I said it when she was warmly hidden in my arms. I said as we drank wine together across the table of the genial table-d'hôte. I said it between the acts of the theater. I said it in the street-cars and in the open country stretches where we walked. Did she marry me partly because of a kindly desire to prove to me that I was wrong? I did all I could to disturb, to wound, to arouse, to make her calm soul discontended and unhappy; as well as interest her vividly and constantly. (1919 ed., 28)

To his credit, Hutchins admits that his need to criticize Neith came partly from his own lack of inner integrity—"the rich peace that did not exist in my soul." He also reports Neith's criticism of him: "Sometimes in her hinting way, she would quietly suggest that if she should try to express herself to me I would run away. She would amusedly call attention to the vanity and egotism in me that demanded above everything else a sympathetic listener" (1919 ed., 29).

Their differences were heightened when Neith became pregnant; she was in despair, while he was overjoyed—and jealous: "If I could only have been with child myself! If we could have been with child together! That would have satisfied my deepest instincts, would have made us one. . . . Is it not a crime for a man to want to be pregnant? To want to be mutually pregnant? Does it not show a passionate invasiveness, an almost incredible desire for violation of another's personality?" (1919 ed., 52–53).

Despite this insight, Hutchins could not control his behavior. When the pregnancy increases Neith's quiet withdrawal, Hutchins responds with hostility. Hutchins also feels ambivalence toward Neith, which he tries to escape himself from her: "Often I want away from her, irritated by her very perfection; by her self-sufficiency and calm; went away from what I loved and what I prized, to occupy myself with transient things, experiences and strangers—with work, with women and with boon companions" (1919 ed., 41).

Throughout the first part of the book, Hutchins casually mentions his interest in other women, his "conventional infidelities," and his jealousy when Neith shows an interest in other men, despite the fact that he has encouraged her to relate to others. He tells Neith about his infidelities but thought that she cared little. In retrospect, he admits: "Perhaps I was wrong in attributing to her that indifference, for at a later time I suddenly realized that these acts of mine had meant more to her than I had thought" (1919 ed., 88–89).

Chapter 6 ends with Hutchins discussing their conflicts over daily life:

> She never yielded to my constant desire for what seemed to her, and perhaps were, the minor moralities of life. . . . By nature she hated housekeeping, and the prattle and needs and noise of small children filled her with a wild yearning to go to the woods and to attain the peace of the savage state. . . . She had wildly vicious moments when the children, cooks and neighbors—whose social calls she never returned, and for whom she generally had a blighting, cold contempt—appeared to her as scorpions made to torment her. . . . I nagged and nagged her, and tried to fit into the world of our meticulous society, and she, like a stubborn mare, kept the bit between her teeth and went her own intolerable way. . . . I dinned nervously into her my demands. I insisted on economy and regularity, an affability towards neighbors and friends. I kept my many engagements with scrupulous care and I expected her, who had no sense of time or punctuality whatever, to keep hers. And when she did not, I fumed and fretted and stormed and acted like a petulant child. For years and years I struggled to overcome her in these minor matters of moralities. . . . and there was constant nervous friction between us. It is possible that the friction helped to keep the spark of love alive; perhaps it was there for some obscure, beneficent purpose. (1919 ed., 93–96).

Notes

1. Letters by Neith Boyce and Hutchins Hapgood are from the Hapgood collection, Collection of American Literature, Beinecke Rare Book and Manuscript Library, Yale University.

2. *A Victorian in the Modern World* (1939; reprint, Seattle: University of Washington Press, 1972), 411.

3. *The Dial*, September 20, 1919, 276.

4. *New York Sun*, September 28, 1919, sec. 6, 1.

5. *New York Times*, September 28, 1919.

6. *Chicago News*, September 28, 1919.

7. *The Nation*, November 8, 1919, 611.

8. *The Liberator*, October 1919, 44.

9. *The Education of Henery Adams: An Autobiography* (1918; reprint, Boston: Houghton Mifflin, 1961).

10. T. J. Jackson Lears, *No Place of Grace: Antimodernism and the Transformation of American Culture, 1880–1920* (New York: Pantheon Books, 1981), 278.

11. *New York Sun*, September 28,1919, sec. 6, 2.

Chapter VII

Spare one another we never did; each struggled to realize his own individuality, his egotistic need. Neither of us was considerate to the other. Those pale renunciations which hold many couples together in fragile relations neither of us would accept. In spite of the manifold connections of a life of work, children and responsibility shared, the deeper relation between us was founded not on compromise, but on attraction and repulsion, on a kind of interesting warfare. In the midst of the complexities of our common life, each of us has stood fiercely for the individual soul and its personal needs. Sometimes she has conquered and killed me, but I have never really yielded, and children, work and impinging society have at times overcome her and forced her warmly from her well of damp, withdrawing comfort; but never with her soul's consent; never merely to be considerate or thoughtful of others. Our relation has been divinely lacking in sentimentality and in that kind of morality which takes the salt out of life. We both passionately demanded that our union should add to, not take from, abundance. So that whenever we have found an adjustment it has been a real one, based on unconscious necessity and not on the minor efforts of the deliberate will.

I have been more of a mother, more of a housekeeper than the great majority of men. This was due in large measure to my indifference to the usual ambitions of the male, to business, to conventional art and literature and to the standards of society; and to my practical lack and inabilities, as well as to her limitations in domestic and wifely qualities. And she has been more of a father than the great majority of women —

she has gone out to the larger world in her thought, her imagination and her work, and has helped to make up for my deficiencies. So that though we never tried to compromise, each has departed in some degree from the conventional sphere and has contributed in the other's fields. Or, more truly, neither of us has felt any limitation of sex, except the fundamental one, and we have worked out our common life as if there were no conventional career for either man or woman. It has been difficult and painful, but it has seemed to us the larger thing to do, the more exciting, the more amusing, procedure.

Amusing! That is the word she has taught me to use in her instinctively Gallic sense. Mentally, emotionally and temperamentally interesting is what she means by amusing, and to insist as we did upon our egotistic personalities as elements in every situation was invariably amusing, no matter how painful it might be. Sometimes the pain seemed almost to break the relation and separate as inevitably, but that which brought us back with a fuller emotion was the impersonal pleasure of contemplation, which to some extent enabled us to see ourselves as if we were others and to be pleased and amused by the spectacle. Art is a significant amusement, and as I have written, there was in each of us, an unconscious attempt to see life as art, impersonally though warmly. That is why we both disliked the sentimental and why we passionately rejected the considerate and the decent attitude toward each other, which was not good enough for our high instinctive resolve.

The deeper disturbance of our mutual life, there from the beginnings as undertones, became more definite as time went on, grew into clear motifs in the symphony of our relation. The essential discord was strengthened, making the harmony more difficult but when maintained rendering it deeper; as it does in the operas of Strauss and Debussy.

About six years after the honeymoon we went, with our two children, to the Middle West where we passed an important year. To make clear the threatening new elements which came into our lives I need to refer to my deepening interest in what is called the labor movement of our day. This interest had grown out of my work as a journalist in New York, and had helped to bring out my natural love for what is called the under-dog. It was a love that had no need of a remoter charm. It had no relation to kindness or philanthropy. It had no pity or morality in it. It was a simple love for the unfamiliar, and for those instincts and basic ideas newly germinating which to my imagination seemed to hold out the promise of a more exciting and interesting and therefore a juster and better society. I was deeply tired of historical, platitudinous conventions and moralities in living and in art, and whenever I found the consciously or unconsciously rebellious I was strangely and pleasurably moved. It was for me an enjoyment second only in intensity to my love for the Woman, and, at bottom, these passions were connected. An intense temperamental element in the love for a woman is the exhilaration of a close relation with the primitive, the instinctive, and the ideal at once. He who has never desired a re-valuation of all values, who in his deeper emotions is not a revolutionist, has never fully loved a woman, for in the closest personal relation there lies a challenge and a threat to all that is meaningless or lifeless in organized society.

I have never been able to learn much from books; or from any other record of human experience. Only when I come in contact with men and women do I seem to myself to think. I then feel the strange inner excitement which is analogous to the thrill of the love adventure. What seems a new conception arouses me as does the kiss of the beloved! My life among the rebellious victims of the industrial system gave me some vital ideas which for a time played an unwarrantably important part in my life and have left a definitely sound and permanent effect. And these ideas deeply disturbed my relation with Her, and, as I now think, enriched and stimulated our lives both together and as individuals.

I saw how deep and all-embracing, and really how destructive of our conventions and minor moralities, the philosophy of the proletarian really is; how it strips society to the essential! It destroys the values we put on personal property as it points out with intensity the enslaving function of possessions. A conception of a social order whose morality, law, art, and conventions are formed about the economic advantage of a dominant few startles the mind and the imagination and turns the strenuous soul to an analysis of the fundamentals. It puts him in a mood where respectability and all its institutions seem a higher form of injustice and robbery and makes him see the criminal, the outcast and the disinherited with a new and wondering sympathy; not a sympathy which expresses itself in benevolence and effort toward reform, but a mental and imaginative sympathy which sees in revolution the hope of a more vital art and literature, a deeper justice and a richer human existence; a sympathy which is in its character aesthetic—the sympathy of the social artist, not of the mere reformer or of the narrow labor agitator.

For a year I was deeply absorbed in these ideas and feelings, new and disturbing and enriching to me. And I, of course, brought them home to her, as I brought everything home to her. I took to her my feelings and my impressions, unbalanced and hot from their source; and she met the men and women who were the incarnations of these disturbing conceptions.

Ideas of marriage and the love relation in general were affected like everything else by this far-reaching proletarian philosophy. To free love from convention and from the economic incubus seemed a profoundly moral need. The fear that the love of one's mistress was the indirect result of commercial necessity aroused a new variety of jealousy! In some strenuous lovers a strange passion was aroused—to break down all sex conventions in order to purify and strengthen the essential spiritual bond!

I met men and women who, with the energy of poets and idealists, attempted to free themselves from that jealousy which is founded on physical possession. They longed to have so strong a spiritual bond that it would be independent of any material event or any mere physical happening. They tried to rid themselves of all pain due to the physical infidelities of their lovers or mistresses!—believing that love is of the soul, and is pure and intense only when freed from the gross superstitions of the past. And one of the gross superstitions seemed to them the almost instinctive belief that a sexual episode or experience with any other except the beloved is of necessity a moral or spiritual infidelity. They traced this feeling to old theology and to the sense of ownership extended until it includes the body of the loved one!

They highly demanded that the love relation should be free and independent, that it should be one in which proud and individual equals commune and communicate, and give to each other rich gifts, but make no demands and accept no sacrifices, and claim no tangible possession in the personality of the other. Only so could each bring to the other his best, something racy and strange because his own, something so personal that it stimulated the other, though it might waylay, disturb, and exasperate. Their voice was that of strenuous and idealistic youth bearing the burden of a general historical disillusionment.

A burden indeed it is! To accept well-marked out conceptions of morality and norms of beauty is the easier way. To try to reconstruct the basis on which our feelings express themselves is a task indeed for the gods. And since men and women are not unlimited, these idealists among them fell frequently and bit the dust of humiliation and despair. Old tradition and old instinct proved stronger than they and, filled with commonplace jealousy, a new pain was added to the old—they were not only crudely and madly jealous but they also hated themselves for being so! Theirs was a new, deep pain indeed! They were no longer comforted by the conviction of being wronged, of their honor outraged, of being soliders, though unhappy, in the cause of morality. They suffered and condemned themselves for suffering. They did not have even the consolation of thinking themselves justified!

These subtly-interested ideas connected with the whole field of the philosophy of total reconstruction with which I came in personal contact through association with expressive personalities among the industrial victims of conventionalized society, had a great and for a time an unbalancing influence on me, and, with my customary need for giving all I had, bad and good, I delivered to her my new passionate perceptions, my disturbing ideals and my fragmentary and idealistic hopes of a superior race of men and women—men and women capable of maintaining beautiful and intense relations and at the same time being superior to the time-worn and, as I thought, out-worn tests of virtue and fidelity.

To try the impossible is the function of the idealist and of the fool. And I have certainly at times been a fool if not an idealist in my demands on myself and on her. She took these my new and excited feelings as she tended to take everything in her moral environment, to make it a part of her as far as she could harmonize it with what she already possessed, with what had gone before. And so she began to make experiments which had been in part instigated by me, but which, after all, was only the following out of her deeper nature, a nature more unconventional than mine, and less theoretical. She tended more than I do to put into thorough practice what she had once mentally accepted. The ease and calmness with which she could take a mental proposition filled me with uneasiness. I felt that if she loved me she would have more in her instincts to overcome.

I encouraged her to have intimate friendships with other men; to be alone with my friends and with hers; but when I saw in her an eager readiness to take advantage of my initiative, the old racial feeling of jealousy would stir within me. When I saw that other men excited her, and that she often preferred their society to mine, deep pain would take possession of me! One day she coolly told me not to come home to luncheon as she wanted that time alone with one of my friends!

That was the occasion of a violent quarrel between us. When I expressed my dislike at being excluded she accused me of hopeless inconsistency.

Inconsistent I was, but not in the way she meant. My inconsistency lay in demanding from her what her nature could not give, even when I knew she could not give it! Perhaps a part of my love for her was this inability of hers to give herself to me, but I always have struggled desperately to secure from her that absolute devotion in passion of which she is incapable—at least to me.

It was not that she lunched alone with another man who was beginning with excitement to see her. It was not that that disturbed me. It was not so crude as that, though she ironically and contemptuously characterized it so. I loved to have her like other men, as I loved to have her like all of life. To taste and to enjoy and to be stimulated to greater thought and understanding and to more comprehensive emotion, I loved to feel that this was for her. It gave me a vicarious excitement, a warm secondary pleasure, and it fed my illusion, an illusion recognized by me as an illusion, of what she might one day be capable of with me.

And to have her know other men intimately, just as I continually wished to know other women intimately, was with me a genuine desire. I saw in this one of the conditions of greater social relations between her and me, of a richer material for conversation and for common life together. Whenever she showed an interest in other men I saw in it what I call the live line; it was to me an exciting sign of imaginative vitality—I saw the life spirit in her!

Yes, but what filled me at the same time with unutterable passionate misery was her tendency at such moments to reject me! That she wanted to see other men alone and intimately squared with my conscious ideals and even with my emotional impulses and with my need of pleasurable excitement. But that this new experience should make the distance between her and me still greater, this was to me the unendurable. For her to tell me she did not want me to be with her and him, when I wanted to be there, this was an intolerable exclusion, and reopened the old periodic wounds.

I dwell upon this seemingly trivial occasion of the luncheon because of its symbolic character. It was typical of much that had happened between us continually. The thing in her which all my instincts as well as all my philosophy and thought rejects is her inability to feel for me at the moment she feels for another! This is the eternal jar, the perception which takes from the harmony of life, from the unity of the universe. As I have written, all through life I have instinctively and consciously struggled to hold all the essential elements of my life together,—not to drop anything out of what has once been seen as beautiful. In this painful effort to maintain our deeper memory, what we call the soul is born.

This demand for an extended harmony is what made the youthful Weininger so bitter towards womankind, in whom he saw an essential limitation of memory, and therefore a limitation of soul. His personal, unhappy fate made him err in making of this truth a merely sexual matter. It is not only the woman but the man, too, whose intensity and concentration are not sufficient to hold enough together on the basis of which the triumphant soul emerges.

I imagine that at the root of every real love is this almost metaphysical passion — this deep emotional insistency on unity. So that when I saw, as I often did in her, transparent forgetfulness, a dry ability to put herself entirely into the interest of the moment, losing the harmonizing fringe of consciousness in which the values of the past are held, it almost seemed to me as if her soul was damned or had never been born, and my whole being wept at the temporary destruction of my Ideal, at the confutation of my philosophy, at the negation of my deepest instinct.

But how often did I try to be as at such times she seemed to me to be! In a kind of metaphysical despair how often did I try to rid myself of underlying memory! to be a rebel to the soul itself, to live in the dry, hard moment, without fringe or atmosphere! — trailing on with me none of the long reaches of the past! And how often has my unconscious demand for unity kept me from realizing my deliberate desire to kill the soul.

In the arms of other women I have attempted to deny the soul. I have longed to live as if I had no essential memory; as if there were no deep instinct in me to build my life of values about a central principle. When I failed — as I always have — I have sometimes wept bitter tears, tears falling because of my inability to break up my own integrity. I have been with women whom I liked and admired, with whom I wanted to have an absolute and refreshing intimacy. I have sometimes felt that my salvation depended on being able to give myself completely to another woman, and I have at times tried desperately to do so, but She always stood between, invisible, silent, representing for me the eternal principle of continuity in emotion, insisting on the Memory-Soul, demanding, without intending to, a monogamy deeper than that based on convention or law.

Demanding this deeper monogamy, not only without intending to, but even without understanding the nature of monogamy when it concerns the spirit. She made the deeper monogamy necessary for me, but she did not understand its nature! How often did she wonder at the character of my love for her! Her large, frank, mysterious eyes glowed with a kind of contemplative examination. I was a curious and interesting phenomenon—sometimes beautiful and attractive to her, sometimes irritating and unpleasant—but always incomprehensible was the nature of my love, perhaps the nature of Love itself!

If she had at any one moment understood this inevitable bondage of my spirit, a bondage which was independent of any of the conventional expressions of fidelity, a bondage bound up with my feeling about myself and all of life, she would have understood the reason for my jealousy.

I was jealous because she was not bound in the same deep, independent way! independent of conventions, bound by the essential law of the spirit. It would have been easy for me to endure what is called infidelity had the real, unconscious infidelity not been so transparently present. A warm friendship with another man involving sexual relationship would have met my growing social rebelliousness, and would have been eventually recognized by me as not inconsistent with our relation, had that relation ever been securely established.

To see in her eyes a temperamental forgetfulness of me and a vague imaginative hope of relationship with an impossibly charming uninjured masculine expression of God brought me back with an indescribable pang to my own inherent weaknesses, my lack of nervous integrity and the impossibility of attaining that spiritual unity in sex which to me my relation to her had always idealistically meant.

I wonder if every lover does not clearly understand me! Am I not here writing the autobiography of every man as concerns his love relation? I think these memoirs are no more true of me than of any one who has felt the full possibility of a human relation with a being of the opposite sex.

Chapter VIII

Our second child, the child of her greatest pain, the child bound up with the sensuous Italian hills, was seriously ill at this period. Almost every moment since that time he has been struggling between the dissolution of his being and its regeneration. The full beauty of Her would never have been fully revealed had it not been for the full pain of this sensitive child! He with his precarious and tremulous marvelousness was a product of her unconscious richness. I have now fully known the hopeless superficiality of the lover who looks to joy as the distinctive fruit of his relation; and of him who thinks himself nearer his childless mistress than to the mother of his children. Every new link of the beloved with the wider life gives her greater beauty and meaning, and the perception of her interrelation with all of Nature lends to her original appeal a deep structural power that becomes identified with the total love of life.

Things grew constantly more complex for us. Practical difficulties and trying illness, my growing relations with the rebels whose philosophy became a disturbing factor in our union, and its consequent effect on her, these weavings and developments seemed to carry us to a point, an infinity of moral distance from the simple sensuous honeymoon—giving, however, to that simple sensuousness a new exasperation and intensity. Especially was this true with her. Her temperamental coolness at times quite vanished in the midst of her deep woe and her growing excitement of life. The possibility of an unknown lover and the tragedy of childhood woke her now to an occasional amorous expression in which she gave herself with the last, sad, wonderful giving!

And thus I reaped the painful joy as well as the pleasurable pain of the new stirrings of her nature toward others! And as those stirrings brought more strenuous disturbance between us, so strenuous that they might have burst asunder the relation, the new additions, the children, the practical difficulties, the growing, deepening relations and experiences brought in a counteracting intimacy which prevented the break between us.

If our relation had remained simple it might not have endured. It could not have endured had it not developed, changed, and taken into it the richness of the outside world. It grew to be so manifold, so connected with all else, that the disturbances of egotistic strife were gathered up, controlled and harmonized by the total structure of our existence—as a sound which may be a harsh discord in a simple harmony is a beautiful part of a more complex symphony.

At the most intense point of my absorption in the rebellious victims of the industrial despotism of our day and in their resulting philosophy of life, she and the two children were away for several months, leaving me excitedly living with my new friends. It was the first time we had been separated for more than a day or two, and in my feeling we were not separated then, for I poured out to her in letters the emotional meaning of my life among the social rebels. These letters were full of an exalted excitement, of a vivid hope for an extended fruitful liberty revivifying and regenerating society, and of a direct appeal and challenge to her, demanding a continuance of the Great Adventure, and exhorting her to live freely and to love me all the more!

With me this time of separation was one of mental excitement and imaginative adventure, adventure with ideas, and with men and women. There was no deep relation, physical or otherwise, with any woman, but I touched and experimented and wondered and glimpsed the human and social vistas that were opened to me. And I passed on my impulsive suggestions to her!

And then, just before I went to her and the children again, a letter came telling of how she had met a man who moved her in a strong, primitive way. He had a root-like, sensual charm for her, she wrote; there was a something in him which needed of her and made her need of him; he was lonely and unsocial and graceless, remote and bad, excitingly, refreshingly bad, and me she accused of being good and that was rather stale and dull, and touched with life's too-refined food and not with the stimulating salt of the earth. In him was the stimulating salt of the earth!

Again, more strongly than ever, there came in me the deep reverberations of a nameless jealousy! How weak were my ideas when my fundamental feelings were aroused! Nameless it was, for we have as yet no name for a jealousy which doubts and despises itself, a jealousy mixed with elation and approval of its cause! In the grip of the pang I tried to justify myself. Oh, why need she reject me at every new out-going? Why compare me unfavorably? Again came to me the old deep wound; she had never seen me! never had liked my real self. Again the intolerable pain of seeing that she had never really given herself to me!

She met me at the railroad station. As she came quietly, calmly and cordially towards me, how wonderful, how strong and self-sufficient she seemed! A new life, which perhaps came from the sense of having a new lover, breathed through her, and lent an enhanced vitality; and to have the new without eliminating the old, this was a fructifying hope in her, a hope I should have welcomed, for it was of the bone of my theory and of my new ideal for civilization. I had the grace at any rate to see her as wonderful. A fresh intensity of liking was added to my love, and for weeks I devoted myself to her with a devouring passion that knew no bounds.

It was a passion full of disturbance and moral agony. Her cool ability to compare him with me, the new with the old, as if we stood on an equality in her feeling, this drove me almost insane!

By nature she was beautifully, cruelly frank; and I with an idealistic instinct for self-torture encouraged and fostered this tendency natural to her. It was an unconscious cruelty, due to that seclusion of her spirit which shut her from a quick, alert knowledge of the state of feeling in the other person. I demanded from her on this occasion an entire, detailed account of her relation with the other man, and she, to my indescribable pain, responded with a lucid exactness which had its fascination, too. Indeed, she never was more desirable to me than when she seemed, through some excluding instinct for another, infinitely remote. I might hate her, but she appeared then as a resplendent being.

I saw from what she coolly told me that she was prepared to give him whatever he needed or asked. Just because of her aloofness she was capable of a rich though cool sympathy which saw him as beautiful partly because he needed—a strong being who needed—who seemed to need her. I felt the beauty of her attitude. To be ready always to meet a need is beautiful. Theoretically and even emotionally I subscribed, but why, oh, why, had she through all these long years never met my completer need with an absoluteness which would have calmed and controlled and rendered for me quite harmless her relations with others?

So I felt the beauty and the limitation at once—the beauty of her feeling for him, and the terrible emotional forgetfulness of me! How the temperamental memory dropped out or had never been for the intenser values of our life together! Before my fierce, uncontrolled reproaches she scornfully called attention to my inconsistency—that made me think and desire in one direction and passionately act in the opposite. She cast up to me my physical relations with women and expressed with cool completeness her temporary contempt for me. He seemed so noble in comparison, for the lover in a much more simple relation, always has the advantage in apparent nobility, over the husband.

And I retorted with what I think was not entire hypocrisy. Despairingly and passionately I insisted that she had as yet shown herself incapable of giving to others without taking from the relation with me that my soul demanded. Never, I repeated, had I been able to forget, even for a moment, even in the arms of another woman, my bond with her; even when I desired to forget it, this spiritual love, stronger than death, was unshaken; its strength was even more conscious to me at such times. I was then more aware if it, of its indestructibility, than ever.

But with her it was different, I insisted. Had she ever loved me in that strange, temperamental way, had she ever had that passionate liking for my real self, independent of my qualities, she would have been incapable of spiritual infidelity; no matter what her friendly actions had been, no matter how technically and conventionally unfaithful she had been, in moments of inevitable sexual movements.

Over and over again I vehemently asserted the difference between the conventions of her sex and of mine, conventions that I hated and wished undone and obliterated from society; but which nevertheless existed and which were a painful element in every human relation. I pointed out how difficult it is for a woman to give herself without the deeper infidelity, for she is told by society that unless she loves when she gives herself, she is evil and unworthy, abandoned; and that that terrible and ugly convention is a corrosive reality even to strong-minded, humorous and emancipated women. I had hoped she, the woman I loved, could rise above this crassly physical measure of virtue, but whenever it came to the test I had seen that when she began to be intimate, or to think of intimacy with another man, she tended to forget her spiritual bond with me. Was it because of this damnable social convention, or because she had never felt that bond? Between these alternatives I passionately vacillated, self-torturing, helpless, morally unattractive, undignified, the ugly incarnation of an extreme unsatisfied need!

One day she asked me, as she had asked me before, not to come home that evening until late. She wanted to spend it alone with him. She wanted a relation in which I could be no part, which could not be if I were there, something excluding me! Dumb rage took possession of me, but at the same time I longed to take the strong and independent attitude, the attitude that might win myself for myself, that might win the greater Her for me—the Her for me that I had never had!

So I went away and dined and spent the evening in a gathering of men and women who lightly talked of love and freedom and society. As I looked on these faces and heard not what they said, I wondered if they felt as I felt, if their lives were as mine, and I knew instinctively that they were; I knew that all lovers understand and that this book is a universal book, that all human beings who felt at all must feel as I feel. In my mind and senses, in my conscious self and in the clearness of my definite thoughts, I was with her and him—not with these my talking brothers and sisters whose faces only I saw, for their faces, not their words, mirrored my soul. Did her being remember me? Doubt of her and doubt of myself came with alternating violence and when I went home I was completely exhausted.

I found her proud and silent, instinct with that torturing and amazing recessional remoteness which was of her inner being, of the inner being of all things. She looked at me with quiet, searching questionings, as if she were looking deep into my nature and wondering if there were any consistency there, anything that remained and endured, anything that was necessary, after all that was conventional and accidental and vain and merely respectable had passed. She was deeply serious and it was with a certain quiet anxiety that she met me.

But the quiet passed into silent reproach as I nervously demanded talk from her. She withdrew into that infinity of distance that I knew and hated, and refused to answer my violent demand to tell me all that had happened between her and him. The strong part for me to have taken was dignified trust, an obvious confidence that the best existed between us and was inalienable. But I did not have that trust. That confidence was lacking in me and I was not strong and clever enough to assume it.

So she with clear disappointment was obstinately silent, and this in spite of my growing excitement and violence. And suddenly something happened which had never happened before and never since, although in after years even more acute crises arose; without premeditation I took her by the throat! I did not know I was doing it until I caught myself in the act. Never had the possibility of using physical violence occurred to me. In my consciousness it was incredible—but here it happened without consciousness! The underlying brute in me terrified me, even in the act itself! At that moment I understood murder, and knew that assassination might become inevitable for any one at any moment.

Terror at myself was followed by surprise at the way she took it. She made no resistance, but in a deep quiet whisper she breathed my name. Her eyes grew big and profound wonder was in that silent sound that seemed to come from all of her. I think the perception that I was capable of absolute unreason appealed in some primitive way to her imagination. Me she had always regarded as a finally civilized creature, analytical, seeking reason and sophistication. The passion which was me she had perhaps never so clearly felt. At any rate I sensed with a kind of shameful pride that she was gazing at me as at an interesting stranger. Not the slightest touch of fear was in her look, but a wonderful quiet excitement dominated her.

Why was it that, in after years, when the waves of passion came on me perhaps even more strongly, I never again resorted to physical violence? It may be the shock to myself when I felt what I was capable of; perhaps it was the contempt that must be ours when we use the uttermost weapon without reserve. To lose all possible control is the final degradation of the soul. And she, too, never again used her final weapon—impenetrable silence to the same terrible degree. Her silence was with her as unreasonable, as much a part of primitive instinct, as was my violence. And she had on that occasion indulged her form of unreasonable violence to the limit. And my violence had been born of hers. I think at that moment a new fear of ourselves was born in each, and that although we did not then know it, we were nearer together than ever before.

At that moment we felt the degree of savageness which each could show the other; and the first symbolic response was a wild, fierce embrace, mordant, painful, without limit, sad with passion, born of the new element of recognized mutual strangeness that had been excitingly revealed to us. And in the languid, unnervous reconciliation that followed, the wonderful complete peace, she quietly and fully told me what I had so fiercely needed to know; and I remember how ashamed I was of my relief when I knew that she had been unable to give herself to him, and at the same time of a certain vague disappointment; perhaps because she was still finally untested and doubt of the inalienable bond continued its periodic possession.

Chapter IX

Then there came three years abroad. Economic necessity was removed to a point where we felt we could devote ourselves for a time to contemplative work—I to those psychological studies of temperament which were so fascinating to me, she to the forming of her experience into stories of human life. Dwelling as we both did in our writing on intimate nervous relations undoubtedly helped to make us more fully conscious of our own relation: and what added still farther to this awareness of our bond was my almost constant presence in the family. This had and has always been so with me, with some brief interruptions. Men who go regularly to their office and are only with their wives and children in the evenings and on holidays do not fully taste the domestic reality nor is made the full test of the personal relation. My being with her and the children was irregular but frequent and extended. All day and all night for weeks and weeks and months and months, then in the house all day and away most of the night; writing, she and I at the same time, I taking my share in care of the children, in teaching them, and in the thousand details of the domestic situation. It was a close partnership, full of variation from the usual, interesting, irritating, and replete with meaning and color.

It was soon after the crisis that we sailed; we were both very tired emotionally, but I think she felt as I did the charm of going off into the unknown together. We had left nothing behind us, not even furniture, and we were taking with us all we possessed, contained in three trunks, with no idea of the future except the decision not to live in hotels and pensions, but to keep house wherever we went. This we always did, no matter how short our stay in a place; we insisted on tasting the life as lived around us, and my domestic partnership with her helped us to get settled as well as unsettled very quickly. That we could bear nothing except keeping house had an inevitable meaning, no matter how exasperating those cares were at times to both of us. We were forced to live together in the external conditions of existence, as in the spiritual bond: it was strong, very strong, whatever it was.

On the steamer we were, I remember, unusually quiet. But I felt in her a new freer interest in other things. She, apparently, thought very little of the lover she had left, but because of him she saw the casual stranger in a warmer, more human light. Her feeling of companionship with me seemed stronger because of the recent experience; the element of additional strangeness added to the color of our common life, although I often relapsed into unreasoning pathos and pain. We were on the whole, however, calmly waiting for the future. We were on a broader base than ever, and resting on our temperamental oars, there was something that whispered to us of exciting, adventurous things to come, for which we were instinctively saving our strength. I saw but not always with pain the fuller appreciation in her glance at other men as they swung freely and picturesquely along the deck. And on my part was unconsciously forming itself the resolution to attain emotional freedom from her by deeper intimacy with other women. Whenever I felt the full pain of my dependency on her, as I did whenever I fully realized her indestructible aloofness from me, I had an excess of hope of attaining aloofness for myself through relations with other women – a hope, however, that has never been realized.

Never, however, even for a moment, have I ever felt any diminution of love for her. Indeed, as time went on and our relations grew more complex, more serious, and at times more painful, that love has seemed more profound, more all-embracing, and to be in a way a symbol of my love for beauty, for Nature, for Life itself.

And now, again in Italy, came another period of wonderful pleasure in her. In the beautiful intensity of an Italian spring and summer we realized ourselves to the joyous full and for a time with no element of interwoven pain. The pleasures of the senses and of the mind, with civilized companions gracefully and indolently living out their unstrenuous lives, dining with them out-of-doors in the long wonderful evenings, and combining the serious languor of passionate Italy with the nervous charm of an epigrammatic Gallic civilization—these pleasures were of a broader, and more intellectualized but not less sensuous honeymoon, rendered all the more poignant by the recent crisis, hinting always of the possibility of volcanic happenings.

Now again began to stir within her the strange unconscious life, and she was pregnant for the third time. At the period of conception we were reveling in a beautiful, full translation into French of the Arabian Nights. Devoted to the sensuous unmoral charm of these gorgeous, colorful tales we lived a life quite out of harmony with Puritanical ideas. The sentimental and the narrowly ethical were far away and this child was started and was born in an atmosphere of mature sensuousness, in a complete acceptance of what is called the Pagan point of view. The tremulous, early lyricism of young love had given place to a rich decided determination to take in full measure the goods the Gods provide!

She was born—this sensitive little girl—on the Arno, on the banks of the stream that runs through Fiorenze, the Flowering City of Tuscany! And her mother this time felt the exhilaration of child-birth, the athletic triumph in the midst of pain, the accomplishment of the impossible with its resultant triumph. And soon afterwards came that full physical beauty, that springing of the blood and of the body, that intense enhancement of color and swelling of contour which gave her the look of a gorgeous Magdalene; more delicate in quality than Rubens or Titian, but suggesting both, richer and more voluptuous than the early Florentine painters, yet having the recessional purity of the Giottesque or Siennese madonna! No virgin could equal her full beauty! No lover could so richly love a maiden were it not for the unconscious purpose of this ultimate fruition!

My feeling for her at that time did not have, perhaps, as much of what is called sentiment as it had before, and was destined to have again; and I imagine it was the same with her. I liked her with an intense and destructive liking because she was life itself, and she had an impersonal relish in existence which included me, the children, the hills, the works of art, the Italian cooking and the witticisms of our aesthetic and self-indulgent friends! Never before had she enjoyed life, never had she trusted and believed in it, so much, never had she been so willing to embrace it!

Yes, she was willing to embrace it! Or, rather, have life embrace her. I saw her in her every attitude. Her feeling about literature and art, about Nature; the love of beauty, always strong and pure in her, was greatly intensified. And there was a subtle sensuousness in her friendly relations with the contemplative men on the hills; a cool freedom from any recognized bond. In her imagination she was as free as air: I could see this in everything; in a glance, in a sensuous movement towards a sunset, the kind of love she showed for a child, as well as her quiet appreciation of the personalities about her. That innate distrust of life which had always been hers, was in large measure displaced by the fully accepted sensuousness of her experience; art, children, the willingness to have lovers, the sense of freedom. The sense of freedom! How vitalizing, how refreshing, how indispensable to the living of every full life!

And this was in part the result of the sex crises we had had together and these were in part due to my interest in the philosophy of the proletariat! What a strange swing it is from the impersonal to the personal and the other way round! How I had fiercely desired this and how I feared it!

And that I feared it with reason was shown by the development of her feeling for me. Her love for me seemed to increase in impersonal warmth; she loved me more as she loved other things more, as she loved life more, and other people more; but at the time there was even less dependency on me, a greater impersonality in her feeling for me! Partly through other men and partly through my ideas she had achieved an even more complete independence of me! This was beautiful: this is beautiful to me now, and the very beauty of it stimulated my emulation. I wanted to be as she was: I want to be as she is!

Let me not be hypocritical enough to say that that was the only reason which now began to lead to more intimate relations between me and other women than ever before. But it was one of the reasons. I was ever struggling to be free of her in order more fully to enjoy her without that intolerable pain. And certainly my deep and luxurious intimacy with her had enabled me to understand other women better and to approach them with greater sympathy – just as her experience with me had rendered her a more attractive object to other men, more subtly sensitive and understanding, more sensuous, with more of that amorous pity which a finely balanced woman feels so thoroughly that she hardly recognizes its specific character and is not inclined to think herself in love.

And a developed sensuousness in all things leading to a general Paganism gives to friendship between a man and a woman an almost inevitable occasional sexuality. It is the condition of a fuller taste of personality. So at any rate I have always felt it to be, and so as I enjoyed her more and more fully, more and more did my friendship with other women tend towards the possibility, but not the realization, of the more intimate embrace! Never have I been able, as I have written, to achieve emotional independence of her, but my social intimacy with other women grew more and more intense and my relations with them were limited not by my conscious will, but by that mysterious bond which held my spirit and made it impossible for me to give my real self to another. It affected even my physical make-up which in amorous play will not respond to the conscious will but only to the unconscious instinct. And she held that unconscious part of me on which even the instinctive movements of my flesh were dependent – that part of me she held in bond! How mysterious is that inevitable monogamy, and how it shows that the real thing in us all is something spiritual! And how it points to the impertinence of law and conventional morality which insists on a condition already inevitable if of the spirit – and if it is not of the spirit it is nothing.

On the top of one of the most beautiful hills of Italy we lived and played, mentally and temperamentally. A few hours of writing in the morning when we tried with sincerity to express our innermost feelings about existence, I in psychological documents and she in fiction, and then the long, late, cool summer afternoons when the sun changed from the white scorching blaze of noon to the luminous ball throwing long, cool shadows made of color and form over the earth, followed by the fresh, warm night broken pleasantly in the early dawn by the noisy nightingale or the shrill, clear clarion of the cock; removed from the urgent call of economic need, with much unnecessary energy, and in such an environment, why not play? How prevent, or why, the inevitable movements of the human temperament, leading to the song and dance of sex? It was this song and dance that sounded and vibrated rhythmically all about, among these sensuous, disillusioned, self-indulgent ones, and among the spontaneous peasantry on the olive-laden slopes.

I think it was her aesthetic sense, that inevitable response in her to form, that determined for her the character of her social pleasures.

There were two men with whom she played in exquisite, amusing ways that had its own subtle intensity, too. There was a passionate, blue flame of a man who loved beauty as Shelley's night loved the morrow, the devotion to something afar from the sphere of our sorrow. She caught and gracefully responded to the aerial nature of his feeling, humorously conscious of his fear of the full emotional or physical caress. And the other was a relaxed sensualist of delicate and civilized character whose French epigrams were the only enticing things about him. Neither of these gentlemen was in deep need of anything except the flitting pleasures of evanescent thought and poetical expression, and she played with them with a smiling and rather slighting sympathy. But the charm was at times great enough to hold her in amusing converse below while the nursing baby above howled in impotent rage because of food delayed. Her need for the amusement of the mind was strong and constant, but I sometimes had sympathy for the child.

And I went off through the wonderful nights to the cafés in Florence to talk to the artists and the women, to taste the Chianti and the Mazarin, and to indulge in that satisfying mixture of work and play — where work is play and play is work, that would be the solution of the labor problem, and is the highest form of an enjoyment that has no sad reaction. But this passion which has followed me always throughout life, to work on my pleasures and to be pleased in my work, periodically ends in an unpremeditated, intenser situation which destroys both work and play.

And in this lovely place I met a lady with whom I played and who played with me. A certain note of frivolity, of the sad Watteau type, however, insists on conveying itself to these pages dealing with this period abroad. The profounder thing in passion is the product of a keen and simple provincialism; where the spiritual lines are long and intense and monotonous. In an old, civilized place, however, full of detailed beauty, passion is broken up into picturesque and amusing half emotions and incipient, laughing ideas which relieve the emotional strain. So I find in writing of our European experience among the completer products of human personality and art that there is an inevitable note of frivolity, even though it has a touch of the sad and the pathetic; it lacks passion and intensity.

We played together, this lady and I, but we were not on an equality, for I was living with my wife — how strange and inadequate it seems to refer to her as my wife — and to this absorbing relation were added my work and the children, and she, the lady with whom I played, was living alone. In every way, except in the deeper need of the soul, I was satisfied, and she was not in any way, and that formed an unfair situation which always leads to pain and regret. Following the conventional episode of sex which of course ensued, there came an inevitable, emotional demand from her which I could not satisfy, try as I might; for that called on instinctive depths which I could not control and I had the humiliation of disappointing her, of leaving her unsatisfied and resentful, and with reason. To arouse and not satisfy a need is the deepest sin of all, and that any one who has experienced knows and bitterly regrets. What I condemn even more strongly in myself is that more than once, with others, I sinned in like manner, not having learned my lesson, or, having learned it, not having enough self-control and genuine kindness to take advantage of it.

I have no intention of going through the list of my experiences with other women, of those warm friendships and impossible hopes of emotional freedom and of periodic belief that never in her could I find the reciprocal passion which my soul needed; with therefore serious movements towards others. I touch and shall touch only upon such aspects of these experiences as help to explain my love life, such experiences as seem to me typical of the love life of all of us. And I bring up especially the memory of the lady with whom I played at that time, and with whom pain was the result, because of the surprising effect that this affair had on Her, on the woman with whom I had been playing for nine years, the complex, perturbed and difficult game of life.

I had never felt it necessary to hide anything from her; I wanted my relations to her to be of that inner truth which was independent of all external manifestations and of all conventions, and her apparent coolness towards me and the quality of impersonality in her feeling gave me a greater fancied freedom both of act and of openness with her. But when she found that I had had this affair, she staggered, slightly, as from a physical blow. I imagine that a part of my instinct in telling her was that desire to disturb her, to make her feel, which is a constant part of my relation to her. I have told how I threw cones at her; but this one was of unexpected seriousness. I felt that something had happened that had never happened before, something that was destined to have portentous consequences; and it created in me a keen sense of my brutality and at the same time a kind of fear, something akin to panic, unfamiliar and disturbing. Never again, I felt, could I be so open with her; for the first time I saw that at some points she, like me, must be spared. Not that my perception had any great influence at that time on my actions, but it did have upon my attitude.

And her gayety was gone. The sensuous lightness and aloof freedom of her life abroad had flown. We were perhaps as close as ever, but it was a sad closeness, with little of the lighter play in it. It was a time of depression with her, and also a time of unconscious preparation for the most serious episode in her life and in mine—an episode that seemed to threaten at one time to put a final term to our relation. She was not aware, I think, of her deep readiness to give to another what I periodically felt she had never given to me; but it was deep indeed in her, this unconscious, perhaps partly conscious readiness to lose her aloofness, to give herself completely away, and the inevitable followed, for that towards which one's whole nature strains, is, in some measure, bound to come.

Chapter X

Again I am aware of the selected character of all writing. No literary attempt, no matter how successful, can do other than trace a thread which runs in and out of a vast complex of experience remaining unrecorded. My sincerity can do no more than catch a small though important aspect of the relations between a man and a woman, and in order to make vivid that aspect all else must fade into a gray obscurity or into a nothingness which is far from corresponding to the reality. That is why the most sincere writing automatically takes on the quality of fiction.

With every deepening addition to our relation there has come to me an ever intenser appreciation of her spiritual and physical beauty. This is true even at the moment of great pain, of disappointment and of anger, showing, perhaps, that my bond to her is aesthetic first and last, a bond of pleasure complete though often unendurable to the point of anguish; yet there was always in it a life-giving something. She certainly came to me that existence might be more abundant. In an indescribable, warm way she has always been for me the Woman, with all the complex marvelousness that that means to the Man.

And in the year that followed, beginning with the shock to her from the projectile of my amorous play, her increasingly alienating depth, her steady recession from me, came to me not as something wrong or ugly. There was a something wonderful in it on which I cannot lay my analyzing touch.

And he, the man, who came at what is called the psychological moment, he, too, now appears to me as even then he seemed, a being of exceptional beauty. He was an old friend of mine from college days, always bitter with nervous unbalance and impatient of the world's futilities, not strong enough to help to set them right, but keen to all hypocrisy and false sentiment, full of ambition to achieve which left him no peace and which prevented any quiet accomplishment. I had loved him for his sensibility and his one-time nervous need of me, and now after long years of separation he came to us, abroad, nervously needing rest, broken down from inner strain and outer fruitless work.

And he loved Her, my Her, of course! And I loved him all the more! Perhaps he liked her—that may be a fitter word to call it; but his liking was that intense recognition of her quality which at the highest point is greater than love; he liked her much as I liked her. She pleased our taste so utterly! And I loved to have him so perfectly appreciate her. She is deeper than either of us, he would say, and I knew full well what he meant: I knew he saw how through her quiet breathing personality all of the elements passed, held by her in solution! I saw he felt her quiet unconscious power, and I felt nearer to him and no further from her on that account.

But then there came the old deep pain when I felt again the excluding movement of their souls. I felt near to them, but their growing affair steadily alienated them from me! He withdrew from me and I was hurt, and she in equal measure went farther and farther into that unknown land in which I had no home, and I was hurt more deeply still. As they came together, each departed from me, and this caused again in me that mysterious unthinking pang which by the shallow-minded is called jealousy; but not to feel that pang when the best that one knows is threatened is to lack life's impulse. Oh, how may we be broad-minded, tolerant and civilized and yet keep our feet firmly on the basic reality of our natures?

They came together as if they were spiritually brother and sister; there is much loose talk about "affinities"; it is a vague word which has become a banality, but between these two there was a spontaneous bond which has never been between her and me. They were drawn together by a nameless similarity; she and I were together, I think, mainly because of my insistent love, perhaps because of a mutual strangeness. I can never understand her and she can never understand me. They understood one another at once; and of course I was therefore on the outside, an interested spectator of a relation I did not understand, but longed for.

When we dwell intensely on any human relation we touch upon a fundamental mystery; but there is nothing more real than the mystery of being in love. And although in after years she did not admit it, and I think does not now admit it to herself even, yet I believe that for the only time in her life she felt the strange, temperamental identity of her soul with another. It is no mere accident that that man, long years before I knew her, and all through our friendship, attracted me; how ironical and yet how natural that the man for whom I felt the most spontaneous liking should be the one for whom she felt the nameless something she never felt for me!

Well, we all met, as I have written, abroad, and her depression gave way at once to a kind of strong excitement – the excitement of finding an affinity! And I in the first stages of their affair played the part of an encourager, of an abettor and promoter of their friendship. Then, as always, I longed for her the fullest life, rejoiced in all that heightened her feeling and caused a warmer glow in her physical and moral nature; in anything that took her from her cooler depths. And my ideas of freedom strengthened this attitude of mine, and both together made it easy, at first, for them to come as close together as their souls desired. I still hoped that she might have the bond with me that was the ideal of my life as it touched the personal relation, and at the same time follow all the inclinations of her temperament which were not easily aroused nor too many. Is it an impossible hope, the sign of a deep-seated idealistic folly? I confess, that as time passed and deep emotional fatigue has come to me in ever fuller measure, that my hope has waned, not indeed for its realization for others in the remoter future, but for me, here, upon this stretch of time, in this our present social state which so stubbornly declines to accept the light of the higher reason.

We played for a time abroad; but it was not a light and cheerful play. Somber and intense chords were throbbing beneath our frivolous talk together in the cafés of Paris, and in and out of our wine suppers there was simmering a more destructive flame than that of the spirit of the grape. We tried to pass it off in external gayety and sensuous pleasure, but sad intensity lived in all of us. In me the deeper jealousy was threatening to overcome my assumed and superficial civilization. And in him I felt the strong and nervous impulse to make a radical break, to insist on a new deal which would nullify the past and open up for him and her – my Her! – a remote and faery life apart from the world! And in her there began a self-destructive schism, an unexpressed struggle which meant for her something far more strenuous than any other situation of her life.

He demanded silently, and more and more in words; it was a fiercely expressed demand, and as his demand grew, mine became definitely aroused, and she was drawn and quartered between the two. This is roughly put, but the expression is not as roughly cruel as the reality. Her nature was made for breathing harmony, for abiding, breathing peace, and here in a deep soul, full of unconventional, sincere feeling, was a conflict which threatened, and later almost took, her life.

We and he separated for a period; he stayed in Europe, and, our time abroad being up, we returned to America, and to a Middle Western town in the midst of those monotonous, passionate plains which so intensely affect the sensitive temperament. Here there was nothing of the civilized charm of the old countries, a charm which relieves the devouring central passions, and renders them relatively harmless.

From the beginning, she hated her environment. She bitterly missed the picturesque detail of Europe, and the long, melancholy lines of the Middle Western landscape fanned her smoldering resentment against me and tortured her with the intense new need which he had aroused, and which his eager, passionate letters sustained and stimulated. It was a baleful music in her soul, and the few people she consented to know in this, her new home, were caught up in the fierce simplicity of the plains and harmonized with and strengthened her mood.

It was a mood of concentrated pain. I felt the inner struggle that was testing her harmonizing resources to the uttermost, and yet I could not relieve her. I could not fail to let her feel my deepening need exasperated by the seriousness of her feeling for him. Scene after scene made vivid to her the reality of my egotistic passion, and his letters were one intense, white flame. When he came again to be with us she could not fail to feel increasingly the sharpness of these two conflicting needs. He then had come to know that she to him was all, and with a beautiful recklessness which charmed and terrified my soul he desired with no retreating doubt to take her completely into his life. It had ceased to be an affair with him and had become the serious business of his existence.

Now, indeed was she disturbed, this quiet and brooding woman! The stronger elements of feeling which I had ever hoped for her and to attain which I had thrown so many cones were now indeed a menace to her very being. She was at last disturbed so deeply that the wreck of all was imminent. When I saw in her lingering look at him the same wondering doubt of what her destiny was to be, sharp memory brought to me that look of hers when I returned long years before and felt her wondering whether after all she destined to live with me!— that look which was the beautiful symbolic forerunner of the honeymoon now and forever a sensuous, lyrical joy to me! And here again her nature was accepting, she was unconsciously prepared to see with sympathy this other man, prepared to give herself again, this time with greater, fuller intensity of the intervening years of experience!

But this time to give herself meant a destructive inner conflict. As he well said, hers was a nature of sincere depth, incapable of frivolity. She could not leave me spiritually, nor could she leave the children; she could not break the interwoven threads of those twelve years of pain and joy together. She could not refuse my demand, nor could she refuse his demamd; she was not capable of the easy relation with him that was not inharmonious with my feeling. For that she cared too much for him. Had she taken him lightly, involving the sexual relation, I could by that time have been reconciled, seen it as not meaning the destruction of the bond I wanted. But this she could not do. She knew as I did that her feeling for him was inconsistent with that she had for me. She was aware of excluding me when with him! It was this awareness that shook her to the depths. She did not want it so! It went against her unconscious will. That she could not fill the deeper need of both of us—and neither of us would accept the lesser thing, even if she could give it—this filled her with a disappointment so keen that it racked her to the uttermost. He wanted all and so did I, and this she knew could never be; and yet she longed for both! She wanted the accepted and redolent past, the old bond, but her temperament eagerly desired the new, the beckoning lover!

Chapter XI

It was him she gave up and then she broke. Ever since the far distant day in Europe when they met, the struggle in her soul had stirred and steadily grown until her nervous system could bear no more. She has often said that in part that terrible situation was due to her physical state, but I think it was the other way round, that her physical state was a result of the unsolvable situation.

At any rate we were all aware that she was very ill. Her calm was gone, and she was utterly disturbed to the very marrow. At last she was what I had so often desired and to attain which I had thrown so many

cones—taken completely away from the reserved depths which so often
had irritated me. Now indeed she talked but her talk to me was torture.
The self-restraint was gone, which had always been hers, and with an
almost terrified fascination I listened to her—listened to her for many
weeks while I helped to nurse her back to life and calmness.

We went on a trip together through the sad monotonous prairie
country, the first time we had been alone for many years, without the
children, with no one else. And she talked to me as if to her own soul.
Never can I forget the terrible, the utter frankness of it. I had longed so
for expression from her—longed all our life together, but when it came,
under those circumstances, it was painful indeed. It was so apparent that
she was shocked so deeply that she hardly was aware of her frank
revelations! She let herself go with an abandonment quite unlike herself,
an abandonment so unlike what had become through all those years the
strongest demand in me!

I suppose that it was the first time that she talked with no reserve;
and she said to me things which she has now forgotten and could never
say again. But to me they live and have taught me much about myself,
about her and about the relation which meant so much of life to me. In
the midst of my utter disappointment I was yet at school. I knew she was
very ill, that she was all unraveled and had for the time given up what
held her life together. I knew it was critical. I feared the result. What she
said gave me constant anguish, but yet it was not all pain. I, the incorrig-
ible, was still at school, still a Pilgrim seeking spiritual progress, seeking
knowledge! It was all so strange! That impersonal love of life which has
been mine in unusual measure persisted, and insisted on making a
spiritual acquisition from my deepest woe.

As we drove through the long-lined, slowly passionate country, as
she lay in restless talk, ever growing more chaotic on her bed of spiritual
pain, some of the things that I must always remember, I have set down.
Extraordinary they are not, for I think they breathe deep in every noble
woman's soul, which is a spiritual abode of deep rebellion against man's
conventional moralities and laws.

In and out of her fragmentary and ejaculatory talk were vivid pictures of why he had appealed to her so strongly, and why I had failed. I
was to her the law. Even in my criticism of existing laws I was still law-
abiding. I was ever seeking a human order. Deep in me the traditional
conventions of civilization lived. I was social; I was socialized. I felt the
slow, painful family structure through the ages. At the thought of harm
to these my soul was ever anxious; I was keen to conscious man's historic

struggle with life and Nature; keen to his protecting artificialities. Family life and children, household cares and anxious economies, fear of the future and prudence, mixed though it were with temperamental generosity, were to her as a prison house. To her I was the symbol of the larger prison, the threatening finger of harsh law, the negator of her primitive imagination and of the impulse beyond good and evil.

But he was different. In him she felt a genuine unmorality, a fresh, refreshing, salad-like unscrupulousness. He was capable of a relation to her which had no law, which was connected with no principle, with nothing beyond itself. The love I bore her she saw as impersonal in large measure: I loved her because she revealed so much to me of beauty; it was really the beauty I loved, not her, something of which she was an instrument, as all other things in life were instruments to me of the Divine Something. She felt I was religious and moral, and he was neither. He took her as she was; he loved her, that particular woman, and asked no metaphysical questions, did not live in soul-torturing and impossible spiritual strainings. His intensity was for her alone, and he was willing to break all else and give her freedom—freedom from morality, from anxiety, from responsibility, from law—from me! It was the eternal advantage of the lover over the husband.

I was too good, she said to me, in constant moving criticism. She meant I was not free to be an exciting self, a pure and life-giving form. I did not make the last appeal to her imagination, for I was bound, she thought, by all things not myself. I was too good! How I longed to be otherwise, and yet how fully I knew I could not be but what I was—not good, but deeply careful, carrying with me all Past, holding all together, insisting on the Soul! It was this, this Soul that oppressed and hampered her. She needed to fly off into mere cool existences, into the soulless placed of the spirit.

And then again I had loved her too much, or at any rate too actively; had not left to her enough to do in our relation, not enough initiative; this was a thought on which she constantly dwelt. Her deepest passion was to construct; she needed to build, to feel that of her own will she was bringing to the relation. Her personal work, her writing, had been the way in which she felt she was herself. There it was all her own doing; if she could have felt that our relation was her construction, not mine, she would have loved me more! She had a need to go out actively to others as I had gone to her! She did not so much want to be wooed as to woo! This was her mood, expressed with passion.

I make no attempt to tell how I suffered at this time. It seems to me my agony went beyond the point of personal suffering and was a quality of external things—that it was a universal pain, deep and full and hopeless. I lost my habitual nervousness and was calm. To see the woman who meant so much to me thus express her deep dissatisfaction and to feel that she was, mainly because of me, almost at death's door—well, I cannot say what this was to me. Each man kills the thing he loves indeed! How this woman, like a fly, had been caught, her free flight impeded, by my all-embracing, passionate egotism! I felt a pity for her that was perhaps more unendurable than all else.

Then there came the hospital, for her life and reason were threatened. For many weeks she lay in danger, feverishly, unconsciously contending with herself, and I, admitted for a short hour each day, sat quietly by her side, hoping, waiting, for returning strength, and self-control. Indeed, it seems to me that it was I who nursed her back to life, for I would not have her go!

It was I and her strong will, for that she finally wanted to live, in part for me and for the children, there is no doubt. Life returned with flickering, hesitating fear, and in tremulous lines she wrote me a note in which it seemed to me a new love breathed! And then, a little stronger, she wrote a poem, a ballad of intense and simple passion, in which is told how a mermaid, loving her native salty substance and the damp sea-weed and the unmoral, beautiful sea, meets one day upon the shore a human man and loves and marries him and has fine children whom she loves. But the sea beckons, and one day upon the shore she meets a salty merman, her old deep-sea lover, and upon a gust of sensuous desire goes with him into her native region, where alone she is at home. But after unthinking satisfaction in the depths the thought of her acquired civilization, of her husband and her lovely, needing children, comes strong upon her, and she seeks the sorrowing human, who, in despairing passion, tries to drive her hence!

Oh, how wonderful, how life-giving is the power of song, of any swelling art! That she could sing, no matter how tragic-wise, showed returning strength, and a strength that bred more strength! Yes, the tide turned and began to flow, and as it swelled, a new hope was born in her—in me!

Chapter XII

She had gone the limit of her impulse leading her away, as far as the sweetness and beauty of her nature permitted her to go. She had gone down almost to death, and when she emerged, it was like the phoenix from the ashes. A new spirit, one of willful lovingness, breathed in all her being. There was a subtle change in her attitude toward the children. She had always loved them, but now her love was unimpeded. She accepted them at last! The grace of her demeanor toward them, those deep, lingering, questioning looks at them, these were instinct with a beauty which really qualified of heaven!

And I had become one of her children! The unsentimental, inexpressive depth of her sympathy had been touched. I knew she loved me, and I regretted nothing of the past; the wonderful, glorious, painful past which had led us both to greater feeling for things outside, for life itself; gave us both a greater impersonal love, a love that lacked more and more of the exasperation of temperament, possessed more and more of the pure classic line of unegotistic passion!

Yes, I knew she loved me, and it gave me deep, but not untroubled peace. I could not forget that I had not had to the full the other kind of love—that she had never been "in love" with me! That need in me had never been and never could be satisfied! I feel sure in my reflective moments that had she had that temperamental dependent love for me, she would not have constantly appeared to me so beautiful, so wonderful! It was in part her inalienable independence of me that filled me with so passionate a respect, even when I strove to break it down! The inevitable quality of her resistance, her unconscious integrity, is the most beautiful thing that I have ever known! What so often has filled me with violent despair and fierce unspoken reproach was perhaps the most necessary condition of my underlying feeling.

And now she had fully accepted me, but in the way in which she had accepted the children, the household, and her lot in life. But she remained herself! She could give us love, but could not give herself away! Always mysteriously remote from us, no matter how tender! Not needing, though infinitely loving. How often when I have seen her slow, quiet, humorous smile have I thought of the Mona Lisa of Leonardo; of that unnervous strength, of the "depth and not the tumult of the soul."

A few months after her recovery the new strange life of another child began to stir in her—a child about whose being she fitted herself with peculiar perfectness. This fourth infant, another little girl, was conceived, nourished and born with no resisting element in the mother's nature. It was as if time and struggle had now fully prepared her to bring forth. Her Pilgrim's Progress was beautifully shown in the new life, which at birth filled her with an exuberance never hers before; an exhilaration more strongly shown and a delighted appreciation without a flaw. And this little girl, now four years old, has had a life of unrelieved, gay joy, taking happiness and health as her native element and spreading joy to others and especially to her mother as the little rippling waves give gay music to the long receding shore.

And so perfect was her adjustment that even another blow from the hand of Nature, coming a few months before the birth, did not affect the unborn child. The little boy, always so sensitive, who had been born following the sudden death of her father, was again taken ill, and for months and years we feared not death but permanent invalidism. It was an intense, sad experience for both us us, relieved by its happy result, but taking from me a certain element of my native spring. I was very close to the boy all through his illness, lasting several years, and one effect it had was to give me a greater need of impersonal activity than I had ever had before.

Her going down into the Valley of the Shadow and the terrible illness of the child affected me more deeply than anything else in my life. I had, in a way, been nurse to both of them; nearer far to each than any one else had been to them, and to see these two beloved beings struggling for life, to feel in each the last supreme effort of their spiritual structure to exist, this was more than I could bear without relief.

And so when he had pulled through his long travail in which, child as he was, he had struggled like a hero for existence, and she had, for the time at least, become adjusted to her lot, and happy with her latest born, I turned to work and outside life with a greater impersonal activity than I had ever shown before.

Then followed three years when to a greater extent than ever, I lived among my fellow men and devoted myself more to the so-called larger social activities of men and women, to the work of the world; and was therefore automatically withdrawn more from the life of the family. These activities mean more to me for what I had gone through in personal relations; I think I saw their meaning better, and was better able to act and think maturely. More clearly I saw, more deeply I felt the necessary needs of men and women and their relation to the invisible reality we call human society. For the purpose and ultimate destiny of society is an organized condition in which the relations between particular men and women and their children shall be fully and beneficently developed, where the architecture of human relations may tower to its fullest and most lovely height.

Not only did I turn to these impersonal activities for relief, but as a natural and inevitable development. I am not, however, here concerned in picturing my life except in so far as it concerns my central love relation. This is the story of a lover. These activities of mine were modified by the experience of my relation with her, and my relation with her was affected by the nature of my activities, and therefore from time to time in this narrative I have touched, merely touched upon them.

In these goings out to the world, one set of experiences are peculiarly connected with my relation to her; affected it and were affected by it; my relations with other women. And here I come to a most delicate situation to explain, where to be truthful is probably beyond my ability, try as I may. Only those who have shared my experience, at least in some measure, will understand, but as many men and women, as all men and women who have the imagination and ambition for love, have in some measure shared my experience, though perhaps only in vague movements and tendencies, there will be some understanding of my words.

I grew constantly nearer to other women. I was filled with a passionate sympathy for them. I felt their struggle and their social situation as never before, and I understood far better what is called their weaknesses; and I saw with greater intensity their unconventional beauty. I saw that beauty in a woman's nature has nothing to do with what is called chastity. I saw how little sexual resistance women have, and yet how much they are supposed to have! How their real virtues are ignored and false ones substituted!

In those years I met several women with whom I desired the uttermost intimacy. I had for them the utmost respect and my instinct told me that they were ready for me, ready to give me what I had never had. How I longed to be able to give myself over completely! I did give myself as far as my conscious will permitted, but always, no matter how deep my friendship, no matter how intimate I was with my appreciated and appreciative friend, the unconscious instinct, that deep uncontrollable imagination kept me bound to Her as a slave is bound to its master. It was often to me humiliating and disgusting that I could not be free of her, that I could not go as far with others as my social judgment and my civilized will demanded.

I met women who were disappointed as I was disappointed; who needed just what I needed—who needed to feel a deep reciprocity in passion, a mutual giving-up to the Beyond in each other's arms. And I could not, try as I might, meet those longing spirits! I wanted to, both for them and for myself. I succeeded in feeling deeply friendly with them and they with me, but underlying our friendship was an irritated disappointment. . . .

I had an intense longing to satisfy longing. My deepest pleasure was to give pleasure. This filled me with strange excitement. It was not the desire to do good to anybody; it was far more real than that; it responded to an egotistic need of my own temperament. And the pain that almost drove me mad at times was that She had no need for me to satisfy!

Other women had and how at times I strove to satisfy them! How I almost wept when I could not! How I hated and despised myself and yet wondered at the strength of something in me that was not myself, a something that held me bound to Her, in a way I did not want to be bound! How I longed to give myself to those who needed me, but how I could not take myself from Her who had no temperamental need of me! In this there was a deep, impersonal cruelty, the irony of life, the laughing mystery of the universe.

I imagine that experience increases one's need to give oneself—to work, to others' needs, to the impersonal demand of Life. At any rate in me this has been an ever-growing passion, and as I felt more strongly about the world, about art and literature and Labor and society, I felt more strongly about women, and loved them always more, and this love was in part a measure of their need of me! I deeply wanted them to take of me all they could—more than they were able! If they could have taken more I would have been more deeply satisfied! It is a strange truth that as I grew older and more impersonal in my passion, women drew nearer to me and wanted of me more, but were able to take of me in minor measure only.

And She who had helped me to be capable of the intenser passion stood between me and its satisfaction! With her I could not satisfy my ultimate longing for she had no ultimate longing to meet mine! But because of her I could not fully meet the need of others and thereby satisfy my own!

I cannot dwell upon these few years of work and of social and emotional attempts at foreign intimacy with my women friends. My affairs were a part of my larger going out to the world and also due to what I at last had clearly seen – that although She loved me, she did not need me in the lovers' relation, and so I could not fully exhaust myself in an attempt to satisfy her, and I needed so much to exhaust myself! – to give myself away without reserve! Important and detailed as these my human relations were, I can here only touch upon them to the degree that they help to show my relation to her – the central relation of my life – for this is the story of a lover, and it is true that I have loved her only – this strange, cool, incomprehensible, wonderful woman, so beautifully aloof from me, yet so loving, and so little in love!

Since we had hurt one another at times so much there had grown up between us a greater reserve. We did not tend to talk so much about others. I was far less of a retriever who brought back rich human stories – when they involved me – to my mistress! But in an impulsive moment I told her of my attempt to meet other women, to satisfy in them a demand that she did not feel, to respond to a feeling in them for me that she did not feel.

And then again, more intensely than ever, she was hurt. What had happened to her abroad was as nothing compared to this. She was filled for months with a deep passionate resentment – something I had never seen in her before. She felt she had given up much when she broke with her lover; she had, she thought, laid aside, once for all, the great illusion, and had done so because of her great love for me and the children. And when she saw I could not give up that illusion, that I was still longing for the intangible reality she could not give me, again there came to her a destructive blow. She had renounced for this!

Once more there were a series of frank talks from her – those rare and wonderful though terrible revelations of an inexpressive soul! I found that during all these years of our married life she had felt my infidelities, not exactly with pain, but that they had caused her to retire more and more within herself. The slight but lovely bud of her affection had never been able to flower. Her love for me was more and more maternal, the illusion of sex more and more absent; the moment came when it seemed to be quite gone. Of course I said it had never been, and I believe I am right, that she had had only the possibility of it, for me or for another, never realized. And I told her over and over again that now she loved me, maternally or otherwise, more than ever – that her conventional disapproval of my acts and her deeper infidelity of thought and feeling had not withdrawn her from me, but had brought her nearer.

She suffered, I really know not why, because of my relations with other women—they were not the relations she wanted for herself, and yet she suffered. And when I saw more clearly than ever before that there was something in her which by necessity was hurt by this my conduct, there came a strange change in me. I hated to lose any shade of her feeling for me, and I closed up instinctively my social sympathy, and my natural intimate outgoing to other women ceased!

But my sacrifice, like hers, like all sacrifices, was useless—nay, more, was harmful. My attitude of receptive openness, not only to women, but to men and work, to life, was in large measure gone. My friends noticed that I had lost the keen zest for experience which had been so characteristic of me. She herself began to see that I was older in spirit, that I was sinking into the reserve and timidity of old age, and that my creative initiative in work and life was less. And I felt it, too. I made no effort to be different. I simply was different, and I saw that my work and my life were more anemic, but I could not help it. Somehow her clearly revealed pain and aesthetic disapproval had for the time at least strangely crippled me. And this, of course, was no good to her. I was less amusing, and still to her the word *amusing* was of all but the greatest moment. She began to regret my virtue and my old age. She saw that one was part of the other, indissolubly connected. She saw that I had done brutal things to others, under her influence, and I think her conscience hurt her, as did mine. But beyond all else she felt that she had invaded my personality and thereby weakened it, and in about a year she withdrew from her position and tacitly gave me to understand that she would be well content to have me go my ways.

During that year she had been consciously willing to have another lover; she had seen beautiful men whom she admired and who admired her, but deeper than her mind was her fundamental disillusionment. She knew that this for her was not to be. I saw that she was on the lookout, and yet I knew that there was nothing deep in her demand, that she was satisfied with life, disillusioned with what is called being in love, but loving more what she had—children, friends, work and me. Yes, me! She loved me more after all this strange and twisted travail! Even when she calmly told me, as she did, that she no longer wanted me in any temperamental way—that the little she had felt was gone—even then I felt a strange certainty of her love for me! For her love for me was of

Platonic purity and strength, unmixed with sex or sentimentality, that seemed to me to be of the essence of tenderness.

She seems now to have given up her futile desire to desire others and to have accepted for herself a deep aloof affection and tenderness for me and for all who touch her. This same she wants from me and only accepts but does not desire my metaphysical needs, my sexual straining toward the universe's oblivion. This she neither understands nor likes. This she feels should be put on other things, on work, on thought and impersonal activity, and she is right, but I, although going in that direction, am not ready—yet.

As yet my soul is not satisfied. It is with a deep unwillingness that I feel her temperamental withdrawal—which in a less degree has always been true of her but never so clearly seen by me. That she loves me more, perhaps, in another way, can never meet the fundamental madness that every lover has. I can never be satisfied until I find the Other—and I know I can never find the Other, and never really want to. I know that what I passionately want is a deep illusion, which can never come. It is of Life's essence, which is to us illusory, as it can never be known and does not respond to our Ideal. It is a passion that leads to death, but, when real as mine is, never leads to satisfaction.

Here I am at middle life living with the one woman I want to live with, hopeful for my fine children, interested in a work I have chosen and which was not forced upon me, rich in friends, in good health, and seeing progressively the sad splendid beauty of Nature and Art, hopeful for man's struggle to break his bonds and interested in cooperating with him, and yet, in spite of all, passionately unsatisfied!

Passionately unsatisfied, and yet to me she is more beautiful, more wonderful than ever! This inaccessible woman, approaching middle age, more loving to me and more remote than ever, consciously rejecting me as a lover and accepting me warmly as a child, her complete and impersonal loveliness, is the one perfect experience of my life, the experience that permeates and affects all others, that has subtly intertwined itself in my love for children and nature, for work and for the destiny of my fellowmen. It has been the sap of my life, which has urged the slender stalk into the full-grown tree with its many branches and its decorative voluminous lines.

The sap till urges its undeniable way; my youthful passion still maintains itself but now more than ever it meets only the rich maternal smile, full of knowledge and a kind of tender scorn. As I write these lines—she, for the moment, distant from me by the length of an ocean— I remember the days when with a certain response she played with me

with a light grace. Two little incidents come back to me from the multi-
tudinous deluge of the past—one, when, with the laughter of unconventionality, we openly and completely embraced on the bosom of a Swiss
glacier encouraged by the full sun of noon! Again, when, in our fancy,
she was the wife of another, and we indulged in sweet mutual infidelity
after a delicious supper in a French garden on the banks of the Seine!
How we talked and smiled, and how we held for the moment aloof the
serious madness that was behind my passion! How we enjoyed the
decorous and polite knowledge of the host who ushered us to the guilty
couch! And how our French epigrams were mixed up with our light and
happy caresses! And at that time, she was beginning to see Him, and I
had thrown my cone—my play with the lady in Italy! And this added
zest, and she threw at me with more joyous lightness a glass of wine
which stained my white immaculate shirt and brought me to her with a
quick reproachful embrace!

Yes, these gestures I must remember, in this the day of the waning of
our lighter relations! The waning, yes, of our lighter amorousness,
indeed the beginning of the day when she pushes me away, but at the
same time the beginning of a love for me that passes understanding, that
has no material expression, that is full of compassion, of a kind of
dignified pity! A love in which the temperament plays no part, but to
which all that has been between us—pleasure, pain, difficulties, work
and infidelities—give an indescribable solidity and depth. Nothing on
earth can separate us. Our relation, indeed, is built on a fortress which
nothing but a double death can destroy, and perhaps not even that!

What is the romance of a young couple with our full experience?
Why do novels, as a rule, end with the first slight lyrical gesture? Why
do we inculcate in the imagination of the young and in our moral code a
false conception of the nature of virtue? Why do we imply that chastity
in woman has anything to do with goodness, or that physical movements necessarily affect a soul relation? I do not know why we have built
up historically these colossal lies which give us pain and unnecessary
jealousy and despair.

But what is to me the deepest mystery of all—and this a glorious
mystery which distils a spiritual fragrance to all of life—is what holds a
man and woman together through an entire eternity of experience. She
is to me the key of existence that opens up the realm of the Infinite
which, though I can never reach, yet sheds upon all things its colorful
meaning. It is only the conception of the Eternal which gives interest to
every concrete detail. God inheres as a quality in all things. Religion is
right when it points the fact that without Him there is nothing.

DIALOGUE AND ENEMIES

NEITH BOYCE AND HUTCHINS HAPGOOD were among the small group of intellectuals who founded the Provincetown Players in the summer of 1915.[1] During its seven-year history "the Provincetown Players grew into the most daring and the most characteristically American undertaking in United States theatrical history."[2] The group functioned collectively so that playwrights also acted and actors served as stage designers and stagehands. Most plays had one act and focused on personal and political experiences common to the group.

The group's first two plays—Neith Boyce's *Constancy*, about the stormy relationship between Mabel Dodge and John Reed, and Susan Glaspell and George Cram Cook's *Suppressed Desires*, on the excesses of psychoanalysis—were produced in Neith and Hutchins's summerhouse. Later that summer they moved their productions to a converted fish house on a Provincetown wharf. In *A Victorian in the Modern World*, Hutchins traces the motivation of those who started the theater:

> The group who started the Provincetown Players in the summer of 1915 and continued the movement in the summer of 1916, was composed of men and women who were really more free than many in Greenwich Village. . . . No one of them had been identified with the theater, and only one had written plays. . . . They didn't even go to the theater, for the theater didn't express life to them—their lives or anybody's lives. Their own intimacies, they knew, were not expressed in the theater. What are we really like, what do we really want, how are we really living, what are the relations actually existing between us? . . . So they wrote, staged and acted their own plays. At first in each little piece there was something fresh and personal. . . . It was a delightful change from the preoccupations of the War and the poison of 1915. It was an escape from that dry poison and also from the meaningless theatricalism of the Broadway theaters. It meant much to us all.[3]

After two summers the Provincetown Players moved to New York City, where in six seasons they produced ninety-seven plays by forty-seven American authors, foremost of whom were Susan Glaspell and Eugene O'Neill.[4]

Dialogue is in the Hapgood collection, Collection of American Literature, Beinecke Rare Book and Manuscript Library, Yale University. Reprinted with permission of the library and Beatrix Hapgood Faust. *Enemies* first appeared in *The Provincetown Plays*, ed. George Cram Cook and Frank Shay, with a foreword by Hutchins Hapgood. Copyright 1921, 1949 by Frank Shay. Used with permission of Janet R. Whelan.

Two innovative theaters of the 1960s, the Living Theater and the San Francisco Mime Troop, trace their roots to this company.[5]

Hutchins describes the writing and production of *Enemies*, the play that he coauthored with Neith:

> It was at Provincetown in the summer of 1916 that Neith and I wrote *Enemies*, a dialogue between a man and a woman. Neith wrote the woman's part and I the man's and we acted it together in the fish-house theater. . . . It was later produced in New York, where it was acted by Justus Sheffield and Ida Rauh. My only appearance on the stage of the Provincetown theater was that one in the fish-house, when, in spite of careful drilling and the fact that I had written my lines myself, I could not remember them but was forced to read from the manuscript. This play had a significance leading into the lives of many of my acquaintances. . . . Neith and I, like many another couples . . . were conscious of the latent feminism urging men to give up the ascendancy which women thought they had, and women to demand from men that which they didn't really want, namely so-called freedom from the ideal of monogamy. . . . [There is] a certain dramatic quality that existed in this little play, though it was nothing but a dialogue. For in it was vividly expressed the man's and the woman's point of view of the moment; the clash of two temperaments in words typical of a general situation. . . . Curiously enough, *Enemies* was one of the first plays to be broadcast on the radio.[6]

Printed here for the first time is *Dialogue* which in all probability is an early draft of *Enemies*. In the quote above, Hutchins uses the word *dialogue* several times to characterize the play, and both pieces consist only of exchange between two characters—Neith and Hutchins in *Dialogue* and He and She in *Enemies*. Both compositions discuss Dostoyevsky; *Dialogue*, in addition, mentions Proust and Synge, while *Enemies* quotes from Wordsworth and makes reference to Dante. *Dialogue* centers on Hutchins's irritation with Neith's love of books; *Enemies* opens with Neith absorbed in a book.

Both pieces discuss the irritations caused by the couple's personality differences but differ in how they conceptualize the central conflict between husband and wife. *Dialogue* is written in a more abstract style and is based on conflict between "the essential male as a wanderer, never satisfied," and "the essential woman, with unfathomable depths, the source and nourisher of life." I believe Hutchins wrote *Dialogue*. His *Story of a Lover* includes comparable philosophical musings, and his a *Victorian in the Modern World* presents similar images of women and men. *Dialogue* also belittles "modern women," while Hutchins's autobiography deprecates feminism. Neith disparaged neither subject.

Enemies is written in a more direct and realistic style and focuses on Neith's concerns with infidelity and male domination of the female psyche. Men and women are still seen as natural enemies, who through "the shock and flame of two hostile temperaments meeting" produce fine children. But most gender stereotypes found in *Dialogue* are gone, as is the attack on feminism. Neith either rewrote Hutchins's draft or prevailed in their joint product. Because she had written a previous play for the Provincetown Players and was the more accomplished and disciplined writer, I believe Neith's style and the issues she saw as important shaped the final draft of the play.

Notes

1. In addition to Boyce and Hapgood, the group consisted of George Cram Cook, Susan Glaspell, John Reed, Robert Edmond Jones, Mary Heaton Vorse, Max Eastman, Ida Rauh, Wilbur Daniel Steele, Margaret Steele, Harry Kemp and, by 1916, Eugene O'Neill and Louise Bryant.

2. Robert Sarlos, *Jig Cook and the Provincetown Players* (Amherst: University of Massachusetts Press, 1982), 5–6.

3. Hutchins Hapgood, *A Victorian in the Modern World* (1939; reprint, Seattle: University of Washington Press, 1972), 392–94.

4. *Jig Cook*, 5.

5. *Jig Cook*, 166.

6. Hapgood, *A Victorian in the Modern World*, 395–96.

DIALOGUE

NEITH: Why is it that you can never sit down quietly, with a book? You are always going somewhere, to see somebody. At your age you should have repose, my dear.

HUTCH: I can understand why you like books. You don't have to do anything about them. They don't interfere with you, or demand anything from you. You don't have to give them anything. It is easy to smoke and read all the time. "At my age" I still like to associate with living things, which remain always mysterious, beckoning, while books are always the same, after one has read a few good ones.

NEITH: No, books are not "the same." A good book is the essence of a human being, the truth about him; it can be read many times, and each time it is new. I am sorry for you: you will never be able to read the eight volumes of Marcel Proust, you will never read his description of a bunch of asparagus, which takes two pages and is like a Dutch painting.

HUTCH: If Proust's books are like Dutch paintings, I will look at Dutch paintings rather than read his books. I like originals. And I think that literature can never equal painting in its own field. Yes, a good book is the essence of a human being, but there are few good books, and most of those express the same essence. It is only once or twice in a century that a book digs down a little deeper into the hitherto unconscious and puts it forth in form destined to become "classic"—something more is told there of the essence of a human being.

NEITH: Proust digs deep. He describes the human heart as well as the asparagus. How much you miss! You will never read *Arabia Deserta*, because you don't like description: that marvelous picture of the sun-soaked desert, the flying nomads. You would like those wild Arabs, they are always hungry and restless, always moving on. They never read but tell long stories over their coffee cups at night.

HUTCH: You like the differences in books. I like the differences in life. I never meet a person who does not mean something different from all others, and something wonderful. You tend to find human beings all the same, and so have little to do with them, except for the satisfaction of vital needs—love, family, a few old friends. I have little to do with books—except to satisfy my vital need of art—and that is done by the few great things, of the past and future. Dostoyevsky holds me or Aeschylus or Shakespeare. How much you miss by not "seeing" the wonderful human beings all around you!

NEITH: I thought we would get to Dostoyevsky. He is the only author of the last hundred years that you have really read. Yes, he is unique. Things happen in his books as they do in life—terrible, cruel, bewildering, with flashes of that light too strong for our senses, that beauty too intense. . . . But books are just as different as human beings, because they *are* human beings—with the advantage that when you are sleepy you can shut them up, and they don't mind. I see many wonderful human beings about me; I like to look at them and hear the sound of their voices. But I don't care much for what they say, unless they are talking straight, either from suffering or from some other strong feeling or direct vision. Then I "see" them and I love them. But I don't like social life, I hate amusements, and I like to be alone.

HUTCH: Books can never mean as much as persons, at any rate to the artist, and by the artist I mean anybody who can read directly from life. The painter does not go to paintings for his inspiration but to the model. The man who sees literature does not go to literature—the real thing is infinitely suggestive. Every book has a form that limits it—and except in the great book a form that is largely a result of an imitation of other forms. People read too much and see too little, love their fellow men too little. As I said, your love of books is partly a love of ease, an attempt to fill a void when you are not actively seeing.

NEITH: You are wrong again, dear: there is no void, when I am not "active," my repose is rich and nourishing. In solitude, with or without a book, I feel the deep sea bearing me up, or I am rooted in the earth and growing quietly like a tree. A tree doesn't have to move from place to place. Some trees grow best in company with their kind; others flourish alone. Sometimes when I am in company with people who are not in relation with me or with one another, I feel a void as though the air were exhausted under a receiver—but never alone. And it seems to me that people are too gregarious, that they huddle together like sheep for warmth and comfort in face of a storm. What are they afraid of? Themselves?

HUTCH: You say so many wrong things at once that the reply though obvious, is not easy. I do not complain about your solitude but why confuse solitude with books? Is reading with you the same as solitude? Rich and nourishing repose is certainly desirable, but you take off its purity and significance by reading—reading at just those moments when the reality of solitude is offered you! Just as you take from the reality of companionship by sacrificing it to a book!—and almost any book at that! Does it add to the treelike growth you derive from solitude to read a book, or to your human growth to read and puff a cigarette when your husband is telling you most eloquently about his wonderful discoveries? Of course, this remark explains what you mean by the "void," but the void may be within as well as without. If *you* huddled with others, I admit it might be a sign of fear. I can imagine nothing less that would drive *you* to it. But to some, people are a part of the material of art and thought and must necessarily be more interesting than books—when one is alive.

NEITH: What a quaint idea of solitude! As though a solitary couldn't read. Of course my solitude includes books, and even people, but with wide intervals. What a delightful feeling is mine when in the morning the children go to school, the man of the house to work or somewhere—when the house is empty and the long day stretches before me in bound-less leisure. There may be household tasks, which I will do or not, as I happen to feel. Certainly I shall spend hours in my garden, happily hoeing out weeds and clipping off the fading flowers. Brutus will attend me—he is a perfect companion in solitude, he is eloquently mute. We lunch together on the sunlit porch, I prop a book against the teapot, and Brutus goes to sleep under the table. The golden afternoon passes all too swiftly, in the peace of nonhuman contacts. The life of trees, flowers, animals existing so curiously side by side with our tormented human life somehow consoles me. We are only a part of the scheme and perhaps not the most important part. . . . And a good book gives me this same feeling of temporary aloofness.

HUTCH: All this, that you so feelingly describe, is lovely enough, but it is the background of human life. You do not seem to feel the essential thing in life for us humans, nor the joy and delight in the color of human beings! How many times, for years and years, have I enjoyed persons whom I happened to meet!—meet anywhere! The romantic expectation, too, as one wanders about, in the country or city—not only the chance meeting but the hope of it. It may come at any moment! Then the reality of such possibilities, coming occasionally and some-times ripening into friendship and love and filling richly the book of your memory with significant figures, profiles, and full busts drawn from the experience of life itself! I am sorry for you—you who live with books—the shadows of life.

NEITH: The world is big enough for us both, and "life" is more various than you seem to think. I have known and loved human beings. . . . I love your restless, seeking soul and temperament; I could not love a contented man, one who was not reaching out for more than he could grasp. The essential male is a wanderer, never satisfied, always going on. Do you remember Synge's play, *The Shadow of the Glen?* The wild tramp comes out of the darkness and woos the woman out of her house away from old settled things to wander with him into the unknown. So long as you pipe to us that strange wild tune, we will follow you through the world.

HUTCH: You will follow us through the world, you say! But you do not. Look around at the modern world and you will find women going more and more their own way, breaking with the traditions. Competing with men in man's own field, demanding that they have the same occupations, the same law, the same morals, or lack of morals. It would look as if woman has renounced the male of whom you speak so eloquently and has decided to be a male herself.

NEITH: That is true—of a small section of the world, the most modern perhaps, at any rate the noisiest. But I said, you must pipe to us, we must hear a voice that is strange, from far away, leading us to adventure. . . . Has the modern man lost his voice, along with his gay plumage, has he lost the magic flute? Has he ceased to be a stranger?

HUTCH: If he has lost this magic flute, it may be due to a change in woman. The essential woman—as man conceived her! how wonderful! She, with unfathomable depths, the Source and Nourisher of Life, full of unconscious faith. She who scorned for herself, while admiring in man the external deeds of heroes and of poets, knowing with deep calm satisfaction the value of her own life and deeds—the creator of heroes and external Doers! How wonderful to man, how strange, this creature whom he wooed with such marvelous results! If he no longer sings, it may be that man no longer has anything so incomprehensibly wonderful to sing to!

NEITH: But let him sing, and see! He must have faith, in himself first of all, he must not doubt, falter, be uncertain. He must do the impossible, or at least attempt it. He must climb Mount Everest, soar miles into the air, find the Pole—he must go forth to conquer. . . . "With your shield—or on it!"

HUTCH: Man always attempts the impossible. That is the secret of his achievement. Now he is trying to overcome himself and his deep-rooted past. This is the most difficult path, the wildest most impossible adventure he has ever set forth on. Wars are nothing in comparison. He has set out to release woman from all of the old obligations! You seem to despise him for making this terrific effort! You do not seem to see the heroism of it; that the male, in a new form, is again fulfilling his destiny!

NEITH: But why, if he found the old type of woman, living in her obligations, so wonderful as you say—why is he trying at such cost to himself to "release" her? Is he trying to kill the thing he loves—and himself, too?

HUTCH: *Es irrt der Mensch so lang er Strebt.* Man errs because he strives! He does not aim to kill the thing he loves nor himself. He is restlessly concerned with enlarging life—he wants to free life and to free woman from all that enslaved her in the past. But he wants her to keep the old beauty. He wants her to keep the old deep brooding charm, but somehow to combine with that free companionship and conscious self-development. He throws out a deep challenge to her: Lo, I will help to release you, but you must know how to use your imagination in realizing your new opportunities. You must not follow blindly along the new path but make the adjustments which deeply satisfy your nature and man's. Even if he is quixotically willing to destroy himself, she must not cooperate with him in his madness but must find the new reserve, the new relationship.

NEITH: Yes, but perhaps he is wrong in throwing out that challenge. Perhaps he would better let woman alone and not insist on her going along with him. In all ages up to the present the functions and activities of men and women have been sharply different, even "taboo," one for the other. Perhaps woman cannot be man's companion. He will appeal more to her imagination if he remains somewhat outside her orbit and makes his visits like the angels, few and far between. He must be something that she cannot be—then she will be content, so nicely, deeply content, to be the matrix, provided she sees him as the precious jewel.

Enemies

A Play in One Act
By Neith Boyce and Hutchins Hapgood

As Produced by the Provincetown Players,
New York City

HE .... JUSTUS SHEFFIELD
SHE .... IDA RAUH

SCENE: *A living room*
TIME: *After dinner*

Produced by the Authors
Setting designed by B. J. O. Nordfeldt

She is lying in a long chair, smoking a cigarette and reading a book. He is sitting at a table with a lamp at his left—manuscript pages scattered before him, pen in hand. He glances at her, turns the lamp up, turns it down, rustles his m.s., snorts impatiently. She continues reading.

HE: This is the limit!

SHE: (*Calmly.*) What is?

HE: Oh, nothing. (*She turns the page, continues reading with interest.*) This is an infernal lamp!

SHE: What's the matter with the lamp?

HE: I've asked you a thousand times to have some order in the house, some regularity, some system! The lamps never have oil, the wicks are never cut, the chimneys are always smoked! And yet you wonder that I don't work more! How can a man work without light?

SHE: (*Glancing critically at lamp.*) This lamp seems to me to be all right. It obviously has oil in it or it would not burn, and the chimney is not smoked. As to the wick, I trimmed it myself to-day.

HE: Ah, that accounts for it!

SHE: Well, do it yourself next time, my dear!

HE: (*Irritated.*) But our time is too valuable for these ever-recurring jobs! Why don't you train Theresa, as I've asked you so often?

SHE: It would take all my time for a thousand years to train Theresa.

186

HE: Oh, I know! All you want to do is to lie in bed for breakfast, smoke cigarettes, write your high literary stuff, make love to other men, talk cleverly when you go out to dinner and never say a word to me at home! No wonder you have no time to train Theresa!

SHE: Is there anything of interest in the paper?

HE: You certainly have a nasty way of making an innocent remark!

SHE: I'm sorry. (*Absorbed in her book.*)

HE: No, you're not. That last remark proves it.

SHE: (*Absently.*) Proves what?

HE: Proves that you are an unsocial brutal woman!

SHE: You are in a temper again.

HE: Who wouldn't be, to live with a cold-blooded person that you have to hit with a gridiron to get a rise out of?

SHE: I wish you would read your paper quietly and let me alone.

HE: Why have you lived with me for fifteen years if you want to be let alone?

SHE: (*With a sigh.*) I have always hoped you would settle down.

HE: By settling down you mean cease bothering about household matters, about the children, cease wanting to be with *you*, cease expecting you to have any interest in *me*.

SHE: No, I only mean it would be nice to have a peaceful evening sometimes. But (*laying book down*) I see you want to quarrel—so what shall we quarrel about? Choose your own subject, my dear.

HE: When you're with Hank you don't want a peaceful evening!

SHE: Now how can you possibly know that?

HE: Oh, I've seen you with him and others and I know the difference. When you're with them you're alert and interested. You keep your unsociability for me. (*Pause.*) Of course, I know why.

SHE: One reason is that "they" don't talk about lampwicks and so forth. They talk about higher things.

HE: Some people would call them lower things!

SHE: Well—more interesting things, anyway.

HE: Yes, I know you think those things more interesting than household and children and husband.

SHE: Oh, only occasionally, you know—just for a change. You like a change yourself sometimes.

HE: Yes, sometimes—But I am excited, and interested and keen whenever I am with you. It is not only cigarettes and flirtation that excite me.

SHE: Well—you are an excitable person. You get excited about nothing at all.

HE: Are Home and Wife and Children nothing at all?

SHE: There are other things. But you, Deacon, are like the skylark—
"Type of the wise who soar but do not roam
True to the kindred points of heaven and home."—

HE: You are cheaply cynical!—You ought not to insult Wordsworth. He meant what he said.

SHE: He was a good man. . . . But to get back to our original quarrel. You're quite mistaken. I'm more social with you than with anyone else. Hank, for instance hates to talk, even more than I do. He and I spend hours together looking at the sea—each of us absorbed in our own thoughts—without saying a word. What could be more peaceful than that?

HE: (*Indignantly.*) I don't believe it's peaceful—But it must be wonderful!

SHE: It is—marvellous. I wish you were more like that. What beautiful evenings we could have together!

HE: (*Bitterly.*) Most of our evenings are silent enough, unless we are quarreling!

SHE: Yes, if you're not talking, it's because you're sulking. You are never sweetly silent—never really quiet.

HE: That's true—with you—I am rarely quiet with you—because you rarely express anything to me. I would be more quiet if you were less so—less expressive if you were more so.

SHE: (*Pensively.*) The same old quarrel. Just the same for fifteen years! And all because you are you and I am I! And I suppose it will go on forever—I shall go on being silent, and you—

HE: I suppose I shall go on talking—but it really doesn't matter—the silence or the talk—If we had something to be silent about or to talk about—Something in common—That's the point!

SHE: Do you really think we have nothing in common? We both like Dostoyevsky and prefer Burgundy to champagne.

HE: Our tastes and our vices are remarkably congenial, but our souls do not touch.

SHE: Our souls? Why should they? Every soul is lonely.

HE: Yes, but doesn't want to be. The soul desires to find something into which to fuse and so lose its loneliness. This hope to lose the soul's loneliness by union—is love. It is the essence of love as it is of religion.

SHE: Deacon, you are growing more holy every day. You will drive me to drink.

HE: (*Moodily.*) That will only complete the list.

SHE: Well, then I suppose we may be more congenial—for in spite of what you say, our vices haven't exactly matched. You're ahead of me on the drink.

HE: Yes, and you on some other things. But perhaps I can catch up too—

SHE: Perhaps—if you really give all your time to it, as you did last winter, for instance. But I doubt if I can ever equal your record in potations.

HE: (*Bitterly.*) I can never equal your record in the soul's infidelities.

SHE: Well, do you expect my soul to be faithful when you keep hitting it with a gridiron?

HE: No, I do not expect it of you! I have about given up the hope that you will ever respond either to my ideas about household and children or about our personal relations. You seem to want as little as possible of the things that I want much. I harass you by insisting. You anger and exasperate me by retreating. We were fools not to have separated long ago.

SHE: Again! How do you repeat yourself, my dear!

HE: Yes, I am very weak. In spite of my better judgment I have loved you. But this time I mean it!

SHE: I don't believe you do. You never mean half the things you say.

HE: I do this time. This affair of yours with Hank is on my nerves. It is real spiritual infidelity. When you are interested in him you lose all interest in the household, the children and me. It is my duty to separate.

SHE: Oh, nonsense! I didn't separate from you when you were running after the widow last winter—spending hours with her every day, dining with her and leaving me alone, and telling me she was the only woman who had ever understood you.

HE: I didn't run after the widow, or any other woman except you. They ran after me.

SHE: Of course! Just the same since Adam—not one of you has spirit enough to go after the apple himself! "They ran after you"—but you didn't run away very fast, did you?

HE: Why should I, when I wanted them to take possession if they could? I think I showed splendid spirit in running after you! Not more than a dozen other men have shown the same spirit. It is true, as you say, that other women understand and sympathize with me. They all do except you. I've never been able to be essentially unfaithful, more's the pity. You are abler in that regard.

SHE: I don't think so. I may have liked other people, but I never dreamed of *marrying* anyone but *you* . . . . No, and I never thought any of them understood me either. I took very good care they shouldn't.

HE: Why, it was only the other day that you said Hank understood you better than I ever could. You said I was too virtuous and that if I were worse you might see me!

SHE: As usual, you misquote me. What I said was that Hank and I were more alike and you are a virtuous stranger—a sort of wandering John the Baptist, preaching in the wilderness!

HE: Preachers don't do the things I do!

SHE: Oh, don't they!

HE: Well, I know I am as vicious as man can be. You would see that if you loved me. I am fully as bad as Hank.

SHE: Hank doesn't pretend to be virtuous, so perhaps you're worse. But I think you ought to make up your mind whether you're virtuous or vicious, and not assume to be both.

HE: I am both as a matter of fact, like everybody else. I am not a hypocrite. I love the virtuous and also the vicious. But I don't like to be left out in the cold when you are having an affair. When you are interested in the other, you are not in me.

SHE: Why do you pretend to fuss about lamps and such things when you are simply jealous? I call that hypocritical. I wish it were possible for a man to play fair. But what you want is to censor and control me, while you feel perfectly free to amuse yourself in every possible way.

HE: I am never jealous without cause and you are. You object to my friendly and physical intimacies and then expect me not to be jealous of your soul's infidelities, when you lose all feeling for me. I am tired of it. It is a fundamental misunderstanding and we ought to separate at once!

SHE: Oh, very well, if you're so keen on it. But remember you suggested it. I never said I wanted to separate from you—if I had, I wouldn't be here now.

HE: No, because I've given all I had to you. I have nourished you with my love. You have harassed and destroyed me. I am no good because of you. You have made me work over you to the degree that I have no real life. You have enslaved me, and your method is cool aloofness. You want to keep on being cruel. You are the devil, who never really meant any harm, but who sneers at desires and never wants to satisfy. Let us separate—you are my only enemy!

SHE: Well, you know we are told to love our enemies.

HE: I have done my full duty in that respect. People we love are the only ones who can hurt us. They *are* our enemies, unless they love us in return.

SHE: "A man's enemies are those of his own household"—Yes, especially if they love. You, on account of your love for me, have tyrannized over me, bothered me, badgered me, nagged me, for fifteen years. You have interfered with me, taken my time and strength, and prevented me from accomplishing great works for the good of humanity. You have crushed my soul, which longs for serenity and peace, with your perpetual complaining.

HE: Too bad. (*Indignantly.*) Perpetual complaining!

SHE: Yes, of course. But you see, my dear, I am more philosophical than you, and I recognize all this as necessity. Men and women are natural enemies, like cat and dog, only more so. They are forced to live together for a time, or this wonderful race couldn't go on. In addition, in order to have the best children, men and women of totally opposed temperaments must live together. The shock and flame of two hostile temperaments meeting is what produces fine children. Well, we have fulfilled our fate and produced our children, and they are good ones. But really—to expect also to live in peace together—we as different as fire and water, or sea and land—that's too much!

HE: If your philosophy is correct, that is another argument for separation. If we have done our job together, let's go on our ways and try to do something else separately.

SHE: Perfectly logical. Perhaps it will be best. But no divorce—that's so commonplace.

HE: Almost as commonplace as your conventional attitude toward husbands—that they are necessarily uninteresting—*mon bête de mari*— as the typical Frenchwoman of fiction says. I find divorce no more commonplace than real infidelity.

SHE: Both are matters of every day. But I see no reason for divorce unless one of the spouses wants to marry again. I shall never divorce you. But men can always have children, and so they are perpetually under the sway of the great illusion. If you want to marry again, you can divorce me.

HE: As usual, you want to see me as a brute. I don't accept your philosophy. Children are the results of love, not the cause of it, and love should go on. It does go on, if once there has been the right relation. It is not re-marrying nor the unconscious desire for further propagation that moves me—but the eternal need of that peculiar sympathy which has never been satisified—to die without that is failure in what most appeals to the imagination of human beings.

SHE: But that *is* precisely the great illusion. That is the unattainable that lures us on, and that will lead you, I foresee, if you leave me, into the arms of some other woman.

HE: Illusion! Precisely what *is*, you call illusion. Only there do we find Truth. And certainly I *am* bitten badly with illusion or truth, whichever it is. It is Truth to me. But I fear it may be too late. I fear the other woman is impossible.

SHE: (*Pensively.*) "I cannot comprehend this wild swooning desire to wallow in unbridled unity." (*He makes angry gesture, she goes on quickly.*) I was quoting your favorite philosopher. But as to being too late—no, no—you're more attractive than you ever were, and that shows your ingratitude to me, for I'm sure I have been a liberal education to you. You will easily find someone to adore you and console you for all your sufferings with me. But do be careful this time—get a good housekeeper.

HE: And *you* are more attractive than you ever were. I can see that others see that. I have been a liberal education to you too.

SHE: Yes, a Pilgrim's Progress.

HE: I never would have seen woman, if I hadn't suffered you.

SHE: I never would have suffered Man, if I hadn't seen you.

HE: You never saw me!

SHE: Alas—yes! (*With feeling.*) I saw you as something very beautiful—very fine, sensitive—with more understanding than anyone I've ever known—more feeling—I still see you that way—but from a great—distance.

HE: (*Startled.*) Distance?

SHE: Yes. Don't you feel how far away from one another we are?

HE: I have felt it, as you know—more and more so—that you were pushing me more and more away and seeking more and more somebody—something else. But this is the first time you had admitted feeling it.

SHE: Yes—I didn't want to admit it. But now I see it has gone very far. It is as though we were on opposite banks of a stream that grows wider—separating us more and more.

HE: Yes—

SHE: You have gone your own way, and I mine—and there is a gulf between us.

HE: Now you see what I mean—

SHE: Yes, that we ought to separate—that we *are* separated—and yet I love you.

HE: Two people may love intensely, and yet not be able to live together—it is too painful, for you, for me—

SHE: We have hurt one another too much—

HE: We have destroyed one another—we are enemies— (*Pause.*)

SHE: I don't understand it—how we have come to this—after our long life together. Have you forgotten all that? What wonderful companions we were? How gayly we took life with both hands—how we played with it and with one another!—At least we have the past!

HE: The past is bitter—because the present is bitter.

SHE: You wrong the past.

HE: The past is always judged by the present. Dante said, the worst hell is in present misery to remember former happiness—

SHE: Dante was a man and a poet, and so ungrateful to life. (*Pause, with feeling.*) Our past to me is wonderful and will remain so, no matter what happens—full of color and life, complete!

HE: That is because our life together has been for you an episode.

SHE: No, it is because I take life as it is, not asking too much of it—not asking that any person or any relation be perfect. But you are an idealist—you can never be content with it—You have the poison, the longing for perfection in your soul.

HE: No, not for perfection but for union. That is not demanding the impossible. Many people have it who do not love as much as we do. No work of art is right, no matter how wonderful the material and the parts, if the whole, the unity, is not there.

SHE: That's just what I mean. You have wanted to treat our relation, and me, as clay, and model it into the form you saw in your imagination. You have been a passionate artist. But life is not a plastic material. *It* models us.

HE: You are right. I have had the egotism of the artist, directed to a material that cannot be formed. I must let go of you, and satisfy my need of union, of marriage, otherwise than with you.

SHE: Yes, but you cannot do that by seeking another woman. You would experience the same illusion—the same disillusion.

HE: How then can I satisfy this mystic need?

SHE: That is between you and your God, whom I know nothing about.

HE: If I could have stripped you of divinity and sought it elsewhere—in religion, in work—with the same intensity I sought it in you—we would not have needed this separation.

SHE: And we should have been very happy together!

HE: Yes—as interesting strangers.

SHE: Exactly. The only sensible way for two fully grown people to be together—and that is wonderful too—think! To have lived together for fifteen years and never to have bored one another! To be still for one another the most interesting persons in the world! How many married people can say that? I've never *bored* you, have I, Deacon?

HE: You have harassed, plagued, maddened, tortured me! Bored me? No, never, you bewitching devil! (*Moving toward her.*)

SHE: I've always adored the poet and mystic in you, though you've almost driven me crazy, you Man of God!

HE: I've always adored the woman in you, the mysterious, the beckoning and flying, that I cannot possess!

SHE: Can't you forget God for a while, and come away with me?

HE: Yes, darling, after all you're one of God's creatures!

SHE: Faithful to the end! A truce then, shall it be? (*Opening her arms.*) An armed truce?

HE: (*Seizing her.*) Yes, and in a trice! (*She laughs.*)

QUICK CURTAIN

Two Poems: "Bird of Passage" and "Hutch"

Neith wrote only a few poems, but the two printed here, like the one reproduced in the introduction to this volume, deal again with her profound affection for Hutchins and a desire to retain her own identity. In 1944—the year Hutchins died at age seventy-five, when she was seventy-two—Neith could still savor Hutchins's charm and warmth. Her poem "Hutch," written in that year, uses "fruit" and "juice" to evoke sexual images. The positive feelings in this poem provide a strong rationale for why Neith stayed in this conflicted relationship.

"Bird of Passage" was written in all probability much earlier (perhaps before the 1915 poem "To H. H. at 44"). Here Neith expresses her ambivalent desire for captivity and escape. Yet the end of the poem also communicates a desire to merge with him—"in the completion of your heart you might forget that I have lived." *The Bond* plays with the same contradictory needs—for autonomy and deep psychological intimacy—that speak to many twentieth-century women.

BIRD OF PASSAGE

You seek to hold me. Alas, my dear,
I shall escape you.
I am a bird of passage;
The blue skies I roam
With never a landing-place, or home.
You see me now; and think this moment, like no other,
May last, but no, alas!
My wings carry me away.
As surely as the sun
Whose clear glory illumines the western height
Smiles and is gone,
So shall my soul be hid from you
By the bulging curve of the eternal world.
If you have me in your heart, there shall I live always

These two poems are in the Hapgood collection, Collection of American Literature, Beneicke Rare Book and Manuscript Library, Yale University. They are printed here with the library's permission and that of Beatrix Faust.

When your eyes behold me not.
Most of all would I wish
That you might hold me so entirely
That in the completion of your heart
You might forget that I have lived.

HUTCH

The tree has lived
It is scared and gray
But still wears its crown of bloom
In May.

Its wealth of fruit
Will last all winter long—
Its jocund mirth
And song.

Juice of the apple
Cooled in drifts of snow
Still makes the heart
To glow.

The apple-tree's old wood
Keeps the heartstone warm—
Flower, fruit and juice
And charm!

LETTERS

The letters—and parts of letters—reproduced here focus on Neith's and Hutchins's relationship. The themes in these letters reproduce many of those in their published and creative works and thus supplement the autobiographical content of *The Bond*, *Enemies*, and Neith's poems. In these letters, however, Hutchins's and Neith's conflicts over infidelity are emphasized and placed in more specific context.[1]

1898–1905: Early Years of Marriage

For the year before their marriage, and for the first six years they were married, only letters written by Neith have survived. These early letters reflect Neith's anxieties about their difference in character, particularly her reserve and his lack of it:

> I miss you and I want you. It's a bondage though and makes me horribly melancholy sometimes. I'm afraid you expect too much of me. You like generic woman—women per se—and I am myself. (HC, March 16, 1899)

> I love to be near you and to have you near me, and I delight in your love, but in my soul I don't like familiarity. I'm like the French populace, ready to raise barricades at a moment's notice. (HC, May 24, 1899)

These early letters also demonstrate Neith's commitment to her work as a writer. In 1898 she envisioned how they would spend their evenings as a married couple: "You can scribble at one side of the table while I scribble at the other" (HC, 1898). Before their marriage she wrote, "When I'm not working I hate the world and myself—when I am I have peace" (HC, February 24, 1899). But after six years of marriage Neith was worried about her productivity, about the negative impact of her marriage on her work, and vice versa:

> I wonder if putting as much energy into marriage as I have done—and acquiring the amount of experience that I have—has not been against me, so far as success in writing is concerned. I think I'm less buoyant, and that counts for a lot! And I do want success, Infant, I want it horribly and money, and I want some gaiety too—now! . . . My own dearest, say you like me a little, still, will you? Or am I too old and dull? (HC, 1905)

In this letter, as in others in these years, Neith often addressed Hutchins as "infant," and in several letters she urged him to "be a good boy" or "be a good child." Thus, the maternal dimension of their relationship was established at an early date, as was their conflict about fidelity.

A letter written in late 1901 communicated Neith's discomfort about adultery, expressed her commitment to fidelity, but indicated her beginning attempts to accommodate herself to Hutchins's style:

> Constancy is the genius and spirit of love – and it does mean strength in the person who is capable of it, and in this sense you are constant to me and I to you. The variety in the genre – is the kind of thing Bob for instance goes in for – and is a weak and empty substitute. Nothing can be so interesting as a relation that has been tried and tested and is still capable of variety and modulation. N'est-ce pas? When you come to me I will try to prove that to you, my Infant. And meantime, don't take my written infidelities seriously. I've been perfectly frank to you, because I see the full scope of whatever feeling I have for another man – see its distinct limit and that it can't carry me far. I know your imagination sometimes works in fearful and wonderful ways. Hence, I assure you that I shall tell you if anything at all occurs beyond friendly and (at times) coolly flirtatious talks – and this latter is a very slight element. (HC, November 9, 1901)

Yet four years later Neith reiterated her earlier beliefs:

> What I said about the varietals out there simply expressed a feeling I have which I suppose is more aesthetic than moral – of the unpleasant-ness of that sort of thing anywhere. I mean of erecting into a principle what ought to be regarded as a breach. There is no doubt in my mind that the ideal on which marriage is based (theoretically) – mutual fidelity – is the most attractive that has been discovered so far and if in the course of human events we temporarily lapse from that ideal, still we ought to recognize the lapse and keep the ideal. But to put up a brazen front of believing that lapsing is the proper thing to do is crude and unlovely, and besides it takes all the zest out of sinning. (HC, Fall 1905)

By 1905 Neith was already nostalgic about the couple's early romance and blamed herself, not Hutchins, for their problems:

I think dearest that we had an awfully good time that year we were so much together before we were married—dinners, theaters, rides in the country and these letters in between. It makes me long for a little of it now, and for freedom from the care and responsibility that these two children have brought—just for a little. Yet of course I wouldn't be without them and the other couldn't have lasted indefinitely—but it was good while it did last. You were a delightful, a perfect, lover, dearest. You won't mind my putting it in the past tense—for though you sign yourself my lover, still it isn't quite the same thing is it? And yet I don't know—we have had some loverlike moments not so long ago. I rather think we might have some more if you were here now. But—but—we are old, sober married people now—with a family and many cares. I'd like to be a bachelor girl again. It's six years ago today that we married. I have never had an instant's regret, nor a single wish to change. . . . I know you will never make me unhappy because of any fault of character. You are a very noble person. I am much more mixed than you, more selfish and self-indulgent. Hence, I have sometimes made you unhappy. I am sensitive to the interest and attraction of other men as (in a different way) you are to women. But I've never seen any man that I could consider in exchange for you, even temporarily. We are really well suited you and I. (HC, 1905)

1907–1909: Sexual Experimentation

During these years, Hutchins and Neith lived in Europe and spent part of their time in different cities—Hutchins in Paris for a while and Neith and the children in Italy. Later Hutchins was in Italy, and Neith and the children were in Switzerland. Hutchins wrote to Neith from Paris while she was pregnant with their third child:

> How mixed we are. I must return. I want to return. And yet I need another relatively deep experience such as I could get here in six months among the people I am just beginning to meet. I love you dear and the children and I want to be with you, but I feel, I think as some women who are constantly pregnant must feel—that something deep in me wants a wide, unknown and profound experience. (HC, March 1, 1907)

Neith responded in anger:

> What do you mean by a wide, unknown and profound experience? Aren't you a little Byronic to be yearning at nearly 40 for a new point of departure? . . . If you mean an emotional experience, look out! Don't go yearning for unknown experiences away from me – don't put me aside as an institution. I'm not yet that – and I won't live in solitude of any sort. I think you have had quite as much experience as is good for you – that's my private opinion – and that you would do well to sit down and read a bit and reflect. . . . At any rate, I don't think we ought to be separated more than we can help. . . . I'm very lonely tonight and restless. Perhaps I too want a wide and profound experience! We might have it together. (HC, 1907)

In a number of letters during the subsequent months, Neith expressed hostility to Hutchins's known or suspected infidelities:

> I have an abiding love for you – the deepest thing in me. But in a way I hate your interest in sex, because I suffered from it. I assure you that I can never think of your physical passion for other women without pain – even though my reason doesn't find fault with you. But it's instinct – and it hurts. The whole thing is sad and terrible – yet we all joke about it every day! (HC, 1907)

> I am enjoying my friend in a thoroughly Platonic pastime, while you, I don't doubt, are on the loose. . . . When you sign yourself, "yours forever," I know it means you are somebody else's temporarily. (HC, 1907)

> I suppose that Florence has warmed up too, now that my eagle eye isn't on her. Confess you have been corresponding hotly? Now tell the truth! (HC, September 6, 1907)

> By the way I hope your "haunting passion" for Italy has nothing to do with Florence. You are not to write her more than once a month, else I shall be angry. She is the one person in the world that I hate! (HC, September 13, 1907)

Hutchins replied: "Of course my haunting passion for Italy has nothing to do with the Florence you mean. In fact, I regard that Florence as an obstacle and you know it" (HC, September 13, 1907). And three days later Hutchins again wrote to Neith:

> Your letter doesn't sound as though you wanted me back at once. Tell me the reason, if there is any. As to "keeping me close" and not letting me have tête-à-tête walks with Theresa, I don't suppose you mean it especially as I always have and still do encourage you to see men alone, except when I'm afraid there's something doing of a dangerous kind. I expect you to be as tolerant as I am. . . . Why insist on anything else. If we do, we'll both feel like slaves. (HC, September 16, 1907)

Several months later Neith responded to what she suspected were Hutchins's continued infidelities: "Your letters are snippy. I believe you're making love to somebody. If not, why not to me? Do you love me?" (HC, November, 1907). Although Neith was angry about Hutchins's affairs, she seemed to feel that, if only she could convince him of her love, he would stop. She wrote:

> I told B the last time we talked together during the drive, of my love for you, that it had never changed since I first really perceived you till now and never would change—that as I felt your essential beauty and charm when I first came to know you, so I felt them now, and that what I most wanted in life was that you should be happy. I told him that I thought you by turns loved me and hated me, took me in and utterly rejected me, but that I had never for a moment rejected you in my thought nor imagined any future for myself without you—that without "making good" in my relation with you, I could never be happy. (HC, 1907)

When her complaints about Hutchins's infidelities seemed ineffective, Neith decided to accept his idea that she too should have flirtations. During 1907 Neith became infatuated with Arthur Bentley,[2] an old college friend of Hutchins's, who was also married. Bentley was the serious threat discussed in *The Story of a Lover*. The Hapgoods returned to the United States in early 1909, but Bentley pursued Neith. Neith finally made a painful decision to break off her relationship to him but then had a nervous breakdown.

Hutchins probably destroyed the letters about the crisis in his marriage created by Neith's and Bentley's attraction, but a long letter he wrote to Mary Berenson reveals his jealousy and contradictory ideas about fidelity:

Dear Old Mary,[3]

Your familiar old letter has arrived, and it is very true, as you say, that, much as we love one another, we can hardly hope to understand one another. But I, too, like you, must have my old say.

In the first place, I hope you will strictly keep all this confidential, you and Bernard, and destroy my letter or letters, as the case may be. . . .

Now for some facts. You say I have demanded the sole physical possession of one woman. That is *not*—true. Neith might have had a hundred physically if she had wanted to. She *has* had several, not indeed in what is generally regarded as the finally attractive act (I don't believe she has ever actually persuaded herself to give herself conventionally), but she has gone as far as she wanted to physically in the case of at least two men, neither of whom you know. I will not be disingenuous enough to say that I do not know physiological jealousy. I do, but yet I have been willing—quite willing—to have Neith get the same attitude as I have—a belief that it is safer and more civilized not to regard the sexual act as of great emotional or ethical importance. I *know* that I have been quite willing, even desirous, that she should go along with me in this matter—and she knows that I could easily have "got over" it and learned to accommodate myself.

But she has never wanted it! Sex with her in the physical sense is a matter of old habit. But what she *has* at times wanted has been what I call destructive, and I will show you why. She has at least once (and I think only once, and that lately) wanted or thought she wanted for a time a life—another life—and this one too. A romantic feeling, that she would like a double life—a double set of interests, complex and long sustained, with two men and possibly two families. I have seen for four or five years this romantic dream in her, generally without an object.

Why do I object to this you will ask. Because, whether egotistically or not, I *want* all *essentially* that there is of Neith, both for myself and the family. She has never had enough energy or excess of strength or of feeling to give out anything important to others without neglecting wholly the individuals whom she has contracted to help and whom she would practically wrong if she did it.

Any pleasure, any freedom, any experience which broadens her, relieves her, amuses her, I have always desired for her and actively helped to get for her. Yet when I have seen that she tended to engage in something which I knew, because I saw it begin, would take away her little energy, would make her withdraw from her little interest in what she was mainly bound to, I kicked and kicked her, I will admit, and I do not and cannot regret it. I have tried to be civilized and tolerant, but I have also tried to recognize the facts of her character, to see that she has no capacity for more than one life, hardly enough for one, and to insist that she lead only one, but that as broadly and pleasurably as possible. I know that she now believes that I am right.

Do you think, for instance, that I could wisely and ethically allow her to go off with another man for six months, live with him, get all kinds of interests with him, and then come back? How could I vigorously lead my life in the meantime? How about the children? How could they not be handicapped in a society such as she and I must live in? Come, be sensible, Mary, and leave aside your academic nonsensical ideas of the general and what ought to be. Think of what is and what is possible—if indeed it is still possible for you attractive Parnassians to really understand what is. . . .

I have tried for a lot. I have tried to hold everything together, things perhaps which cannot go together. I have seen Neith's unwillingness from the start to meet a necessary situation and with her attitude of mind I can see how unnecessarily great the strain was. . . . I therefore tried (not being clever I didn't do it well) to combine all I could for her, enough freedom to satisfy her temperament and yet not too much to endanger the unity of our life together. I had to try, for she would try for nothing.

My sexual adventures were of the slightest kind—and Neith recognized that I was *all the time* devoted to her and the family, that all else was nothing but dissipation and amusement. I don't defend it—but I say that no deep interest was thereby taken away from her and her interests. And yet Neith, whenever she thought I had a sexual interest (and merely that) in some women whom she recognized as an equal, was very jealous and much more unkindly (to the other woman) than I have ever been in a like situation.

Now, another thing in this haphazard letter may be said. I have always loved Neith in every way—and in my love has been a deep element of passion. She has, I think, loved me and more now than ever, but she has not had this feeling of passion. (I don't mean mere sex; she has that for me.) If she had that, I would have been in every way willing for her to have had the utmost sexual freedom. I would have known then that I and mine were safe, that nothing would ever lead her away from the center. But I do know that this element of temperamental passion often destroys everything in the way of a relationship complexly lived together—and I feared that such a thing might come to her and destroy what I was most deeply interested in. If she had been actively interested in our life, or had had this passion for me, I would not have acted as I did, in any case. Now, this my dear, is as you can see a very intimate if not humiliating confession—and if I felt less for you and Bernard I could not write.

Please destroy this letter.

Affectionately, Hutch

As I re-read this, it seems I have said so little. I think when we can talk again together I may make even you, you old dear feministe, understand (March 6, 1909)[4]

In the summer of 1909 Hutchins wrote several letters that document his attempts to normalize the relationship between Bentley, his wife Anne, Neith, and himself. Hutchins wrote to Bentley:

Dear Bentley,

I fear we shall not be able to get to Chicago after all. . . . I think our meeting—the four of us—if it had been practicable would have been desirable—not only for the pleasure of it—but also, to serve to convince all of us of the well-being of all of us. I shall leave here for the East a week from Friday. But after I have gone, if there is any vacation coming to you, I know that Neith would be delighted to see you both (of course if you could, as I suppose you cannot, come before I leave). If these are not possible, why should not whatever is to be accomplished be done by letters between you, Anne and Neith? I can now see no reason why there should be any difficulty in anything any of us want—since we all want the best.

Sincerely, Hutch

(HC, June 23, 1909)

But in July Hutchins wrote to Neith:

I think it would have been better to have written Bentley at once, than to have waited and then have written a propos de rien. He, as usual in his relation with you, has scored—as he did once before when you refused to write him, against my advice. I was much pleased by your expression of affection for me. I hope your letter to him showed it—though the account you sent me did not seem to indicate so. In fact, though I wanted you to feel that I had no objection to you not showing me his letter of some time ago—and yours to him now, I should yet have been deeply touched and pleased if you had done so. I should have felt better—surer. But of course I don't blame you. I wanted to get as near your feelings as I could—and I imagine I have succeeded better in understanding than if I had tried to induce you to lay it all before me. Life is cruel and yet I love, and must love, to the end. (HC, July, 1909)

Evidently, Hutchins's and Neith's friendship with the Bentleys settled down. The archives contain a number of chatty letters written to Bentley by either Neith or Hutchins in the 1920s and 1930s, expressing sympathy at the death of his wife, trying to interest him in a new woman, congratulating him on his remarriage, and inviting him to visit for the holidays.

1911–1913: Greenwich Village Affairs

After their return to New York, Neith and Hutchins became involved with the circle of Greenwich Village radicals who also spent their summers together in Provincetown. To accommodate their four children, Neith and Hutchins (with help from his father) bought a large house outside New York. In her autobiography Mabel Dodge observed:

Neith didn't come in town much. They had a large, red brick house with porches around it on a hill in Dobbs Ferry, up over the Hudson River, and as they didn't have very much money, Neith did nearly all the housework. They had no servants but Elina, a small, ugly Italian woman like an electric spark. With four children, Boyce and Charles, and the two girls, Miriam and Beatrix, there was a lot of sewing and other things to do.[5]

Hutchins, however, often spent several nights a week in town, an arrangement that perhaps encouraged his wandering eye. Emma Goldman, whom he met about this time, wrote him an affectionate letter, that commented on his reputation but also expressed her dislike of infidelity because of its negative impact on women:

My dear Hutch:
     Let me congratulate you on your splendid review in *The Bookman*. It is the first thing you have written about me which is free from the

ordinary journalistic tricks. I am indeed very grateful that it is so, not so much for my own sake as for your own. You are altogether too fine, dear, to write cheap things. I know one cannot escape it in a cheap world and yet it seems a pity, especially in your case. You have such a store of human sympathy, something so warm and glowing, that it is often a marvel to me, how little it asserts itself in your criticisms or reviews of people. In your Bookman article, you cease to be Hapgood the newspaperman. You are Hutch the very human, tender Hutch who thrilled me so the night at the Boulevard, and many times before at 210. I cannot begin to tell you how happy that tone in your write-up has made me—not because of whatever praise it contained, really not. Rather, is it because I felt that you have at last looked to the soul of E. G. the public character. It took you many years to do it, old man, but I am glad you got there at last. Possibly, a few years longer, will bring you still closer to E. G. I hope so anyway.

Don't you think we are rather slow in knowing each other, Hutchie, dear? We two, with such a world-wide reputation for getting sweethearts. It seems to me it's harder to live down one's reputation, than to live up to it. . . .

Tom is a wonderful chap. What a pity the men I might love have wives I like. You may ask, what difference does it make? Well, if I thought the wives free it might not matter. But somehow I hate to get my joy at the expense of others. Or possibly it is arrogance, a very selfish reason: I hate to be an incident in a man's life.

Well, if I could explain motives I should be a very wise woman. As it is I am a woman alright, too much for my own good, and not wise.

Affectionately, Emma

(HC, January 31, 1911)

In 1912 Hutchins met Mabel Dodge,[6] a wealthy woman who attracted dissident intellectuals, writers, artists, and activists. She soon opened her mansion on lower Fifth Avenue for a weekly salon. For several years large gatherings of people from diverse political and intellectual milieux debated politics, modern art, Freudianism, feminism, birth control, and other controversial topics of the day. Writing to Hutchins in the mid-1920s, Mabel Dodge Luhan reflects on his influence:

I want to tell you that it has meant a lot to me to see you again and be in your neighborhood. Ever since I have been back I have been looking and looking for some person or group where I could feel satisfied. . . . But I haven't found any rest with any one here. . . . But I—feel it again with you just as I did eleven, twelve or thirteen years ago when I came back from Europe and wanted some kind of medium. Lately—when many people have been speaking to me of 23 Fifth Avenue and the particular thing we all created there for a moment, I have been looking back and realizing that after all it was *you* who really started it there, for you first gave me a sense of renewed life and then you brought people to me that I liked—Steff[7]—and all the others really. I met Reed[8] through you. . . . I feel, therefore, you are an important person. You were so to me—and coming back now after years in an environment [Taos] that makes everything except the truly living values seem valueless—I find you just the same in your reassuring quality. . . .

Yours, M. L.

(MDLC, 1920s)

Early in 1913 Hutchins had an intense relationship with Mabel that may or may not have involved physical intimacy, but which soon evolved into a friendship. Writing to John Reed in 1915—in order to help Mabel end her unsatisfying affair with Reed—Hutchins drew an analogy between their experiences:

So, to me, Jack, I feel sure of one thing. Mabel will never again be to you what she was. If I know her at all, I know she cannot repeat an experience, a feeling, that is gone. She felt for me once, I think, and I would just as soon try any impossible thing as to try to get it back. The feeling she had for me has now changed into a deep and I think permanent friendship. It is just what she and I want. I wish something of the same kind might be between you and her. But she thinks you cannot do it. I don't know. (MDLC, 1915)

Earlier in the same year Hutchins had written a philosophical letter to Mabel signifying the end of their affair and the start of a friendship:

When I write to you, I would like to be all temperament and flirtability, but I have little of either.

But my "reason" tells me—and truthfully, strange to say, that I have a deep, unalterable feeling and affection for you. I do not know what it is, whether founded on similarity or difference, or disease or health—on our dislocation or our integrity—but I know somehow we have managed to build something very real between us. I don't know what to call it, except an Existence. It is not characterizing to call it love, or friendship or hatred or attraction, or interest, though it includes some of these things—but many other things, not it, also includes these things. So they do not help to characterize or explain or state it. It is merely this specific relationship, without analogy or prototype. It is like a work of art in that no other work of art and no category of art will explain it. It belongs nowhere, but is. It is no class or classification, in no planet or constellation, but it *is*, is simply *is*. That is all. . . . I have a great desire to write you a real letter, but I evidently don't know how anymore. I do know, however, that something significant happened during these last five months in New York. I am too tired to know just what. Do you? But I am sure it was something real. . . .

Yours, as he has been to you, H
(MDLC, June 24, 1913)

At the end of a chatty letter written to Mabel a month later, Hutchins reasserted his commitment to Neith:

Neith and I talk about you frequently. She wrote you a long letter the other day. It seems to me that she and I are even closer than ever. It is wonderful how, if love begins a relation, how richness is constantly added, just through common experiences of all kinds, painful and delightful. I do not think she and I could be so close now, if we had not had all kinds of difficulties in common, as well as all kinds of delights. (MDLC, July 24, 1913)

But in August Hutchins ended a similar letter to Mabel: "I am quiet, unreal and about to go to sleep in your bed! Yours, with old affection. H" (MDLC, August 6, 1913).

Did Neith know about the sensual relationship between Hutchins and Mabel? Maybe not, for Neith and Mabel became good friends, taking a trip to Europe together in the summer of 1914 without Hutchins. Later, in 1915, when Neith became very troubled about Hutchins's new affair with Lucy Collier,[9] it was Mabel to whom she turned as a confidant.

1915-1916: Battles about Infidelity

A letter that Hutchins wrote to Neith in May, 1915, set the stage for a new crisis in their relationship:

> This the month of May. Perhaps there is fitness, though cruel fitness, in the month of May. Now in calm mood, I recognize that I feel to you quite differently than in any other month of May since we met. I am expressing this because I have always expressed myself to you. These last days and nights I cannot work, nor sleep. I feel an unreasoning resentment, not against you, but against the fact that my constructive energy with you—on you—is gone. When I am tired, there is nothing going on independent of me. I must work in the creative sense or else there is nothing between us. I want help when I am dead and you will not give it to me.
>
> I am like the artist who sees his work forgotten and obliterated by new waves—as soon as he pauses in his energy. I am to blame for having called on those depths in you of which you yourself are ignorant and—cannot control. But I can call no more, and I must—leave these depths untouched, or to be touched into independent and creative life by someone else, by something else.
>
> But I must, when Life again comes to me, call on Somebody or Something, possessed by the eternal illusion of creating, of hoping to inspire Something that will go on when I am tired. I do not know who it is, or what it is, but I must, if real life remains, begin again my work—Somewhere, with Someone.
>
> In the month of May the old illusion, the old hope, the old creative instinct returns to me. But I feel that I must suppress it all, for the present, until Something new—Someone new—beckons to me in mysterious kindling hope.
>
> You have been all to me. But I can construct with you no more. The instinct, the hope is gone. Although we shall live together with the children, and do our best, and I hope cheerfully and amiably—yet I feel we are separate. What is to come I do not know, except that I have the old, terrible longing for intense companionship, for Sex, for Self-oblivion, for impelling Something into life which will independently carry on my life. I am tired. I cannot work. (HC, May, 1915)

Five months later both Neith and Hutchins corresponded with Mabel Dodge about their conflicts. On October 31, 1915, Hutchins wrote:

Dearest Mabel,

I got your letter last night. . . . Now where you are mistaken is here: It is true that I am disturbed about everything, about my work, about what is *value*, about Neith, about life in general. . . . It is Neith rather than I who is deeply disturbed. I do not know whether it is the approaching change of life in her or what. She loves me – I know that – but I believe it is increasingly difficult for her to be near me. I am waiting with a deep anxiety to see what will happen to her. She is away to rest – in any way she can. I feel that she will have to work out her problems alone. Perhaps I ought to take care of her, as I did once before, but I feel this time, cost what it may, that I must not. I want with the greatest intensity for her to be adjusted and happy with me. Anything that you can write me about her, that you observe, that will help me to understand, I will receive gratefully. I am trying to "let go," as you once told me to, but not through indifference. Far from it – but through a feeling that that is all I can now do. I have my fears, but I hope all will turn out well. Do not imagine anything: There is no other man for whom she cares much. It is far deeper than that. It is that impulse in her that demands isolation, solitude, that is at present most intense in her.

I love you, Mabel, and I want you to show your love for me now by being entirely frank with me, and in not talking about me and Neith to anybody.

Devotedly, Hutch.

(MDLC, October 13, 1915)

Neith also described the friction to Mabel:

I knew we were killing one another. It was the culmination of long years of strains and of savage intensity in which I was expressed much more than he was – which I insisted upon against what he wanted and struggled for. We both wanted to get away at times and tried to but couldn't. At last it got to a point where the only way out seemed to be physical murder. Things happened several times approaching that – getting nearer and nearer. We both lost hold of ourselves. . . . I knew something had to break. I thought perhaps he would never come back and I deeply wanted something to happen that would free him, make him himself again—that would get him out of that misery and give him peace and happiness. I wanted this even if I never saw him again. In will and desire, I took my hands off his throat and let him go. I wrote him that I wanted him to do *anything* that would keep him. Whatever it was. And I did honestly deeply want it because I knew otherwise he couldn't go on at all. [Hutchins left for several days.] He came back full of love for me—the old love and more, only without the violence, the desperate need—ready to give anything. . . . Something had broken in me too and I completely loved him. . . . I don't mean there haven't been some shadows. What happened cost us something—cost me something. . . . And I cried most of one night because I regretted the old fierceness and wildness—which something perverse in me wanted, perhaps the red Indian. (MDLC, 1915)

In all probability, this crisis arose from Hutchins falling in love with another woman. Sometime in November or December, 1915, Hutchins wrote to Neith: "I have fallen in love with Lucy Collier, but not in the way I am with you. I'll tell you all about it when we meet" (HC). Neith replied: "So you confess to being 'in love' with Lucy! Suppose I told you I was 'in love'—oh, what thunder, sighs, sobs and curses you would emit! Well, you ought to be very tolerant toward me now. After all, we can't love our young friends as we do one another can we? So we might as well do what we can" (HC, 1915).

Neith tried to accept the affair. She wrote to Mabel in December:

As to your famous question. "Why do we want men to be monogamous?" I should respond: Do we? So long as they won't be, why should we want them to be? Why want anybody to be what they are not? Perhaps we like the excitement of catching them in flagrante delicto—and their excuses are so amusing! An absolutely faithful man, but what's the use of discussing him—he's a mythical creature. . . . I don't want any mythical creatures. I like them as they are. (MDLC, December, 1915)

Hutchins reassured Neith that this affair with Lucy Collier did not threaten their marriage:

I had a long talk with the Colliers yesterday—part of the time alone with her and part alone with him. They are deeply in love with one another and love each other deeply – or rather they love each other deeply and she is much in love with him. His nature is impersonal and aloof. . . . Lucy told me that she has always longed for a more intimate personal relation with him. He has given it to her at times, but seems to want to use it for something else – rather ashamed of it for its own sake. . . . In a way their relation is rather like that between you and me. You are very different from him, of course, but you are aloof like him, and I am like her in my demand.

She said a curious thing about you. She said she admired you more than anybody that she had ever seen – thought you disturbingly beautiful. That when you walk, it is like music to her – and that she wants to look at you all the time. But she said when she left you after that day at Dobbs Ferry she was all broken up, that you seemed to destroy her – to do something terrible to her. . . . I think she has for you something awfully strong, but very disturbing, and that from me she hopes for peace. Isn't it queer. I really wish I had something for her. But I can never see anybody again except in terms of you. You are between me and all others. (HC, December, 1915)

Neith was skeptical about the effect of all this talk and analysis. She wrote:

Perhaps I was too hasty in what I said about Lucy C's letter. I reread it afterwards and thought some thing in it very interesting. She is an unusual girl. But I stick to my opinion about analysis. I believe psychologically it is a bad thing for any person to put their emotions and life under a microscope and in the hands of a third person. I do hope you won't give her our book [*The Story of a Lover*], which Hutchins wrote in 1914]. . . . After all, whatever our troubles and misunderstandings, our relation is ours and nobody else can do anything about it if we can't. (HC, December, 1915)

Neith tried to lighten things up a bit in a letter to Mabel:

There's been such a *lot* of solemn letter-writing lately! It doesn't suit my temperament and I always feel like adding a postscript to take off the effect. And now I feel like writing you a mischievous letter – but I suppose I mustn't. Let's all be solemn for a while yet. . . .

But I *do* wish you could have seen Hutch the last three weeks here – with two women making love to him – one by letter and one in presence—and how he liked it! He was perfectly darling! And he told me as he was leaving that these three weeks had been the *sweetest* time. You can't quite get that, can you? If you can, you won't feel bothered about *us*.

You seem I'm writing a sentimental letter instead of a frivolous one! No, I don't feel frivolous—but you know the old Eve dies hard—and I'd always rather laugh if I can! Oh, life—life—life! (MDLC, January, 1916)

A month before, however, in another letter to Mabel Dodge, Hutchins confesses that Neith had not taken his affair so lightly:

Neith and I have had a very emotional time. Perfect frankness has brought us nearer together. I think everything will come out all right all around. I told her I told you much and that you have guessed the rest. But that you will not tell anybody. So when you come you and Neith will be able to talk freely. She feels that nothing has come between her and me. And she is right. She has been wonderful about it. Deep pain, but much more. (MDLC, December, 1915)

Hutchins also tried to explain his side to Mabel:

There is one thing I will tell you now—which *please* do not tell to anybody. I do *not* think that Lucy loves me or needs me more than I do her. She loves me and needs me, but she loves Love more and what I cannot give she will get from others—as you did! I do not think I shall hurt her. She is young in spirit, *must* love—And I love her *very much* and am much in love—And I wanted you to realize that without my *saying* it to you—or to *anybody*.

And Lucy *loves* John and I *love* Neith. You ought to see that it is hard for all of us—except for John, and it is hard for him, but not so hard because he loves pain and impossible self-transcendencies and metaphysical difficulties.

I love you too, dear Mabel.

Hutch

Please do not tell this! You understand why. (MDLC, March, 1916)

A series of letters Neith and Hutchins exchanged with Mabel Dodge in early 1916 indicate that both Neith and Hutchins got angry at Mabel's interference. Neith wrote to Mabel:

Now I have a small bone to pick with you. I was surprised and not very pleased to receive here from Lucy C a private, personal letter which I wrote to you. Can I not write confidentially to you without having it go the rounds? There has been entirely too much public discussion of H's love affairs, anyhow, for my taste. Lucy is a sweet thing, but a perfect baby. If you understood the whole affair you would understand too my feeling about it—which is very tolerant and not disturbed—except about the practical aspects. For example, she thinks she is going off on a trip with H—going to Europe later with him etc.—which of course is absurd—and has been talking about it—and of course I don't like that and neither does he. But these are superficial things. I am really deeply happy in reaching a deep understanding and peace with Hutch. (MDLC, January, 1915)

Later Neith revealed more of what had transpired:

Dearest Mabel,

I have just come back from seeing Hutch off to New York and find your letter to me. Am forwarding yours to him to the club. He and I had expected to go to town together about Feb. 1st—he to straighten things out with Lucy and other business and I to see some other people. But this morning came letters from her which shocked and grieved us both—he felt he ought to go at once and I agreed with him. I feel *terribly sorry* about her if this last mood of hers is at all durable. But she has had so many moods and feelings that I hope this one will pass—and that she will accept the situation as it is and not be unhappy about it.

I don't think you as yet understand it completely—but you know so much that you ought to know all—so far as anyone can. Hutch will talk to you about it, I know, and his point of view and mine are the same. What you don't realize yet is the changed situation between him and me—which inevitably affects everything. You say I "don't want him"— Well, I *do*—completely, absolutely—and he knows it and for the first time we have had a completely happy and satisfying relation together— and this cannot pass or change. I can't tell you why it is so or why I know it is so—but it is. And it is a free relation—I haven't got him "by the throat" any more.—He doesn't suffer any more with me.—He is happy and peaceful and satisfied in *our* relation. Now if he can settle his relation to Lucy it will be all right. The only thing that will make the situation "impossible" is if she feels her relation with Hutch to be *primary* in her life—for with him it must be secondary, as he has told her and as he felt it from the first. That means a lot. It means that she *can't* have him "completely" even while he is with her. The understanding between them was—at least *he* so understood it—that it *must* be a secondary relation and that she wanted to maintain a primary relation with John as he did with me. She herself wrote me that—but now she seems to have lost sight of it—to want to make Hutch her main passionate interest—her lover. Well, he can't be that, because he is *mine*.

Short of that, I see no reason (unless in her feeling) why they shouldn't have the relation that he wants—a sweet, undisturbing one, involving intimacy of all kinds, perhaps, but *not* passion, which he has never felt for her, he says. But Hutch and I feel that we are free to love other people—but that nothing can break or even touch the deep, vital, passionate bond between *us*—that exists now as it always has—only now it is happy instead of unhappy. I see no reason why he shouldn't love Lucy, and she him—in fact, it *ought* to be so. But she *can't* be happy unless she loves John *more*—or somebody else. At times she has said she *does*—seemed quite sure of it.

I wish you'd write me what you think—especially after you've talked to Hutch—and tell me about Lucy. I feel awfully cut up about her—I *hate* to think she's suffering. I do hope she will feel differently soon.

Dear Mabel, I'm not "more or less content"—I'm content as I never was in my life before.

Neith

(MDLC, January, 1916)

About the same time Neith answered a letter from Hutchins:

I am sorry indeed that Lucy is ill as your telegram says. I wrote her two letters which you have probably seen. I meant what I said about accepting whatever arrangements you and she make. There's only one thing I feel like saying before I know more definitively what you have settled— which is that I hope it will be arranged this way: That you shall be perfectly free as to the time you spend with her and the time you spend with me. That is that she shall *not* demand you when you are with me— as she did this time—but will wait until you go to her freely. I shall try to leave you perfectly free—for I want to feel that when you're with me it's because you *want* to be and I don't want any impatient female dragging at you when you are with me. Make this clear to her as you can—make it clear that I shan't try to keep you away from her, but that she mustn't break in your time with me. She will have to have patience and self-control too—if any such arrangement is to work as you and I talked about.

Dearest love & complete trust, Neith
(HC, February, 1916)

Neith's tone had been much different when she answered a letter from Mabel some weeks before:

Oh, that certainly *is* a "croak," yours of Wednesday! Is it really as bad as that? Why *will* people flop as Lucy seems to have done? Why *can't* they know where they are? It isn't very long since she wrote me that her "all-in-all experience was with John, and always would be"—that she "could never give up her place on his breast"! And now she wants to break with him and thinks "Hutch is her mate"! (Hutch couldn't live with her a month—her volatility would drive him crazy.)

And you picture her and me fighting over Hutch's body! How enchanting! But I really think you're wrong there. I don't care so much about the sexual act as you think—it's not of primary importance! If she wants that with him she can have it, naturally. Nor do I care about Hutch being always in my presence—whenever he *wants* to be with her, he will be.

Really, Mabel, I decline to be regarded as fighting with anybody about Hutch! I've told you how I feel about him and about his relations with other people. I can't get down into the dirt about it!—If you persist in picturing Lucy as a "predatory" female determined to snatch Hutch from me—why of course, I can't help your view. And you may be right about her. I'm sure I don't know. Of course, I don't think he'd like being snatched. But I may be wrong about that too! Perhaps she's destined to bear him off in triumph! Well—well—it's all a bit sad, considering that he says he only wants peace and liked Lucy because she was so peaceful and there was nothing passionate about it! But can't she do anything about it except go to Japan—leaving her children loose around the place? (Did you know she proposed to drop one on Dutchy and one on me for the summer?) Confound it, why does she have to be quite so irresponsible, not to say nutty?

And how about John? Nobody says anything about him! The few letters that I have seen from him and all I have heard about him indicated a deep feeling about Lucy and belief in their bond—and are they now so ready both of them to chuck it? Can't understand!

Mabel, you've taken a very primitive view of the situation—of what started out to be a very civilized arrangement! (I think you do take a very primitive view of the love-relation anyway.) In this case you may be quite right as to Lucy—I don't know. But Hutch isn't primitive and neither am I. I think we could both swing such an arrangement, if the third person were all right for it.

And you're too hard on Hutch now. He *isn't* selfish and egotistic— he wouldn't want the relation with her at all if he thought it would harm her. He said that he wouldn't have it anyway except on his own terms—on the basis of what he thought right all round. He isn't any more snatching at his own satisfaction. He'd like to have Lucy in his life as a "luxury" but not if it's wrong for her. But you can't expect him to take absolutely *your* view. After all, I suppose he knows more about it than you do!

But I am more and more sorry about Lucy. To live with a man eight years, to bear him three children, and *then* to discover you're not mated! That, if you like, is a tragedy. But the longer I live the more I'm struck with the unrooted character of most people in their human relations. The way they change, and don't know their own minds, and fly from this to that. I begin to regard myself as a rock! Do you think I shall be split asunder? It will take a heavy charge of dynamite!

Well, I suppose it's all a mess, like most human affairs. I'd love to have a long talk with you about everything.

Yours, Neith

(MDLC, January, 1916)

A few days later Neith wrote again to Mabel:

Dearest Mabel,

Just reread your letter and find I misread one word. Instead of saying "you don't want Hutch," you said "you *both* want"—quite a difference! I'm glad you realize I *do* want him! But I don't think you realize just *how* nor what I want *for* and *with* him. It isn't any more a simple elementary business of trying or wanting to corral a man and shut off his interests in other women. Hutch and I have lived through too much for that. When I said I wanted him "completely and abso- lutely," I meant in *our* relation. You know he has never felt before that I *did* want him that way—but he knows now I do, and I feel I have him. So there can't be any business of "struggling" with another woman for him (as if he were a piece of goods at a bargain counter!) or of "agoniz- ing!" It isn't necessary—and I want him to have what he wants and to be right for himself with other people as well as with me. I really have some impersonal feeling for him now, as well as a very deep personal one. I particularly want him to get right with Lucy just now—because from everything that happened he *needs* to, for his own sake. He can't bear to feel that he has hurt her or that he has taken anything from her without making return—this quite aside from his strong feeling for her. You see, when they met in New York, it seemed like an even exchange. They were both unsatisfied and rather desperate and Hutch, feeling a kind of despair about *our* relation, could let himself go. That's the really terrible thing about it—for now the situation is changed. Now he feels that he can get what he has always wanted from me—can get it from me instead of from her—and for all reasons he prefers to get it from me—so he can never be again what he was to her then. And *that's* what she wants. I think if things hadn't changed between Hutch and me, he might have given her what she wants—but now he can't. Now he feels that the condition of his having a satisfactory relation with her is that she shall be satisfied emotionally with John—or with someone else—just as he is. His feeling for her is strong, real and deep—but she can't build her emotional life on it or about it—it can never satisfy her.

The trouble is that she doesn't know herself or where she is—she changes from day to day—and isn't in our class as regards experience, naturally. I think that when Hutch left she tried to get nearer to John, really wanted to—perhaps found she couldn't and had a violent revulsion of feeling about Hutch, a demand for him. This is what her letters indicate.

I hope she won't have to break with H. or go away—for then it would be a failure, and I should hate that—and he would feel it deeply. He wants a relationship with her and I want him to have it. And it wouldn't be any question of his "oscillating" between her and me! What he wants with her and what he wants with me aren't in the same class and needn't conflict. I hope she'll be able to meet what he wants.

Love to you, N.

(MDLC, January, 1916)

While confiding in Mabel, both Neith and Hutchins soon began to resent her active intervention in the triangle, which they felt was producing more tensions. Neith wrote:

Mabel,

Didn't you do me rather a bad turn with Lucy? Her letters to me and mine to her have been very nice. But I'm *sure* you put the idea into her head or at least gave her the phrase about my still "having Hutch by the throat!" I know you did! I really feel very kindly toward her and don't want her to hate me—and why should she? I've behaved extremely well, to her and everybody. And Hutch was very very anxious that we should all be friends. Don't represent to her that she and I are natural enemies! She's very impressionable and you know you're impressive! But in this case don't put your oar in—unless you can help it—and it *doesn't* help to make people feel bitter and suspicious. Please don't make her hate me!

    N.

(MDLC, February, 1916)

Neith was more conciliatory in another letter to Mabel:

Poor Hutch! His letters are puzzled! Between what you tell him about Lucy and what she wrote him—and what she says now he's with her— he doesn't know what to think! He says she's "perfectly reasonable and sweet about everything"—and he things you're too tragic about it. It's really difficult for Hutch to think that any woman has a devouring and undying passion for him—and he thinks Lucy will "get over it" soon!

    I suppose the truth is Hutch and I are a couple of hard old nuts and it isn't good for the young and tender to associate too intimately with us—though we'd like to think it is—good for them and for us too. We want everything!

    N

(MDLC, February, 1916)

Hutchins was more angry about Mabel's interference and her resistance to his ideas about the affair:

Dear Mabel,

    There is no need of a long reply to your letter. It is hopeless. You now have a need, under your present fad of "analysis" to immolate yourself—and others, on the altar of self-sacrifice. . . .

    You are so sure about everything! For instance, you are sure that Lucy needs me more than I do her. *I* am not sure of it. That is all I care to say about that. How do you know I didn't feel what she was thinking when I was away?

    I never said to you or any living soul that "Lucy needs to have her body loved." That is a coarse and untrue report of anything I said and I *forbid* you ever to repeat that statement to anybody. If you do, I'll never speak to you again. You are simply an abominable reporter and you ought never to trust yourself to quote anybody—not even their meaning.

You have acted in a really unfriendly way to me. I am willing always to have you or any friend tell *me* what you thing about me—but to go to others and talk to them about me in the way you have, about matters in which I am deeply concerned and which you cannot know much about—is genuinely unfriendly. I could never have acted in that way to you. . . .

You say I ought not to accept when I cannot give. Even if that applied in this case (I mean even if Lucy needs more than I do) I am not sure that the principle is sound. You have given some people much more than you received. Was it wrong for them to accept? If your principle is good, there would be *no* giving or taking. There is never an equality.

Unselfishness! Egotism! Really I am sick of the words. What they really do for us is to blind us to the real character of our needs. I won't split hairs with you there. But, from you I cannot be deeply moved by a charge of egotism. Egotism is shown quite as much by what it lets go of as by what it "holds on to."

You are not, at this moment, frank enough to admit that what love you had for me is gone. Love interprets in some favorable measure. I am frank enough, however, to admit that I have "let go" of you—and I suppose that ought to give you unselfish pleasure.

One of your past experiences, Hutch

I could go through a long list of your absoluteness in criticism. . . . You are always harsh and one-sided because you see only abstractions of people and never people. (MDLC, February, 1916)

We have no evidence about how Mabel reacted to this angry letter, but Hutchins's threat to end their friendship did not lead to a permanent rupture. But a series of letters from Hutchins to Neith in March, 1916, demonstrates that he had decided to end the affair and try to reestablish a friendship between the two couples:

I had a long talk with Lucy this afternoon. She is not quite well yet and is melancholy. It seems to me that I have known her for years—a sort of settled relation. But to you, love of my life, goes the root and the soul of all things. Lucy reread *The Story of a Lover* and it made her feel the deep passion I have for you. With eternal love, H. (HC, March, 1916)

Dearest,

I am sorry it looks as if you would not see much of Lucy and John which was as important as anything else. All things are well here. I wrote you yesterday. . . .

But as John and Lucy go to the country today, I hope you deferred your other interests and got in all the time you could with them. I supposed that was the main purpose of your trip. . . . A letter from Lucy tells me that you are to spend the evening with John. I am glad of that.

I love you tenderly, and I want to take full care of you, emotionally dear, dearest one.

H.

(HC, March, 1916)

Neith wrote back to Hutchins:

Yesterday I did errands in town—saw Mary, Jig & Sue, supper with F. and the evening with John till 11:30. . . . I found John very tired, but in a cheerful mood. Was relieved to find that he and Lucy had come together before she left and that she had gone away feeling happier. He seemed very confident that all would come out right between them. . . . He talked much as you and I have talked about our situation—In many ways he and I are much alike, except that he is much more up in the clouds, less yielding, more theoretical than I am! Partly, because he is younger and lived less—he is really less human, more remote. I understand him, in feeling, but I see rocks ahead where he insists the sailing is good. (HC, March, 1916)

Perhaps the sailing was good. The affair seemed to have ended amicably; the archives contain friendly letters John wrote to Hutchins from 1939 to 1941. Lucy also wrote to Hutch in 1939, telling of her continuing dissatisfaction with John, but her tone was comradely and not romantic. In 1941, after asking Mabel to send copies of letters they had sent her over the years, Neith wrote back, commenting on her own response to the Collier affair: "How noble I was. How patronizing. And of course all the time I was nothing of the sort" (MDLC, October 8, 1941).

In letters written in the months just after the affair ended, Neith wrote to Hutchins with a sincerity that undoubtedly expressed her real feelings about infidelity:

I have told you exactly where I stand and what I want with you. I can't say any more than that. The rest you must settle for yourself. I want you as near me as you can be happily. I don't want an intimate, emotional relation with anyone else. I don't want you to encourage in yourself an emotional attitude toward someone else. It won't give you peace, it will only distract you. I love you deeply, quietly, surely. I am not disturbed by anything except your disturbance — and I feel that must pass and soon. Cannot you cease tormenting yourself and me — my dearest in the world? It seems so strange to me that you cannot be sure of my love for you.
Neith
(HC, April 6, 1916)

Dearest —
    . . . What I have in mind and heart now between you and me is a *real marriage* — not an arrangement! It is not "pity or compassion" that moves me, but a strong instinctive feeling for you which has survived everything. My idea is that we shall not be too hasty about it — that we shall test ourselves by living in sin together this summer! Then if we find it satisfactory, we'll marry one another — with the understanding that it means absolute mutual *fidelity* in every way, physical, spiritual and everything else. I believe that's the only way we can be happy together & I believe we can be happy that way. I have doubted at times if it wouldn't be best for *you* to get clear away from me — if you could ever be really happy with me — and this is one thing that makes me say now we had better test ourselves this summer. I want to be quite sure of our basis & I want you to be. But I believe myself it is *there*. I think you and I have got down to bed-rock — and that what holds us together is as strong & firm as the rock — in spite of all we've done to smash it.
    I have been looking back over our emotional history & I think I see one or two things about myself which may interest you! In the first place I think it's true that I am "primitive" — that is, very instinctive. This is covered up a good deal by my strong unwillingness to be hurt, or if I *am*, to show it, or admit it even to myself. I *know* that your physical infidelities (beginning very early) hurt that instinctive feeling

for you in me – that I wished to be reasonable about it – that I therefore tended to be more aloof in my feeling about you – because otherwise it would have hurt more – that I accepted your feeling about such things as reasonable – didn't blame you – but shrank from it. That as time went on I didn't feel it less – but came more and more to feel that you didn't belong completely to me *nor I to you* – that this gave me a more disengaged feeling to other men – that after the Indianapolis episode [with Bentley] I did return to you in my feeling, bore you a child and did not think of any man for seven years – that the discovery of your long-continued secret relations was a blow to me deeper than you could realize – that I *did* then in my feeling really withdraw from you and by last summer had got so far away that I could live without you, that after our break I felt free of you and could really love another man. This is my side of it. I know your side too – my failings toward you – and that's why I've never *blamed* you – why I really have no resentment. I know I am just as much at fault as you and very likely *much more* – but it won't help us now to try to fix the blame exactly. It will help us to feel we've *both* been wrong – for we have – we have both been ignorant and careless and reckless about our relation. But it is so deep & vital in its root, that though we have cut it to the ground it will grow up again – so I believe. But if it *does* – and if it is the close relation we both want, there must be no more playing with it – no more theories about double relations. I come back again to that first letter I wrote to Lucy. I told her that no one could maintain two complete love-relations at the same time. She has lost John's instinctive feeling for her – and hers for him – at least for the time. You and I lost ours for one another, to some extent – but I think it's clear that it isn't gone completely. It's *there* and now we have to find out if it's a strong enough basis to build on. I think it is. And I believe it will be a better relation than before – more completely accepted by me – more understood by you – sweeter and more satisfying to us both. This is my hope. We can forget the past – no, not forget it, but forgive it! – Fulfill our real obligations to others – and be happy *together*.

Neith.

(HC, May 16, 1916)

The summer of "living together in sin" was perhaps a success – but not on Neith's terms – if we can judge from a letter Hutchins wrote to her in July, 1916:

I am longing to hold you in my arms tonight. . . . I'd like to forget worries in a passionate embrace. I am full of lust and love and desire to talk and hear you talk. I don't know how I can go to bed alone. Send me a gossipy letter. Tell me you love me and also tell me about the flirtations you are having. Have you been unfaithful? Have you sinned? Did you like it? Come and hug me and confess it all. Do you like me better than ever? What shall we do when we meet so as to take another step? Do you think I am a disturber? You wrote that I am turbulent. Are you sorry that I am? . . . I am naughty tonight. I wish you were here for many reasons, some unprintable. Your old goat.

If you were here I'd kiss you first, before I talked. I am uncomfortable. I need you. I want you. Tell me who it is you like now. Is he younger than I? Warmer? Handsomer? How many letters have you received from Brother? You are the only woman I ever loved or could love. Why is that? There are so many others who are attractive, but my imagination and my nervous system don't seem to fit in with them. Since I have known you I have been a spiritual monogamist, and now I am an actual, literal one. Isn't it strange and a little enslaved.

Dear, why are you not here? I'd try to give you a good time. Did I ever give you a good? Did any other man ever do as well? Better? Do you love me? Will you always love me? Well, why don't you say so? Kiss me, hug me. Closer, closer. Ah! Ah! Ah! I am quite wild. I don't dare go to bed. This is like my early youth. (HC, July, 1916).

1917–1918: Hutchins Falls in Love Again

In the fall of 1917 Neith decided to rent a farm in New Hampshire, ostensibly so that their oldest son (then sixteen) could have a horse and revel in his love of the outdoors. Hutchins, restless as ever, spent most of the fall and winter in New York. Here he fell in love with Mary Pyne, a young actress with the Provincetown Players. She was twenty-five years younger than Hutchins and married to Harry Kemp, a Greenwich Village poet. In *A Victorian in the Modern World*, Hutchins discusses the "spiritual intimacy" between Mary and himself, although in all probability it was also a physical affair: "Harry Kemp realized that there was something strong between Mary and me; he didn't like it, . . . [and] he was continually threatening to beat me up."[10] In contrast, Hutchins claimed, "the deep and beautiful Neith understood

it perfectly, and never had a word of objection."[11] The few letters that
remain from this period say otherwise. In September, 1917, Neith
wrote to Hutchins:

> I am sorry you are still sad and that my letter disturbed you – Don't see
> why. I certainly didn't want to interfere if you are making love to Mary!
> Only you better not tell me about any more of your affairs of that
> kind – then I shall be sure not to disturb you! I wish you didn't always
> need to have a woman around, though. – For my own idea of you, I
> would prefer it, apart from any jealousy. It is better to be able to get on
> without them. But perhaps you are one of the men that can't. I
> wouldn't mind if it was only amusement with you, but I don't like to
> think you're dependent on female companionship. Now write me a
> scorcher. I can just see you getting mad! Don't get mad, darling. I say it
> for your good. If you really love me as you say you do, get a job and
> then I'm sure we can live in peace together. You see you have too much
> energy for my meditative temperament, but you ought to put it into
> work and not into other females if you want peace. I shall always be
> jealous of you, so you might as well make up your mind to it!
> Yours, lovingly, N.
> (HC, September 17, 1917)

In February, 1918, Neith wrote again to Hutchins:

> I wish that there could be now between you and me, deep affection and
> friendship, that we could help one another, not hurt, that we could
> forget the storms of the past and be peaceful. Perhaps, it is impossible –
> but you know I think this is the best there is. I wish we could rule out
> the element that has made so much trouble. I would like to be your
> best, dearest, truest friend – your confidant and stay in time of trouble.
> I think I am capable of being good in that way. But I know I wasn't good
> to you in the way you wanted. I remember long ago my Danish friend,
> Laura, said to me, "You will be a good mother, but a bad sweetheart,"
> and I guess she was right. I have not the amorous imagination as you
> have – so I couldn't be what you wanted. I am so sorry for you, poor
> infant, but it has been bad for me too. I wish I could do something now
> to keep you and comfort you. I can't bear to feel that you are sad and
> lonely and that you are not using the rare gifts of mind and spirit that I
> know so well you have.

Bless you, dearest, with all my heart.
N.
(HC, February 15, 1918)

In another letter to Hutchins in 1918 Neith found his brother's remarriage threatening because it implied that "beginning again" was possible:

I have an instinctive feeling against beginning again. I can't feel that they [Norman and his second wife] are married or that anybody can be, more than once. Reason tells me that when Norman was deserted, it was right for him to start again with someone else. But I have an almost religious feeling against it all the same—and I would rather struggle forever with you, if it had to be, than try to be happy with anyone else! I couldn't think of that sort of relation with anyone else and never did. I can understand breaking a relation that was too painful, but not replacing it, and certainly the beauty is, as you say, only in an enduring thing. (HC, 1918)

The death of Neith and Hutchins's seventeen-year-old son in the summer of 1918 in an influenza epidemic during his stay at a Western ranch effectively ended Hutch's affair with Mary. The next year she was diagnosed with advanced tuberculosis and died sometime later. Upon receiving word of Mary's illness, Hutchins left to see her, and Neith wrote:

After you'd gone, I repented as usual that I hadn't expressed what I really felt. Last night after the message from Harry, I felt great sorrow and a longing to send a message to Mary. The way it came to my mind was: "I want to give you *strength*." Whether it was strength to live or to die I didn't know—didn't know which was best for her—but I did strongly concentrate on that message to her. And I felt how harsh life is to the best among us—how lovely things are created and then, it seems, roughly and carelessly used.

Then this morning I didn't want you to go—though I think you were right to go. Just before I came downstairs I said to myself, "Now be decent, you mean old pig!" And then you see I wasn't. Forgive me.

Love to you and to Mary and poor Harry.

Neith
(HC, Spring 1919)

Later Years

A few letters written after 1920 illustrate the continuation of unresolved personality conflicts between Hutchins and Neith, although infidelity no longer seems to be an issue. These letters depict Neith's commitment to the relationship despite frustrations, her maternal tolerance toward Hutchins, and her self-blame. But they also indicate that alcohol was used by both Neith and Hutchins as a means to escape from conflict or pain.

Neith wrote to Hutchins in the 1930s, when they were both in their sixties:

> I'd like to say one thing about the origins of this (and many other) quarrels. Your feeling that I hurt you with the children. It's hard for me to realize that feeling of yours, in spite of the way you show it, because I know that I couldn't do it if I tried. I don't think you realize how deeply they all feel toward you. . . . You are much more to them than I am. What they get from me, I think is important, but it is almost passive on my part. I am just there, like the soil—a rather stony and arid soil too, I fear. But you are the sun in their lives, the vital warm principle of growth. . . . Therefore, I think your resentment against me on their account is terribly exaggerated. You need not fear anything in your relation with them—it is too deeply rooted. They love and respect you far too much. I am very well aware of my failings toward you, and I would be glad to make amends at once when I cause you annoyance. But your violence often prevents that and causes resentment in me, because of what seems to me your unjust overstatement of my wrong behavior. I know you have good grievances against me, but you state them in such a way as to aggrieve me. I wish I could be more patient. I wish you were not so restless and irritable and I wish the summer here could be for you like the first few days when you seemed content and happy. It's my fault I know, but not all my fault. (HC, 1933)

In 1944, three weeks before his death, Hutchins wrote to Robert Lovett, a classmate from Harvard, a leftist professor at the University of Chicago, and an editor and contributor to the *New Republic*:

> I am otherwise just the same as I have always been, full of love for that incomprehensible life in which we somehow are engaged. I drink every-thing I can afford to get and much that I can't afford, and the women

attract me as much as ever although I am afraid to manifest this in any obvious way, for fear of humiliating consequences. On this point Neith is very sympathetic, and although she is very far removed from wanting any part of it, she seems genuinely sorry that I don't go out in the world and behave as usual. (HC, October 29, 1944)

A letter from a friend, John Cowles, to Arthur Bentley painted an interesting portrait of Neith and Hutchins in their later years:

I feel I must go back to the picture of Neith again and describe the conditions under which it was taken. About the middle of April, 1940, and the day they were leaving for the trip home, we went around to their house to help get them packed and started and found Neith completely ready to go, having arranged herself the night before, while Hutch was bumbling around up and down stairs stuffing his dirty underwear and shoes against his clean shirts. To maintain the calm which is always demanded in the vortex of a hurricane, Neith poured herself a good go of gin and was quietly consuming it while the burley hurleyed. We got them and the bags settled in the car, but suddenly Hutch thought of something else and went for a last look. In a moment he returned triumphantly, on high in each hand a bottle of glue and a bottle of ink, telling Neith: "I knew you would forget something." Neith to Elizabeth, soto voice: "I thought I had them hidden from him. Now they will surely break on the trip and make a hideous mess." Elizabeth tactfully removed them from his grubby fists and persuaded him we needed them for our own use. In his perfect generosity, he relinquished them both and everyone was happy. In Neith's lap was the bottle of gin with one drink gone; between her feet a bottle of red wine and grasped firmly in her hand the drink which is shown in the picture. That was the winter that through some heinous misdemeanor which Hutch must have committed, Neith packed a bag and said she was leaving him forever and for good and he need not bother to try and stop her; just get the car out and take her to a railroad station or any other means of far transportation. Though Hutch seemingly persuaded her that his need for her was greater than her desire to get rid of him, she did keep the suitcase packed for the ensuing two weeks and Hutch under reasonable control during the interim. As you gather, we loved them very much and always feel so warmly attached to their fond memory (July, 1954).[12]

I conclude this portion of the book with comments on Neith and Hutchins by two of their children. First is an excerpt of a letter written by their son, Charles, in the 1970s. This letter was written to a publisher (put perhaps never sent) to tell him about *The Story of a Lover*:

> My father's personality was most unusual, he knew an enormous number of people, and he influenced them and had important effects on the life of his time. He had brilliant imagination, a warm sympathy with people of almost every sort, a remarkable ability to express himself in words. He was an artist in ideas.
>
> But there was a hidden weakness in his personality. Behind the facade of outgoing activity, there was an inner feeling of weakness. He has said in his longer Autobiography, that he always felt somehow "wrong" inside. . . . [But] he never arrived at an understanding of himself: he did not know where this weakness came from.
>
> . . . My father was really, despite his brilliant intellectual independence, what we call a dependent type. Some factor or factors in his early life had injured his self-esteem, undermined his sense of security, so that he had, emotionally, to find strength outside himself. We see this work out in his life. His father said of him, that he would always need financial help; he would not be able to make his way alone. And so it turned out: despite the brilliant endowments, father was not ambitious. He was not aggressive or assertive about his own career. I can remember that this was a disappointment to me as a boy. Other boys' fathers went to work, mine did not. The fact that he inherited money was not the cause, for Norman [his brother] also inherited money, yet he went on to earn larger salaries than anyone in American journalism except Brisbane.
>
> His book, *The Story of a Lover*, is the story of the attempt of a brilliant man, whose emotional life was incomplete or immature, to find a protective relationship in marriage. Unknown to himself, he was seeking in my mother someone upon whom he might depend emotionally.
>
> But this was not the only complication: he had been conditioned in a way which is not altogether clear, to emotional denial . . . through relationship with a denying woman. It should be understood that when the phrase "denying woman" is used, it does not denote a woman who denies others to please herself. It denotes a woman who denies herself and others as well. . . . Under the surface of a calm mind, and many attractive and unusual traits, my mother was a denying person. She did

not wish to deny anybody anything. But within her was a deep conviction that life was not really worth living, that she herself was of no
moment.

. . . What is now evident to me is that my mother had rejected my
father as a romantic figure (although she loved him as a person). . . .
How could he be an effective romantic figure, if his own emotional
nature made him seek dependence? For the romantic figure must be
strong, independent, dominant. . . .

. . . My parents were not exceptional. There are millions of people
with the same problems. What is exceptional is that the relationships
were on an extraordinary level, and both documents are written with
consummate literary art, astonishing depth of feeling and utter
honesty.[13]

Charles is now dead, and only one of Neiths's and Hutchins's children, Beatrix Faust is still alive in 1990. She read and responded to
Charles's letter for the first time in October, 1990:

It must be remembered that Charles was not really qualified to psycho-
analyze anyone—what he knew (or thought he knew) he learned from a
woman friend of his whose main occupation was analyzing her friends
and sometimes her acquaintances, like my parents whom she had met
several times, briefly. Miriam and I asked him to read our parents'
letters before passing judgment; but Charles was very busy with his
own work and never got around to reading them. . . .

While Charles approached this subject from a Freudian point of
view, my own is that of a feminist. In short, I think that the relations
between men and women (including our father and mother) are
deformed by the centuries of belief in dominance on the one side and
subservience on the other. . . . I loved my father but could not agree
with his view of women, even before I knew anything at all about his
extramarital affairs. . . . When father called himself a Victorian in the
modern world, he was bang on target. And Charles had essentially the
same point of view toward relations with women. This comes through
very clearly in the letter, where he speaks of the importance of the male
being "dominant" as well as the very conventional attitude he took
toward father's lack of "success," as though making money was the sign
of a man's being nondependent. . . .

Mother, of course was a far stronger person, as women in general
are, I think, because they have had to be in the life they have lived over

the centuries. Father was perhaps more brilliant in some ways, but mother was more logical and intellectually more disciplined, and far more courageous. . . . Charles speaks of mother's inability to give the children a feeling of love and security. In this he speaks, perhaps, for himself, certainly not for me. I thought she gave us a great deal of love and, as far as the females in the family were concerned, a person to look up to and to consider (as they now say) as a role model.

Miriam and I both felt that they were wonderful parents and that we were more fortunate in having them—in being brought up by two such people.[14]

I agree with Beatrix that both Hutchins and Charles held sexist attitudes toward women. And I concur with her that Hutchins's and Neith's deviations from these sex-role norms make them positive feminist role models. Yet, I believe that Charles put his finger on a problem in his parents' marriage—and in modern marriage, more generally—when he characterized his father as a dependent man who sought a protective relationship and his mother as emotionally aloof.

We live in a culture that values individual autonomy, now for both women and men. Yet we desire satisfying intimate relationships, if not in marriage, then in alternative family and community forms. We await the movement for a personal politics that will make any woman's or man's struggle with these issues less isolated. In the meantime, we can gain personal sustenance from the writings of Neith Boyce and Hutchins Hapgood: they managed their disappointments and compromises in a way that dignified their struggle without a nostalgic return to conventional gender roles. Their example indicates that our search for meaningful work and love in egalitarian relationships is not apolitical, ephemeral, or self-centered. Like them, we are still intimate warriors in a pivotal cultural conflict of the twentieth century.

Notes

1. All letters between Hutchins and Neith are in the Hapgood collection (abbreviated as HC) in the Collection of American Literature, Beinecke Rare Book and Manuscript Library, Yale University. The letters to and from Mabel Dodge are in the Mabel Dodge Luhan Collection (abbreviated as MDLC) in the same library, with some copies in the Hapgood Collection. Miriam Hapgood DeWitt (since deceased) provided me with a typed copy of many of these letters, which made them much easier to read. Some of the letters have exact

dates, but in most cases the dates are approximate. Letters and excerpts from letters are printed here with the permission of the library and Beatrix Faust.

2. Bentley (1870–1957) received a Ph.D. in sociology from Johns Hopkins University in 1895. He taught for a short while at the University of Chicago (where he met John Dewey) then spent fifteen years as a reporter and editorial writer for Chicago newspapers. Bentley always had serious philosophical interests. His first book, *The Process of Government*, was a work in political philosophy drawing on European (George Simmel, Emile Durkheim, and Ludwig Gumplowicz) and American (John Dewey) thought. Hutchins wrote Bentley some prepublication comments and tried to be polite, but the book was too academic for his taste. In 1910, when he was forty, Bentley retired and settled on an estate in Indiana where he wrote a number of books and articles, including some he coauthored with Dewey. His papers ae in the Libby Library at Indiana University.

3. Mary Berenson was the wife and collaborator of the brilliant Jewish-American art historian, Bernard Berenson. The Berensons lived on an estate in Italy where they accumulated a fortune through his work as an authenticator of European art purchased by American millionaires. During their years in Europe, between 1906 and 1909, the Hapgoods often rented a villa near the Berensons and became friends.

4. This letter is in the Berenson Collection, Collection of American Literature, Beinecke Rare Book and Manuscript Library, Yale University. It is printed here with permission from the library.

5. Mabel Dodge Luhan, *Movers and Shakers* (1936; reprint, Albuquerque: University of New Mexico Press, 1985), 47.

6. Born Mabel Gamson in 1879, she grew up in an extremely wealthy and unhappy family in Buffalo, New York. During a European sojourn from 1904 to 1912, after the early death of her first husband, Mabel was introduced to an intellectual and artistic world by Leo and Gertrude Stein. Mabel Dodge was one of the organizers of the 1913 armory show in New York where Picasso and other European abstract artists were first shown in the United States. She was also an organizer of the large workers' pageant in Madison Square Garden that year to support the Paterson (New Jersey) strike by textile workers. Mabel was on the advisory board and a contributor to the *Masses*, a supporter of the Women's Peace party, and an early populizer of Freudian psychology in a weekly column for the Hearst papers. In 1918, discouraged by a growing conservative political climate during World War I and by the disintegration of the Greenwich Village circle, Mabel Dodge moved to Taos, New Mexico. There she started a campaign to preserve Native American culture and institutions and to attract artists and writers (including Georgia O'Keefe and D. H. Lawrence) to the Southwest. Her commitment to this new cause was solidified by marriage in 1923 to a Pueblo Indian, Tony Luhan, her fourth and final husband, with whom she lived in Taos until her death in 1962.

7. Lincoln Steffens was a famous journalist (the first "muckraker"), who employed Neith and Hutchins in their early days in New York.

8. John Reed graduated from Harvard in 1910 and became a well-known radical reporter, poet, and political agitator. During the Russian Revolution, Lenin and Trotsky received him as a brother. His most famous book, *Ten Days that Shook the World*, is an eyewitness account of the revolution. Reed was one of the founders of the American Communist party. He died of typhus in Moscow in 1920.

9. Lucy Wood Collier was a Smith College graduate who was a journalist, but she is best known as the wife of John Collier. John, a social worker, became the head of the People's Institute in New York in 1908, which provided help for new immigrants to the United States but also helped them preserve their native culture. In 1919 John became the head of adult education for the State of California and taught anthropology at San Francisco State University in the 1920s. Mabel Dodge interested him in the plight of Native Americans, and he became the commissioner of Indian Affairs in the Roosevelt administration in the 1930s. John and Lucy divorced in the early 1940s.

In *A Victorian in the Modern World*, Hutchins draws this picture of the Colliers:

> John Collier was married to a woman who was in some respects the exact opposite. He was interested passionately in the abstract and impersonal, and she was interested exclusively in the human and in the sensuous values of life. The contrast was so marked that it sometimes created profound maladjustments between them, especially in her feeling, for John understood the situation I think from the beginning. . . . Her warmth and physical nature, physical in the largely temperamental and human way, gave his roving spirit a tangible home (Hutchins Hapgood, *A Victorian in the Modern World* [Seattle: University of Washington Press, 1972], 413

10. Hapgood, *A Victorian in the Modern World*, 429–30.

11. Hapgood, *A Victorian in the Modern World*, 430.

12. A copy of this excerpt from a letter was provided to me by Miriam Hapgood Dewitt (now deceased).

13. This letter was given to me by Charles's sister Miriam after his death in the late 1970s. Excerpts are printed here with the permission of Beatrix Faust.

14. Letters from Beatrix Faust to Ellen Kay Trimberger on October 2 and November 11, 15, and 17, 1990.

AFTERWORD

> The marriage of a woman and man of talent must constantly be reinvented: its failure has already been predicted by conventional society, and its success is usually . . . disbelieved or denied.
> —Carolyn G. Heilbrun, *Writing a Woman's Life*

What is perhaps most striking about the forty-five-year marriage of Neith Boyce and Hutchins Hapgood is not just its struggles or each partner's search for fulfillment and self-expression within its bonds. These are the features of any long-term relationship. As remarkable are the writings it produced, writings in which their marriage underwent intense scrutiny. In their novels and plays, Neith and Hutchins invented marriages that mirrored their own union. In poetry, autobiographies, letters, and journals, they documented the psychosocial dynamics of their most intimate relation. They revealed themselves to and for each other, each serving the other as reader and respondent. But these were not merely private exchanges, a dialogue between lovers. They were also public acknowledgments of marital pleasures and pains, its risks and rewards.

We cannot underestimate the bravery that sustains both the marriage and these portraits of it. To our contemporary sensibility this bond of love and desire is both modern and impossibly outdated—not because Neith Boyce and Hutchins Hapgood were themselves too much the products of their late-nineteenth-century Midwestern upbringings but because the institution of marriage that they endeavored to refashion according to the measure of their lives is no longer recognizable to us. Today marriage is the name we give to serial monogamy, where partners "bond" for shorter or longer periods of time before moving onto another coupling. That is, marriage as a social and cultural institution has lost its power to hold and mold lives.

While marriage provided the bourgeois model of family life for Neith's and Hutchins's generation, it was a model rejected by many of the young Greenwich Village intellectual radicals who were their friends and colleagues. *La vie de Bohême* was defined by its rejection of middle-class values and goals, especially economic gain and conventions of marriage and family life. Shifting sexual alliances and "free" love were thought to enhance artistic and intellectual creativity. Thus, it is surprising that Neith and Hutchins decided to marry, especially since Neith, in order to pursue a writing career and maintain her independence, had planned not to marry. Although not a marriage in "name" (like many contemporary feminists, Neith Boyce retained her family name), theirs became a marriage in both the spirit and letter of the law. Neither did the couple marry in order to have children: Neith's first pregnancy (three years after the marriage) was unplanned, and, as she describes it in *The Bond* and Hutchins observes in *The Story of a Lover*, the pregnancy created conflicts in the marriage and within Neith herself. She fell in love with her first child, however, discovering unexpected pleasures in motherhood. Later she took refuge from the strains of the marriage in close relationships with her children. At these moments Hutchins both desired her more (he was sexually attracted to the maternal in her) and resented what he perceived as her withdrawal of affection and sexual attention to him.

Behind the many issues that emerge from their separate and quite different accounts of the marriage, then, is the fundamental question: why did they marry? Although this question is never answered (or even openly addressed) in their writings, one might conclude that Neith and Hutchins were as committed to marriage as marriage—a lifelong bond to be broken only by death—as they were to each other as persons. Their very identities became inseparable from the marriage, and they were unable to leave one another and escape the marital bond, despite various attempts to do so.

Marriage provided the plot of their lives and the narrative of their fictions. It was an intimate partnership defined by their separate struggles to balance connectedness and individuality. It was also a passionate commitment, and in this it broke an unspoken rule of letters, if not of life: marriage kills romance. For this reason, we are told, most romance fictions of the eighteenth and nineteenth centuries end with the wedding, never following the bride and groom beyond the threshold of their marital existence.[1] Neith and Hutchins broke social, cultural, and artistic bonds merely by addressing these issues. Their writings explore the emotional economics of marriage, revealing the flexibilities and subtleties, its ability to support passion and pain and to serve as a source of creative and intellectual inspiration. Marriage became the measure of their world: desire and love, fidelity and intimacy, creativity and domesticity, sex and work, productivity and sacrifice, individual freedom and coupling, political engagement and intellectual separateness.

The Literature of Marriage

Fiction has largely rejected marriage as a subject, except in those instances where it is presented as a history of betrayal—at worst an Updike hell, at best what Auden speaks of as a game calling for

"patience, foresight, maneuver, like war, like marriage." Marriage is
very different than fiction presents it as being. We rarely examine its
unromantic aspects.[2]

The literary and cultural contexts for Neith Boyce's *The Bond* (1908)
and Hutchins Hapgood's *The Story of a Lover* (anonymously published in
1919) are characterized by an emerging artistic experimentalism that
produced radical changes in both the subject matter and styles of modern art.[3] The artistic groups that grew up in Greenwich Village and in
European expatriate communities such as the Paris Left Bank shared a
common interest in establishing new modes of artistic expression and
breaking free of the cultural and social conservatism of late-nineteenth-
century United States. Resisting conventions of decorum and social
propriety, women and men refused the "work ethic," with its emphasis
on economic gain, and often joined together to produce communal art;
their artistic and political endeavors sometimes included group living
arrangements and sexual experimentation across class and race lines and
among same-sex couples.

The collaborative work of the Provincetown Players, for example,
had its counterparts in Natalie Barney's Paris *académie des femmes*, which
performed original dramas by group members and provided occasions
for writers to read and discuss their work, and also in Peggy Guggen-
heim's Hayford Hall in the English countryside, where in the 1930s
artists and writers reinvented family structures in a supportive, communal environment. While Barney's academy was dedicated to the support
of women in the arts, the Hayford Hall "family" included both women
and men, most of whom had suffered severe emotional damage as children and young adults. In the lush Devonshire environment, Djuna
Barnes, Antonia White, and Emily Holmes Coleman (who in 1931 had
served as secretary to Emma Goldman while the political activist was
completing her autobiography, *Living My Life*) attempted to heal the
effects of childhood sexual abuse by telling their stories in plays, poems,
and novels. The men of the community included some half-dozen writers, editors, and a filmmaker. Traditional sexual and companionate
arrangements were restructured within the group, which collectively
took avid interest in Freudian psychoanalysis. For the women especially,
Hayford Hall provided an enriching environment for their literary
work: Barnes was able to complete *Nightwood*, which is both the record
of her nine-year love for the American artist Thelma Wood and a map

of the sexual-cultural-political coordinates of expatriate literary modernism.[4]

The literature of this period reflects the growing awareness of Freud's discoveries in psychosexuality and efforts by the medical community to understand and treat neurosis, depression, and sexual "dysfunctions" such as frigidity and homosexuality. Havelock Ellis's work in sexology and S. Weir Mitchell's treatments for neurasthenia and anorexia nervosa influenced literary subject matter, and philosophers as different as Henri Bergson and William James examined the role of human consciousness in constructing external reality.[5] A new openness about intimate relations was joined to literary explorations of dreams and fantasies; the psychic, sexual, and emotional dimensions of the *experience* of reality replaced the traditional emphasis on the external dimension of social customs and conventions, mores and morals.

By comparison to many of their contemporaries, especially those who chose to live outside the United States, Neith and Hutchins lived rather conventional lives, and their literary accounts of their life together meditate on subtle nuances of the shifting balances of their individual strengths and vulnerabilities. From our late-twentieth-century perspective it is easy to miss all that is revolutionary about their lives and works because their writings focus on marriage, a traditional social bond that many of their counterparts quickly discarded as they set about establishing an intellectual counterculture. Some women of this period, for example, saw expatriation to Paris or London as the *only* escape from the marriage-motherhood plot and the only way possible to maintain an active life of creative expression. Neith and Hutchins on the other hand, were drawn to the experiment of balancing family life and literary productivity, even instability of gender roles. Their domestic arrangements, however, respected middle-class conventions and the moral imperatives that underwrote conformity to social mores. The value of monogamy and the virtue of fidelity were of primary concern to them; their extramarital alliances (whether sexual or intellectual) constituted real threats to the fragile equilibrium of their relationship. That is, the tensions within their intimate union arose not so much from the pressure of social conventions but from desire for the trust and loyalty that these conventions were meant to sustain.

These differences are more readily apparent when we read Neith and Hutchins alongside other writers of the period. Their work contrasts sharply, for example, with that of Djuna Barnes, who acted in and wrote plays for the Provincetown Players, which produced three of her plays in 1919 and 1920. Before moving to Paris to continue her work as a journalist, Barnes lived among the Greenwich Village group. In her early years with them she was close to Mary Pyne, who later became Hutchins Hapgood's lover. Barnes's complex literary works constructed a critique of gender roles that was also a bitter attack on patriarchal power structures, kinship and family alliances, and sexual mores. Treating taboo subjects through the guise of richly allusive and arcane language, she also challenged literary conventions. Mary Lynn Broe writes that "Barnes alone among the 'new women' playwrights dared to introduce vampirism (*The Dove*), incest (*Three from the Earth*), and various radical sexual ideologies in her work. . . . Barnes mimed romantic conventions at the historical moment when the small time husband-and-wife acts of the Provincetown Players—those of Neith Boyce and Hutchins Hapgood or Jig Cook and Susan Glaspell—were forging an uneasy link between Freud and feminism."[6] Even the titles of these plays suggest predictable Freudian-familial subject matter: *Fidelity*, for instance, or Boyce's *Constancy*, which examined the relationship between Mabel Dodge and John Reed, or Glaspell and Cook's *Suppressed Desires*, which looked askance at psychoanalysis. Just at the moment that sexologists were attempting to catalog and categorize forms of sexuality and in the wake of Freud's theories of infant sexuality and the oedipal complex, Djuna Barnes's visual and verbal art exploded the conceptual premises on which such categories rest. As Broe suggests, she "encode[d] complex modes of eroticism for which we as yet have no literary typology."[7]

Barnes represents one register of the preoccupation with the sexual and social power structures that define human relationships within families and between sexual partners. Twenty years younger than Neith and Hutchins, she belonged to the generation of modernist writers who not only redefined the boundaries of acceptable subject matter for literature but revised writing genres in an effort to join form and content, subject and style. *The Bond* and *The Story of a Lover* herald this new era, especially as they elaborate a poetics of intimacy that is later expanded in works by Anaïs Nin and Henry Miller and presage the socialist-feminist perspectives of Rebecca West, Katherine Anne Porter, Kay Boyle, and Lillian Hellman.[8] Among women writers, Neith Boyce and Susan Glaspell advance an already emergent tradition of candid and critical portraits of marriage by Kate Chopin, Charlotte Perkins Gilman, and Edith Wharton. Hutchins's treatise on love belongs to another, longer literary tradition in men's writings. Anaïs Nin would soon radically revise this genre in fictions of feminine desire that portray women as subjects of their own desires rather than objects of men's fantasies. Nin's discourses on love, especially works like *House of Incest*, challenged Freud's definitions of phallic sexuality.

The Bond continues a genre of writing on "women's issues" that became popular in the nineteenth century.[9] Many of these earlier works, although read with enthusiasm at the time by women trapped in dull and constricting marriages, are no longer remembered. They responded, however, to needs of a domesticated, middle-class reading public that later writers such as Edith Wharton were able to tap. The major themes of Wharton's novels and short fiction concern relationships between women and men as they are bounded by social expectation and cultural narrowness. Although Wharton has most often been defined as a satirist of social class and convention who captured essential character traits in quick, deft strokes, recent feminist research has discovered in her writing rich psychological portraits of women and men struggling to break through the forms and norms of social rituals to attain emotional intimacy. Indeed, this was the drama of Wharton's personal life, and her writing reflects her own experience of the patriarchal family and also reveals the dark horrors that its facade of respectability can often hide. Her works explore paternalism and materialism, wealth and poverty; courtship, marriage, and divorce; child abuse, incest, illegitimacy, and illicit sexuality; women's friendships, motherhood and childlessness, stepparent relations with orphaned children; and mental illness and suicide.

Wharton's best-selling second novel, *The House of Mirth*, was published in 1905, three years before Neith Boyce's *The Bond*, and sold 140,000 copies in the first three months after publication. The reading public was drawn to its analysis of the corrupted values of rich, worldly New York society where privilege no longer entailed social responsibility. The fate of Lily Bart, the novel's central figure, depends on her ability to manipulate this society for her own ends and to negotiate successfully the reefs and shoals of its sexual-social politics. Hers is not a search for intimacy and emotional connectedness but rather a desperate effort to secure economic security and social status through marriage. Lily fails in her efforts, refusing finally to marry for economic gain or to accept a marriage based on friendship and mutual respect rather than sexual desire. In this, as in many other Wharton fictions, marriage is observed from the outside; only rarely, as in *Ethan Frome*, do we gain an insider's view of marital relations. Moreover, in the privileged society that Wharton most often examines, extramarital relations for both women and men are tacitly accepted, provided they are conducted within the terms of decorum and discretion. Perhaps because Wharton never achieved a fully satisfying intimate union in her own life, she was never able successfully to portray it in her fiction. (In *The Children*, her 1928 novel about the effects of divorce on children, Martin Boyne muses: "If love couldn't be friendship too, as he had once dreamed it might, the only thing to do was to make the most of what it was.")[10] That she desperately wanted to achieve such a relationship is everywhere apparent in her private and published writings, but marital intimacy for Wharton existed as a desired dream or a fragile reality that impulsive human desires, if not social circumstances, soon destroys.

Discourses of Desire

Historically, the discourse of absence is carried on by the Woman: Woman is sedentary, Man hunts, journeys; Woman is faithful (she waits), man is fickle (he sails away, he cruises). It is Woman who gives shape to absence, elaborates its fiction, for she has time to do so.

—Roland Barthes, *A Lover's Discourse*[11]

The unenthusiastic literary reception of *The Bond* and the condemnatory reviews of *The Story of a Lover* were due not so much to their focus on marriage or the exploration of sensuality but to their intense focus on the psychology of the intimate partners within the relationship. Reviewers agreed that the central character of each work was "neurotic." In the *Dial*, William Morton Payne complained that he was "getting a little tired of the neurotic young woman who makes unreasonable demands upon life, and is unhappy because it turns out to be less exciting than she would like to find it."[12] His reference is to Teresa Ransome, the heroine of *The Bond*, but his wider subject is a genre of works by women writers that examines the psychosexual effects of social constraints of women's lives. He might be speaking of Kate Chopin's Edna Pontellier, the heroine of her 1899 novel, *The Awakening* (which, like Hapgood's *Story of a Lover*, fell victim to public censure) or to Edith Wharton's Lily Bart. It is perhaps not surprising that male reviewers were put off by the self-regard of women characters who struggled with unmet needs and the desires for autonomy, recognition, and creative self-expression—what today we would call subjecthood or "agency." Moreover, Neith's subject was not ordinary middle-class marriages but a union of two artists, whose conflicts around issues of domesticity and creativity, monogamy and sexual experimentation, could be dismissed as peculiarities of the "artistic temperament."

Hutchins's *Story of a Lover* focuses more directly on the psychosexual dynamics of the marital bonding. The social and economic coordinates of their daily lives, even the historical frame of the story, disappear into the background as the memoir traces the emotional equilibrium of the relationship. This is indeed a discourse on love, and while its roots can be traced to ancient literatures (the Song of Solomon, Plato's dialogues, Ovid's *The Art of Love*), it also prefigures radically experimental modern texts (Barthe's *A Lover's Discourse*, for example) as well as Anaïs Nin's *Henry and June*.[13] It has the quality of confession, but it is also an adventure, an exploration of the affective life of the kind most often undertaken only in the privacy and safety of psychoanalysis. It opens onto an intensely private world, exposing its wounds to the public eye.

The speaker, a man, admits to being "sensitive and passionate," subject to ill health (1919 ed., 7–8), referring to himself on several occasions as a "neuresthenic" and punctuating his frequent expressions of joy or sorrow with exclamation marks. That is, the speaker presents himself in the feminine, thereby inviting the charges brought against him by reviewers and critics, who called him a "sexual psychasthenic," a sentimentalist, and a "pathetic philosopher." Moreover, his love of domesticity, his ready acceptance of household duties, and his expressed desire to experience pregnancy itself seemed to emasculate him. Indeed, the traditional masculine-feminine roles are reversed in the relation between the lovers. The man is sensual and passionate; the woman is "cool, unconscious, poised—cold, the ignorant would call her" (1919 ed., 13). Nonetheless, the speaking position of this memoir, the place from which the lover is constituted *as lover*, is masculine.

This philosopher of love recognizes, of course, the necessary role that "talk" plays in intimate relations ("most misguided busy men avoid talking life to their sweethearts and wives," he observes—1919 ed., 21). He awakens his loved one's sensibilities, which she protects by composure and reserve, through conversation: "I talked about everything—literature, art, sex, wine, people, life—especially about life! . . . She liked my talk from the start" (1919 ed., 21, 22). He mistakenly assumes, however, that the woman's self-possession signifies a lack of passion in her innermost being. Thus, he begins to reproach her: "I said she had no soul" (1919 ed., 28); he tests her commitment to him and tries to arouse her jealousy by taking lovers. He also encourages her to expand her emotional horizons by experimenting with relations outside the marriage. In the end he remains "passionately unsatisfied" (175), but he has succeeded in turning her inaccessibility into an idealized form of all-encompassing mother love. She is Madonna and Mona Lisa in one, radiating a maternal, spiritual mystery through which he glimpses eternity (176).

Her self-containment and need for long periods of solitude simultaneously ignite his passion and frustrate its fulfillment. He complains: "She needs to be emotionally alone, most of the time. Why cannot I endure it?" (1919 ed., 55). His desire, which he calls the lover's "madness" (174), exceeds hers. In language that anticipates Jacques Lacan's theories of desire as the basis of human subjectivity, the lover confesses, "I can never be satisfied until I find the Other—and I know I can never find the Other—and I never really want to" (174). The woman represents fullness and plenitude, and he worships her most when she is pregnant. On the other hand, he figures the lack and insufficiency Freud (and later Lacan) ascribed to the feminine, his persistent sexual drive, a reminder of his failed efforts to fulfill his desires.

We know from Neith's letter to Hutchins's mother on the publication of *The Story of a Lover* that the memoir represented for her "a very different truth from *my* truth." She did not recognize herself in his portrait of a woman who withholds herself in autonomous isolation and yet represents spiritual plenitude. Neith's novel, which provided the unacknowledged background against which Hutchins drew his own self-portrait, presented an altogether different view of woman's struggle for independence and identity. Early in the novel, Teresa reveals to Basil that he has awakened in her another woman (her "Other" within):

> You are responsible for that person—she never existed till you insisted that she should be—and she makes me very uncomfortable. She's responsible for my moods and silly jealousies of women that I know you don't care for. I am rational, but she is blind instinct. I know you belong to me, but she doubts it. I believe that even if another woman had a physical attraction for you, it wouldn't touch your feeling for me—but she would go wild at the thought of it. So look out for her. *I* am reasonable, as I said, but *she*—. (1908 ed., 97)

Basil laughs away her confessions ("Are you trying to make me believe that there's primeval passion in you? I know better"), but from this moment on he tries to incite the passion of this Other, to call her forth, to unsettle her complacency. He succeeds in exposing Teresa's needs and dependencies and in so doing to turn her away from her work as a sculptor and jeweler, handing over to her his own insecurities and passions.

If there is a "primordial passion" in Teresa that Basil desires, there is cruelty and jealousy in him that she fears. The delicate balance of their relation shifts constantly, and its turn toward self-destruction—of the individuals and the relation itself—is foreshadowed early in the novel:

> Teresa's life was full, and, on the whole, free and happy. She desired nothing more for herself, except that it should not change. . . . She saw that she herself changed, that her love and need of Basil deepened. She saw that he changed—that he became more tranquil toward her, and more interested in the play of life outside than he had been during his year of absorption in her. And this shifting balance frightened her. If she should come to need him more than he needed her, it would destroy their first relation, in which he had given to her out of a free abundance of life and joy, and she to him calmly, tenderly, and with a smile on her lips, and in her heart. And this change, too, would destroy her own poise, and leave her at the mercy of chance or fate, in a dependence on Basil which she obscurely dreaded when she thought of it. (1908 ed., 122)

What Teresa fears comes to pass, as if her fears (unknown to Basil) and his self-doubts (unknown to her) predict their future relation. Unpredictably, their bond is not broken; instead they are further entwined in its sinews. The question of whether this alliance is for the best or not remains unresolved at the close of her novel and his memoir. There is an inevitability to their bond, and also an immutability that harmed—and also engaged—both partners.

The Writing Couple

NEITH: The essential man is a wanderer, never satisfied, always going on. . . .

HUTCH: Look around at the modern world and you will find women going more and more their own way, breaking with the traditions. Competing with men in man's own field, demanding that they have the same occupations, the same law, the same morals, or lack of morals. It would look as if woman has renounced the male of whom you speak so eloquently and has decided to be male herself.

—*Dialogue*, 184[14]

Literature by men in the first half of the twentieth century focused insistently on the situation of the artist. James Joyce's *A Portrait of the Artist as a Young Man* (1916), Thomas Mann's *Tonio Kroger* (1903), Henry James's *The Middle Years* (posthumously published in 1917), André Gide's *The Counterfeiters* (1923), and Ernest Hemingway's *The Garden of Eden* (posthumously published in 1987) examine the artist as projection of a (male) self.

Less often do women writers examine the nature of the artistic temperament or the social and cultural influences on the artist. Kate Chopin's treatment of these questions in *The Awakening* (1899) incorporates the traditional subject matter of women's fiction (the domestic scene and relations of husbands, wives, and children) into a novel of artistic and sexual awakening. Sexual desire and artistic creativity are viewed as mutually reinforcing, and they lead Edna Pontellier, a painter, farther along the path of self-knowledge, independence, and emotional liberation. That her new life may bring loneliness and social alienation can be seen in the character of Mademoiselle Reisz, the concert pianist, whose art requires that she renounce marriage and motherhood—or, more likely, that her art exists in lieu of the possibility for familial attachments. The same dilemma is posed by Virginia Woolf in *To the Lighthouse* (1927): the sad and solitary existence of the painter Lily Briscoe is contrasted with Mrs. Ramsay's life of domestic responsibilities. Each woman longs for an aspect of the other's life: Lily to experience the fullness of Mrs. Ramsey's domestic existence and Mrs. Ramsay to find an artistic form in which to express her sensual reactions to the world in which she lives. The clear message is that, for women, the commitment to art means the renunciation of affectional bonds, especially the claims of marriage and motherhood, with their attendant domestic claims.

If portraits of the woman artist are rare in the fiction of this period, even more difficult to find are portraits of artist couples who must balance their roles as loving partners and parents against the priorities (and potential competition) of their art. Neith Boyce's *The Bond* stands alone as an early exploration of a subject for narrative art that is in our present moment the predominant subject of women's writings. That is, Neith was several decades ahead of her time. Since the eighteenth century women's letters and journals have addressed these questions, but only in the twentieth century has it been possible for women to comment publicly on the tensions between domestic and artistic desires. Virginia Woolf spoke directly to the issue in *A Room of One's Own* (1928), but we are just now learning of the broader pattern of women's efforts to achieve the delicate balance between "life" and "art."

The focus on the balancing act of work and love is the distinguishing feature of *The Bond*, setting it apart not only from other writings of the period but from Hutchins's later memoir. Positioning himself as the lover in that work, he redomesticates his loved one. He engages her desires with his "talk" (the social expression of his artistic leanings), but her artistic longings do not engage his desires. She does not exist as an artist in his text but, rather, as the subject of *his* desire even, or especially, when he makes direct reference to their working lives. Describing their revision of traditional domestic roles, he comments: "she has been more of a father than the great majority of women—she has gone out to the larger world in her thought, her imagination and her work, and has helped make up for my deficiencies. . . . Or, more truly, neither of us has felt any limitation of sex, except *the fundamental one*, and we have worked out our common life as if there were no conventional career for either man or woman" (*The Story of a Lover*, 141, emphasis added). Her work, apart from domestic duties in which he shares, is never brought into the text as a central feature of her life and selfhood. To have drawn the realistic dimensions of their life work together would have detracted from the central premise of his memoir: "Life had prepared me to love" (1919 ed., 7).

That Neith Boyce's artistic desires and her need to work were difficult for her husband to understand and accept, despite his many disclaimers, can be seen in the play they wrote together, *Enemies*, and its probable early draft, *Dialogue*. In *Dialogue*, Neith speaks to her need for solitude and her desire to read. Here and in *Enemies*, her desire to read

stands for her artistic inclinations, her longing to separate herself sometimes from communal and social engagements in order to turn inward
toward her *own* desire. Reading incites Hutchins's anger and jealousy.
Seeking her attention, he accuses her of domestic failures. In *Dialogue*
she tries to explain to him the pleasures reading brings her:

> Of course my solitude includes books, and even people, but with wide
> intervals. What a delightful feeling is mine when in the morning the
> children go to school, the man of the house to work or somewhere—
> when the house is empty and the long day stretches before me, in
> boundless leisure. There may be household tasks, which I will do or
> not, as I happen to feel. . . . Brutus [the dog] will attend me—he is a
> perfect companion in solitude, he is eloquently mute. We lunch
> together on the sunlit porch, I prop a book against the teapot. (183)

Many women, enclosed within the domestic environment, know these
pleasures occasioned by the daily absences of husband and children. But
for Neith Boyce (as for Teresa Ransome in *The Bond*) these periods of
solitude are not merely resting places in the turmoil of daily life but
moments when the artistic impulse makes itself known. In *Dialogue*,
however, Hutch defines such moments as "the background of human
life" (183), a turning inward of the feminine spirit, and Neith responds
that women "must hear a voice that is strange, from far away, leading us
to adventure" (184).

Hutchins mistrusts this adventure of the spirit; indeed, it incites his
jealousy more quickly than the knowledge that Neith has taken a lover.
A competitor in love excites his sexuality, while the inward turning sets
a match to his rage. In *Enemies* he links her literary work to sexual
infidelity: "Oh, I know! All you want to do is lie in bed for breakfast,
smoke cigarettes, write your high literary stuff, make love to other men,
talk cleverly when you go out to dinner and never say a word to me at
home!" (187). The scenes of her unfaithfulness are the bed (where she
reads and, according to his accusation, takes lovers) and the dining table
(where she talks cleverly to others and later ignores him). Her complaint
against him is that he runs after other women; his retort is that those
women ran after him. But the charges and countercharges of infidelity
and inattention to domestic duties draw a veil across a more fundamental resentment: his jealousy of her creative spirit (which somehow
excludes him); and her anger at his refusal to grant her subjectivity—
that is, to acknowledge that she has desires of her own.

The art of marriage and the place of art within marriage constitute the double bind of Neith's and Hutchins's union. Their writings do not reveal disputes about the quality of each other's work or the opposed perspectives their art expresses (Anaïs Nin records many such disagreements with Henry Miller on these issues), nor does Hutchins serve as mentor and silent coauthor of Neith's writings (as Dashiell Hammett served Lillian Hellman). That is, the central tension of their artistic coupling is not what constitutes good art or which of them is the better writer. Rather, the tension radiates from the place of art itself within their coupling. They do not record the familiar contemporary complaints about balancing work roles within the marriage. The problem their texts pose is more fundamental, and more complex. It strikes at the heart of subjectivity and desire. That is, the "bond" that enfolds them and which they try to understand has to do with more than sex roles or social conventions. It has everything to do with the intractable pull toward self-realization and artistic expression.

Jacques Lacan describes this defining feature of human subjectivity as a "knot of desire" that projects its dreams and acts out its tireless longings on others.[15] In relationships, the individual desires of subjects cross, intersect, and deflect one another. They are intractable, resistant to the social codes that would domesticate them or the cultural forms that might release their energies. Neith and Hutchins grapple with these dominant (and dominating) primordial forces, silently acknowledging their failures to conquer them. Sexual desire that breaks across the bounds of marital arrangements is only one example, perhaps the most banal, of the constitutive elements of subjectivity. In *The Story of a Lover*, Hutchins refers to this bond of selfhood when he writes: "Spare one another we never did; each struggled to realize his [sic] own individuality, his [sic] egotistic need. Neither of us was considerate of the other. Those pale renunciations which hold many couples together in fragile relations neither of us would accept" (141). In one of Neith's earliest letters to Hutch she foresees what will be the most persistent tension between them; she expresses their bonding in terms of *bondage*: "I miss you and I want you. It's a bondage though and makes me horribly melancholy sometimes. I'm afraid you expect too much of me. *You like generic woman—woman per se—and I am myself*" (March 16, 1899, emphasis added). She recognized his resistance to her individual subjectivity, and in a letter written a few weeks later she comments, "I delight in your love, but in my soul I don't like familiarity" (May 24, 1899). Neith did not yet realize that her creative gifts—her "soul" in all its self-reflective solitude—were both the focus of Hutchins's desire and the measure of their separateness.

The lifelong efforts of Neith Boyce and Hutchins Hapgood to define (and refine) an intimate partnership produced literary achievements that are unique in twentieth-century letters. From a contemporary post-modernist and feminist perspective, these accounts surprise us not only by their frankness and patient honesty but by their desire to extend and enrich our understanding of intimacy. Ours is a culture that speaks openly of sexual matters but cannot comfortably discuss (much less participate in) the emotional connectedness and enduring closeness that intimacy implies. The modern marriage that Neith and Hutchins struggled to create was one that privileges proximity, where partners must negotiate the relation of individuality to bonding over a long period of time. The potential for failure, whether by the collapse of the relationship or the collapse of individuality *within* the relationship, is everywhere apparent. Psychoanalysts and therapists who specialize in "couples counseling" can attest both to our desire for such unions and our despair at failing to achieve them. Ours is also a society in which the responsibility for tending to relationships usually falls to women. Even in families where men share domestic chores and parenting duties, the emotional "business" of the family is left to mothers, wives, and sisters. Neith Boyce and Hutchins Hapgood sought to avoid this unequal division of labor. They were both attuned to the relationship, bringing to it energy, intelligence, and a large measure of stubborn persistence. Their writings reveal not only the successes and failures of their emotional bond but also the double risks of intimacy: the potential loss of individual selfhood within the relationship or the perseverance of one partner at the expense of the other.

Shari Benstock

Notes

1. See Laurie Langbauer, *Women and Romance: The Consolations of Gender in the English Novel* (Ithaca: Cornell University Press, 1989).

2. Carolyn G. Heilbrun, *Writing a Woman's Life* (New York and London: W. W. Norton, 1988), 87–88.

3. Selections from *The Bond* (New York: Duffield, 1908) and *The Story of a Lover* (New York: Boni and Liveright, 1919) are reprinted in this volume.

Unless otherwise indicated, page numbers are from the Feminist Press edition of the works.

4. Shari Benstock, *Women of the Left Bank: Paris, 1900–1940* (Austin: University of Texas Press, 1986); Mary Lynn Broe, "My Art Belongs to Daddy: Incest as Exile. The Textual Economics of Hayford Hall," in *Women's Writing in Exile*, ed. Mary Lynn Broe and Angela Ingram, 42–86 (Chapel Hill: University of North Carolina Press, 1989); see Karla Jay, *The Amazon and the Page: Natalie Clifford Barney and Renee Vivien* (Bloomington: Indiana University Press, 1988).

The men at Hayford Hall included would-be writers and editors: the Russian emigré William Gerhardie, whose study of Anton Chekhov was published by Scribners at the suggestion of Edith Wharton, George Barker, John Ferrar Holms, Douglas Garman, Silas Glossup, Peter Hoare, and Humphrey Jennings.

5. Charlotte Perkins Gilman, Edith Wharton, and Virginia Woolf underwent, for varying lengths of time, S. Weir Mitchell's treatment; Gilman's short story "The Yellow Wallpaper" examines the effects of the treatment. Literary modernism was characterized by its exploration of psychosexuality in everyday life. James Joyce, D. H. Lawrence, Ernest Hemingway, F. Scott Fitzgerald, Henry Miller, and others examined the intersections of desire and domesticity within heterosexual relations; Djuna Barnes, Virginia Woolf, H. D., and Anaïs Nin reconfigured desire to include male homosexuality and lesbianism; Gertrude Stein and Natalie Barney critiqued (but also imitated) the power structures of heterosexuality within woman-to-woman bonding.

Lisa Ruddick examines the influence of William James's and Sigmund Freud's theories in *Reading Gertrude Stein* (Ithaca: Cornell University Press, 1990).

6. See Mary Lynn Broe, "Djuna Barnes," in *The Gender of Modernism*, ed. Bonnie Kime Scott, 25 (Bloomington: Indiana University Press, 1990); and Ann Larabee, "The Early Attic Stage of Djuna Barnes," in *Silence and Power*, ed. Mary Lynn Broe (Carbondale: Southern Illinois University Press, 1991). See also Jane Marcus, "Laughing at Leviticus," in *Silence and Power*.

7. Broe, "Djuna Barnes," 25. Broe's claims that the subject matter and style of Barnes's plays are more radical than the coauthored productions of Boyce and Hapgood and Cook and Glaspell direct us to an important, and often overlooked, question: what *are* the lived and literary coordinates of the "uneasy link between Freud and feminism" among members of this group?

8. Bernard Benstock examines the personal, professional, and political ties in the thirty-year intimate relationship between Lillian Hellman and Dashiell Hammett in "Non-Negotiable Bonds," in *Significant Others*, ed. Isabelle de Courtivron and Shari Benstock (forthcoming).

9. Nina Baym, *Woman's Fiction: A Guide to Novels by and about Women in America, 1820–1870* (Ithaca N.Y.: Cornell University Press, 1980); and *Novels,*

Readers, and Reviews: Responses to Fiction in Antebellum America (Ithaca, N.Y.: Cornell University Press, 1984).

10. Edith Wharton, *The Children* (New York: D. Appleton, 1928).

11. Roland Barthes, *A Lover's Discourse*, trans. Richard Howard (New York: Hill and Wang, 1978), 13-14.

12. August 16, 1908, 91.

13. This text, based on expurgated portions of Anaïs Nin's diaries, was published in 1984, after the death of her husband, Hugh Guiler.

14. Page numbers for *Enemies* and *Dialogue* are from the Feminist Press edition of the plays, reprinted in this volume.

15. Jacques Lacan, "The Subversion of the Subject and the Dialectic of Desire in the Freudian Unconscious," in *Ecrits: A Selection*, ed. and trans. Alan Sheridan, 292-324 (New York: Norton, 1977).